Blood
on the
Doorposts

William and Sharon
Schnoebelen

CHICK PUBLICATIONS

ISBN: 0-937958-43-3   *5th Printing*   169/D

Chick Publications
P.O. Box 3500, Ontario, Calif. 91761-1019 USA
Tel: (909) 987-0771 • Fax: (909) 941-8128

Outside the U.S. call for a distributor nearest you or see our entire listing on the internet at: **www.chick.com/distrib.asp**

www.chick.com
E-Mail: orderdesk@chick.com

Printed in the United States of America

Though all incidents in this book are true, virtually all names and minor circumstances have been changed to protect confidentiality.

Conversations were reconstructed as well as memory allows or case notes permit. However, the essential substance is accurate to the best of our human ability.

God bless you!

Contents

1

"The Sweetest Screams"

> "And they caused their sons and their daughters to pass through the fire, and used divination and enchantments, and sold themselves to do evil in the sight of the Lord, to provoke him to anger."
>
> 2 Kings 17:17

MILWAUKEE, 1979

The phone call was frantic! The mother on the other end of the line could scarcely restrain herself from weeping.

"Our little girl's in the hospital! She's so traumatized she doesn't even recognize us!"

"Why are you calling us?" I asked.

"I got your name from..." The distraught woman named the man who ran the occult bookstore in Milwaukee.

"He said you knew something about Satanism."

"You could say that..." I ventured.

As a matter of ironic fact, my wife, Sharon, and I were deeply involved in hardcore Satanism. My involvement extended to the practice of animal sacrifice and vampirism. Additionally, we had as a house guest a fellow named Orion, a Satanic high priest and the representative of the hierarchy of the Satanic Brotherhood for the Midwest.[1]

"May I ask what Satanism has to do with your daughter?" I pressed.

"You must understand," she cried. "My parents took my 9-year-old daughter for a weekend, and when they dropped her off she was like a zombie!"

The woman was overcome with emotion.

"What happened?"

"All she could say was that she didn't want to go back to the black room."

"I thought something was wrong, so I suggested that she take a hot bath and get into bed. When she didn't respond, I started to help her undress and she fainted and fell on the floor like a rag doll!"

"I undressed her to get her into bed, and her body was covered with bloody designs, bruises and burn marks! Someone had drawn a star on her chest in blood and burned her bottom. Her wrists were torn and bruised like she had been tied up and struggled, and there were also needle marks in her arms—as if she had been injected with drugs."

I felt my mind whirl. Although I was a Satanist, I had never seen such things done—except to adults who were more or less willing victims. I had heard vague rumors about the torture of little children from Orion, but it wasn't discussed much.

"The doctor admitted her to the hospital, but she is almost like in a coma. Our doctor says she has been sexually violated. She won't eat or talk, and she doesn't recognize us. When the nurses try to help her relieve herself, she starts screaming about the black room. Can you help us?"

Hysteria put a keen edge on the woman's voice. My mouth was dry.

"What would you like us to do?"

"Is this some sort of satanic spell? I called my parish priest, but he doesn't want anything to do with this. He just said he would pray for us. Can you bring our daughter back?"

"What do the doctors say?" I asked, stalling a bit as I tried to think of ways to help.

"They say that she has probably experienced something so horrifying that her mind and emotions shut down."

"What do her grandparents say?"

"They deny anything happened. They say she had a fun weekend and was fine when they dropped her off. They are trying to make it look *as though my husband and I did this!*"

Anger was now mingled with fear in her voice.

"Is this some kind of curse, or what?"

I was in the middle of getting a Masters degree in theology and pastoral counseling, so I had a few graduate level courses in psychology under my belt.

"That's hard to say. It could be a curse, or it could be a normal psychological reaction to being horribly mistreated. It could be a combination of both."

Back then, there wasn't much in print on the sexual abuse of children, and virtually nothing on Satanic Ritual Abuse (SRA). The idea of adults torturing and sexually molesting children was beyond comprehension. It was even a stretch for someone as immersed in perversity and evil as I was.

"Please, is there anything you can do?" the mother's voice intruded upon my shocked reverie.

I felt a terrible mixture of emotions. Part of me was disgusted by the tale. But another—very dark—element within me felt intrigued and even sexually stimulated by the child's plight. IT whispered, *"I wish I could have been there!"*

I fought it back, and realized, with an uneasy shudder, that I—myself—was not that far away from doing such atrocities. It was incredibly incongruous that this woman was seeking my help.

"Well..." I finally managed to stammer, through a mouth dry as cotton, "we could certainly do some rituals in our Circle to heal your daughter, and hopefully we could break any curses which may have been placed upon her."

Privately, I wondered about these grandparents. If they were into something this vile, they might be more powerful than our covens could withstand. It would depend upon how large their coven was, and who else I could enlist to our side.

"How much do you know about your parents' involvement in this?" I probed.

"Nothing! I never had a clue! They're church-going Catholics! Could they have been deceiving us all these years?"

"It's possible." I admitted.

"How long have you been married and away from their home?"

"About ten years. Terri is our first child."

"It may be that your folks were into this all the time, or maybe they got into it after you moved out of the house. Did any dramatic changes take place in your folks' life in the last decade?"

I thought perhaps that something had forced the parents into getting "in debt" to a satanic coven. My covens had taken out "contracts" to curse people to death, and usually it cost the "client" some money.

"Well," the woman sniffed, getting some of her composure back, "my dad's business started going under about five years ago. Then all of a sudden, a huge infusion of money came from someplace, and it pulled out of its dive."

"You don't know where the money came from?"

"No. Dad just said it was a silent investor who wished to keep a low profile."

"Was it a lot of money?"

"I believe it was more than a half-million dollars."

I sighed. "It could be that your dad—or both your folks —made a pact with a satanic group. They would have that kind of money without a problem."

"What do you mean?" The woman sounded intrigued.

"He may have signed a kind of blank check with the Brotherhood without fully understanding what was involved." Then when your daughter reached age nine, they may have demanded that she be turned over to them and dedicated to the devil."

"I can't imagine my folks agreeing to such a thing."

"That's just it. They wouldn't have known at the time what they were agreeing to. Then, when the Brotherhood called in its chips, they'd have no choice."

"I don't understand."

"The way these things work is that Satan would threaten to take his entire family—you, your siblings, their children, **AND *your daughter,*** unless your folks let the coven have their way with your daughter."

"That's monstrous!" she finally breathed. "Such people exist?"

"I'm afraid so." I admitted, carefully concealing that I was one of them.

"So what can be done?"

"I'm not certain. We will definitely need a lock of your daughter's hair and some fingernail clippings —and at least one piece of her clothing."

The woman sounded even more incredulous.

"What for?"

"Ma'am, we are white witches—Wiccans," I lied.

"We need those things for object links—ways that our good magic can have a more powerful impact on your daughter and her health. Also, if it's alright with you, we would like to know where your folks live."

"You're witches?" she gasped.

"Yes, ma'am," I explained patiently. "That's what you get when you go to an occult bookstore for help. But we are GOOD witches. We don't hurt people. Only white magic can counter black magic," I said, lying again. Lying is necessary when you serve the Father of Lies.

I continued. "It may be that we can talk to your folks and see if we can rescue them from this group— talk some sense into them. Otherwise, this sort of thing will go on."

"What do you mean?"

"Satan is like a blackmailer. He never stops with one request. If what I think happened to your daughter really happened, he now thinks of her as his personal toy. He will want her back—again and again—until she is entirely his—body, soul and spirit."

This elicited an awful cry over the receiver. *"You mean the devil is after our little Terri?"* Faster than I could grab a pencil, she blurted out the name and address of her folks.

A day later, I took Orion and drove out to the fancy suburb where the offending parents lived. Orion was along because he was a much higher level Satanist and thus supposedly had more power. He also knew more about the inner workings of the Brotherhood. He claimed to have sacrificed animals and people to the glory of Satan.

We pulled in the driveway of the parents' large ranch home. It was very nice, but hardly a mansion. After much trepidation, we rang the doorbell, but found no one home.

Orion, who was a short, dark, wiry fellow with the demeanor of a weasel and the manners of Attilla the Hun, chortled under his breath, "Let's check out the back."

The place was a fairly unremarkable suburban home. However, both Orion and I could sense an evil energy around the backyard. After making a circuit of the property, Orion led me back to the rear of the house.

"Check it out, little brother," he smiled, gesturing towards the basement windows. One of Orion's more irritating habits was calling me "little brother," although I was a full head taller and probably seventy-five pounds heavier. It was something one had to put up with from an "Ipsissimus High-Priest King of the Morning Star," Orion's official title.

Looking down, following Orion's pointing finger, I saw that all the basement windows were sunk below ground and that huge, sturdy bars guarded the little window-wells which allowed light to get to them. And the windows were painted with opaque black paint.

Orion snickered. It sounded like air escaping from a motorcycle tire. "You could cut up anything or anyone you wanted in that basement, little brother, and no one could see in."

He turned and with his arms took in the entire two acre lot.

"Not only that, there aren't any neighbors near. Screams wouldn't carry too far from these windows —especially if they used the right kind of sound-proofing."

I shook my head. "Does stuff like this really happen?"

Orion nodded sagely. "Believe it… some of the sweetest screams come from little girls."

In an oddly anti-climactic ending to the entire affair, we left the house without further incident.

I never got the hair and nail clippings from the mother, and was never contacted by her again. The media was surprisingly silent on the subject. Perhaps the mother got some better advice and decided not to try and fight "black" magic with "white" magic.

It would take Sharon and me five more years to truly escape from the clutches of Satan and become Born Again. Only then did we fully understand that white and black magic were two sides of the same satanic coin, and that all the coin bought us was a one-way ticket to the lake of fire (Rev. 21:8). We don't know if Orion ever got out of Satanism, because he was taken out of our lives before we were saved.

However, this disturbing and bewildering incident left us wondering. Did the woman find help elsewhere—hopefully from Christians? Did the Brotherhood get to her and silence her with threats? Was this truly a case of Satanic Ritual Abuse (SRA) which emerged a year or so before the book, *Michelle Remembers*, which first discussed it publicly, made it on the popular scene?[2]

We didn't know how prophetic that brief brush with Satanic abuse would be to the thrust of much of our later ministry as Born Again Christians!

Today, fourteen years after "Terri's" tragic story, SRA is showing up in countless pastors' studies and counseling offices, all over the world. Thousands of adults and a significant number of children are coming forward with stories similar to Terri's mom's account. We have prayed for dozens—perhaps hundreds—ourselves!

While some in the helping professions think these people are reporting genuine experiences, others feel that these are "mentally disturbed" people. They believe the stories are either made up to elicit sympathy or are conjured up by therapists who ask leading questions or even hypnotize clients into thinking they have been ritually abused because the therapist (or minister) has a vested interest in believing that such abuse is wide-spread.

This book is not the place to debate the truth of abuse accounts.[3] But the clear testimony of the Bible is that throughout the pagan world parents were driven by demon gods such as Molech or Ba'al to offer their children in ghastly rituals of torture and murder (See Leviticus 18:21, etc.).

However, it is our intention here to suggest ways in which these people might best be helped. We have ministered to far too many survivors to reduce their turmoil to an academic debate.

Whether or not their "memories" or abuse are actual fact, the point is that these people are in pain. Only Jesus Christ can really minister to that pain. Ultimately, psychiatrists cannot help. Counselors cannot help. Even pastors, unless they deal with the spiritual warfare dimensions of the person's problem, will be limited in their effectiveness.

It is only through the Liberating Power of the Lord Jesus Christ that these people can be healed, restored and freed. This book concerns the subject of accessing that Power to help those in pain—and to free them for worship, service and joy in the Lord!

2

"If You Don't Leave, I'll Call the Police!"

MILWAUKEE, 1985

Now true Christians, Sharon and I stood on the front stoop of a small apartment house, trying to see the most powerful witch high priestess in the city.

The woman stood at the door, imperious and threatening. Sharon spoke to her:

"Cathy, I wonder if we could come in and talk with you about Jesus Christ."

Before any of us could react, Cathy was on Sharon like a junkyard badger. Cathy was bigger, and had her hands around Sharon's throat. With a furious snarl, Cathy smashed her into the stairwell wall, picking her up slightly off the ground. Sharon's face actually started turning purple from the force of Cathy's vice-like grip.

How did we find ourselves on the landing of an apartment building grappling in a life-and-death struggle with a demon possessed woman?

Several months earlier, in the final months of 1984, we had the blessed opportunity of leading our second witch/Satanist to a saving knowledge of Jesus Christ. Gary had been one of our occult pupils in Milwaukee for many years, and now he was a Christian.

We were living 170 miles away in Dubuque, Iowa. Because of our friend's conversion, we made occasional trips to Milwaukee to help disciple him. On this occasion, we learned some distressing news.

Gary still had some contacts in the Craft, thus he was a pipeline about our old "colleagues" in Satanism and Wicca.

When we were first saved and renounced the occult, we spoke to or wrote as many of our old coven members as possible, to tell them the wonderful liberty we enjoyed after being saved. We wanted them to be Born Again!

Most of our letters were answered with stony silence. A few were nice enough to write back or call, although our relationships had become strained.

A more unique response was from Cathy. She was one of our most astute priestesses, and was involved with us in some of the most dangerous and perverse aspects of magic. She was fully committed to Aleister Crowley—a leading satanic figure of our century—and considered herself a Satanist.

Like us, she had become involved in black magic, voodoo, vampirism and even Nazi magical rituals. Also, like us, she had invited demons into her body by the score.

A few days after she got our letter presenting our testimony of Jesus Christ, we got a very disturbing phone call from Cathy. She informed us in furious tones that she was going to catch the next bus to Dubuque and bury an emerald dagger in my heart!

Needless to say, we spent a few anxious days in prayer, trusting in the Lord to protect us. After all, we were still fairly young Christians. However, to the best of our knowledge, Cathy never made it to Dubuque, with or without her dagger.

Now, however, we had come to Milwaukee. As we sat in Gary's living room, we learned that Cathy had been getting increasingly bizarre—even by occult standards.

Gary heard that she was unable to keep a job and that she sat around the apartment she shared with her high priest companion. She was losing weight at an alarming rate, was known to sit for hours and watch television without the set being turned on, and was pulling parts of her hair out by the roots.

Gary asked if we thought she was demon possessed. We said that it would be astonishing if she were *not* demon possessed, considering her extremely high level of involvement in black magic. Whatever her situation, it was extremely desperate. It was reported to Gary that her high priest was thinking about committing her.

We looked at each other and felt as if this was on our shoulders. Most of this woman's black magical activity came from her following either our advice or the advice of the "spirit guides" (actually demons) who had spoken through us. Thus, if there was something we could do, we should do it.

We had studied enough of the New Testament to understand that, as Christians, we all had authority given to us by Jesus over evil spirits (see Mark 16:17). We felt that if we could get her to sit down and listen to reason, it was possible that she could be reached for Jesus Christ.

But neither Gary nor I were overly anxious to make the contact. We were more than a little nervous about trying to do an "exorcism"[1] on probably the most powerful and experienced Satanist high priestess in Milwaukee, even if she was an old friend. However, Sharon took the part of "Deborah," exhorted us big, strong men to enter the battle (see Judges 4:4-9). After all, our friend's soul was at stake—to say nothing of her sanity.

After an impromptu but lengthy prayer meeting, we set off for Cathy's apartment. Gary agreed to come along to be prayer support.

So it was that Gary and I stood there dumb-founded as Cathy picked up Sharon by the throat and shook her head until her teeth rattled. It seemed like a terrifying eternity, but it was only a couple of seconds. Finally, Sharon managed to croak breathlessly "Satan...the Lord...rebuke... thee... in Jesus' name..."

Sharon didn't even have time to gasp out an "Amen." Cathy gave out a brief cry like a cornered animal and crumpled back against the opposite wall. It was as if all the strength had run out of her like water. Sharon fell back, coughing. Before any of us could move, Cathy was up the stairs with the speed of a cat. She whirled into her apartment and slammed the door.

Even from the bottom of the stairs, we heard the chain being slipped into place on the door. I helped Sharon to her feet. She indicated with a gesture that she was reasonably alright. Between breaths, she managed to wheeze, "We need to get up there and get her to open the door."

We ascended the stairs and knocked on Cathy's door. Absolute silence.

"Cathy, we aren't trying to hassle you. Please let us in," Sharon ventured.

Still no response, although there was a sound emerging from the other side of the door which sounded like a seven-hundred pound cat purring.

"Let's pray!" Gary suggested, looking at me. Sharon nodded in agreement. We held hands and began to pray.

"Lord, we know it is Your will that Cathy hear

the gospel of Jesus Christ. We also know that Satan will do anything to prevent her from hearing it. In Jesus' name we ask that You would bind the power of Satan to influence Cathy in any way. In Jesus' name we ask that You would give Cathy the freedom to make her own choices and be able to admit us if she wishes. Father, please clear Cathy's mind and heart so that she can hear the Good News about Jesus Christ. In His name we pray, Amen."

We continued to pray in that vein for about three to four minutes. Suddenly, we heard the sound of the chain being slipped off the door. Our hearts beat faster. The latch clicked and the door swung wide. Cathy stood there, her hand on the doorknob, her eyes down-cast. She would not look at us, nor did she speak. She looked almost demure.

Uncertainly, we entered the apartment. It didn't look substantially different than the last time we had been there. A sofa sat facing away from the door, toward two massive stereo speakers and a highly sophisticated music system. Cathy's high priest companion was quite an electrician and audiophile. Two chairs sat facing the sofa by the windows.

A year earlier, Cathy was running her own coven, a daughter-coven of the one Sharon presided over. Thus, our eyes were drawn to the right—to a doorway which we knew led into Cathy's Temple Room, where dozens of witchcraft circles and many even more incredible rituals of power and pain had been performed. The door was shut, and we could only wonder what now lay behind it.

The apartment hadn't changed, but the three of us had! The last time we were in this room, we were witches. Now, we were servants of the living God.

Cathy sat down on the sofa as the silence grew thicker. We sat opposite her. Sharon finally spoke. "Cathy, we appreciate your letting us come in. Do you understand why we're here?"

She nodded. "We understand," she said in a serene but metallic monotone. We recognized it as the voice of one of her supposed "spirit guides."

Sharon persisted. "We need to speak to Cathy."

"She isn't here," the voice responded.

"That's a lie," Sharon said quietly. "Cathy IS here, and she has a right to hear about Jesus Christ."

Cathy sighed a cavernous sigh. "Speak if you must. I have a few minutes to spare you." Her voice sounded more normal. Gary was praying furiously.

"You know what happened to us, Cathy." Sharon continued, "We found what we were seeking for all those years! You walked through many of those years with us. You're one of our oldest and dearest friends. Won't you give Jesus Christ a chance?"

Cathy smiled, but it was a brittle smile which did not engage her eyes. "What makes you think I am not a Christian? Am I not a member of the Church of Jesus Christ of Latter-day Saints?"

I sighed, "I know you joined the Mormon church at our leading, Cathy. But the Jesus it offers you is a false Jesus. He cannot save you."

She snorted softly. "So there is more than one Jesus? Picky, aren't we?" The sarcasm dripped from her voice like poisoned honey.

"You need to be picky when it comes to the fate of your immortal soul," Sharon pointed out.

"The Christ who has spoken to you in trance—the Christ who is in the Mormon church—the Christ in the New Age Movement—these are false Christs."

Cathy sat forward. "Who are you to tell me I worship a false Christ!" she spat.

"We're your friends. We got you into much of this mess, and we want you to see that there is a way out."

"Friends?" she laughed sardonically. "You left this city when I needed you most! You deserted me when I was in darkest despair!"

"The Lord had to get me away from Milwaukee so I could finally discover Him," I confessed. "Now that we understand who Jesus really is, and what He is offering—we came back to share Him with you."

"I spit on your crapulous creeds," Cathy quoted from Aleister Crowley's obscene revelation, *The Book of the Law.*[2]

"You are fools, and your gods are fools." The venom in her voice was palpable. It hung in the room like fetid fumes.

"Don't turn your back on Jesus," Sharon insisted. "He can take away your pain."

Cathy rose abruptly from her sofa. "My pain is all you have left me. I believe I shall keep it." She walked to the door and opened it. "I think you all had better leave now."

We looked at each other uncertainly.

"If you don't leave, I'll call the police," she declared, her voice rising subtly.

We stood up and filed out. Cathy glared at us, her face an iron mask. Sharon smiled slightly. "We will be praying for you."

Strange fire came into Cathy's eyes. "WE'LL be praying for you, too!"

Thus ended our first attempt at a deliverance. It will not go down in church history as a mighty victory. However, we did learn some valuable lessons which would serve us in good stead later on.

First, we learned it was normally a mistake to try and do this sort of ministry without LOTS of serious prayer in advance. We also learned that it is easier to do it on "home ground"—either a church or some other setting where you know that the environment is free of defilement and soaked in Godly prayer.

Finally, we learned that while we DID have authority over evil spirits, there were limits to that authority circumscribed by the person's free will— i.e., their human spirit. If a person WANTS their evil spirits, it is nearly impossible to set them free.

Little did we know where this humble—even humiliating—beginning in ministry would lead us.

3

On the Couch with Dr. Frankenstein

"...forgetting those things which are behind, and reaching forth unto those things which are before, I press toward the mark for the prize of the high calling of God in Christ Jesus."   Phil. 3:13-14

Whenever counseling with SRA survivors comes up, another subject is usually not far behind. That is the issue of a psychological syndrome known as "Multiple Personality Disorder" (MPD).

Though this book makes no pretense of being a work of psychology *(praise the Lord!)* it is necessary to dip into the murky waters of psychiatric study to be able to minister to people who come to the church for help. For too long many pastors have "referred" their people to "professional counselors" rather than minister to them themselves in a Biblical manner.

Sadly, though, psychology is at best a *very soft science*. It's an idol frequently worshipped by Christian pastors, teachers and leaders. A critique of the *"science falsely so-called"* of psychology is beyond the scope of this book. Many authors, writing both from within and without the fields of psychiatry, clinical psychology and counseling, have already done an admirable job of showing the many fallacies of so-called "Christian" psychology.[1]

Certainly there are genuine brain disorders caused by biological illnesses which can be helped by psychiatrists and their medications. However, the VAST majority of what is done in the counseling office could better be done in the pastor's study! There are not always clear answers, and what we are about to discuss is one of the more difficult areas in which one can draw clear-cut lines.

It is important for the Christian to understand what the MPD person feels is happening, because many SRA survivors are told (usually by psychotherapists) that they are suffering from MPD. Thus, whether or not the Christian worker or pastor believes that MPD is genuine, it is vital that they be able to meet the distressed person "where they are" with some comprehension of what is supposed to be happening and what the person's expectations are.

The psychiatric world recognizes MPD as a genuine disorder. The "bible" of American psychiatry, the DSM-III-R, has this definition of MPD:

> **"...the existence within the person of two or more distinct personalities or personality states (each with its own relatively enduring pattern of perceiving, relating to, and thinking about the environment and self). At least two of these personalities or personality states recurrently take full control of the person's behavior."[2]**

MPD is classified as a type of "Dissociative Disorder."[3] This means that it is a disturbance of memory, or of the person's sense of identity and consciousness. Psychiatrists feel that all people dissociate to some extent. Daydreaming is a mild example. However, the way dissociation is used here, it refers to a splitting or segregation of a group of mental processes in such a fashion that their normal relationship to the rest of the personality is lost.[4]

MPD is felt to be a "super-dissociation," in which entire, fully developed personalities exist side-by-side within a person, usually ignorant of each other's existence. It supposedly occurs mostly in childhood, although it is not discovered until many years later. Studies indicate that in nearly all cases the disorder is preceded by a childhood abuse (usually sexual), or some other early childhood trauma. It is diagnosed three to nine times more often in females than in males.[5] Because of the preponderance of female victims, we will use the feminine pronouns in this discussion. This does NOT mean that men or boys are never victimized or suffer from what is called MPD. It is just not as common.

Supposedly, when one "alter-personality" ("alter" for short) is in ascendancy, the other personalities are submerged and have amnesia about what happens during that time. Thus, MPD people allegedly suffer from memory black-outs and have a great deal of anxiety from these unknown elements of their life.

A true Christian who had no knowledge of this psychiatric concept would probably think a person displaying MPD symptoms was demonized, or at least suffering from what the "layman" would call a split-personality.

WHAT CAUSES MPD?

It has already been mentioned that psychiatrists feel that child abuse or some other extreme trauma from childhood is the predominant cause of the MPD phenomenon. Beyond that, there are different theories. The most common one is as follows:

A child is severely traumatized, say by sexual abuse. The experience is too overwhelming to handle, so she "escapes" by "dissociating," which psychologists define as a "defense mechanism." It is a coping device the mind uses to deal with stress, fear or other unwanted stimuli. Supposedly some people are more gifted at dissociation than others.

Most MPD people are alleged to be victims of repeated abuse—dozens, if not hundreds of occasions of severe trauma. The theory is that when the child dissociates, it's like part of her personality is split off—the part which "takes" that particular episode of abuse. Since the child's "core personality" (the original, "un-split" personality) is kept insulated from this dissociated fragment which split off, the girl herself has no recollection of the abusive episode. It is sealed off from the main memories of the core personality. Thus, an "alter" is created.

If the child is horribly mistreated many times, there might be many "alters," each frozen at different ages and stages of personality development, according to when the abuse occurred. Thus, in a 30-year-old woman, there might be four-year-old alters, seven-year-old alters, and even teen-aged alters.

It gets even more complicated because (according to the theory) if the child is creative and imaginative and there are many alters, she will unconsciously create "alters" which keep the abused "alters" organized, or protect some of the more fragile personalities. Some of these cases have twenty or thirty alter personalities, and they have alters that control which alter emerges at which time, and which alter submerges—kind of internal traffic cops.

These alters assume names and identities, sometimes based on the traumatic experience, sometimes based on fictional characters, or upon their function. Many MPDs have a "tough" alter which exists solely to "take" any abuse which comes their way. They will also have a nurturing, loving alter and an alter whose sole function is to keep the core personality from finding out about the abuse, to "protect" her from that knowledge.

Some will be male, and others female. Some might not even be able to verbalize because they were "split off" at an early age. Some might be chaste and demure, and others wanton. Some might possess skills which the core personality does not have (i.e., speaking in a foreign language) because the "alter" learned the language when the core personality was submerged.

Usually, these people live a normal life, but with a sense that something is not right, especially if the alters have learned to function well together. Most MPDs have alters that talk to one another, and often agree which alter does which tasks. Thus, the theory goes, a child can grow up without knowing that: a) she was abused or: b) she has many personalities living within her mind. She will just have this vague sense of anxiety and unease, but will not be able to pinpoint its cause.

Something usually happens to precipitate the discovery of alters. A crisis in the woman's life jogs something loose in the normally smooth routine— the death of a loved one—or an involvement with a man. Sometimes the woman gradually becomes aware that there are parts of her life missing, or that she is experiencing memory blackouts. She goes to a doctor or therapist and is diagnosed as MPD.

A TREATMENT WORSE THAN THE DISEASE?

Depending on the therapist, there are several courses of treatment. Sadly, among secular (and even some Christian) psychologists, the therapy of choice is frequently hypnosis. Most therapists are careful to not immediately diagnose MPD, and *a sizable number don't even think the disorder is genuine.* But, if an "alter" emerges during sessions, hypnosis will usually be used to supposedly facilitate the process of healing and recovery.

Sometimes, the therapist will not even share this discovery with the woman immediately. Sometimes the alter(s) will request that they not be revealed to the woman's core personality until they (the alters) feel she is ready. It is felt that many of the alters have expended a tremendous amount of time and energy protecting and insulating the woman from the knowledge of what was done to her. Thus, they often think that keeping *"the secret"* is best for her.

However, those who treat MPD feel that, except in mild cases, so much emotional energy is used to maintain all of these different personalities that the woman would be better off dealing with the pain which the personalities conceal.

Therefore, the goal is usually to "arm-wrestle" the alters into revealing themselves to the client and then begin a process of *integration.* It is believed that through various psychodynamic techniques, including insight-oriented therapy frequently bolstered by hypnosis, these different alters can gradually blend back into the core personality.

This is accomplished as the agonized shards of her life are exposed, run through "catharsis" in which the painful memories are relived (sometimes *quite spectacularly)* and lanced—like a hidden psychic boil—so they can heal.

Hypnosis (and occasionally certain drugs) are used primarily to reduce the anxiety and stress of these encounters between the different personalities, enabling them to emerge and talk with the therapist. In chapter 7, we will examine why hypnosis is probably *the worst* technique to use on an MPD client.

Aside from that issue, this kind of therapeutic procedure *takes months, if not years of counseling.* Some therapists counsel each "alter," spending week after week helping them work through and deal with the painful episode which created them. Obviously, this can run into a huge operation!

Some Christian counselors I have spoken with endeavor to get each "alter" to be Born Again. Others believe in praying for deliverance with each "alter," until everyone is integrated and cleaned up.

I would not deny that these therapists are fine men and women who work for the betterment of their clients. And I am sure that those who are Christians are fine Christians! Evidently, what they are doing is helping some people. But is all this really necessary? More importantly,—is it Biblical?[6]

WHAT ABOUT THE CROSS?

I am not going to waste my time discussing the unsaved therapists who are trying to hypnotize and counsel their clients into "wholeness" and "wellness." These clients will emerge with their fractured selves patched together (perhaps) and probably with several thousand dollars lifted off their wallets. They will emerge satisfied with themselves (and their therapist—hopefully), feeling that they have achieved a great personal victory. They will also emerge heading straight to hell faster than a greased ball-bearing sliding down a water-pipe.

The problem with all human-centered therapy is that—no matter how grievous the original hurt done to the person —the therapy is nothing more than a band-aid on the tumor of sin. Sadly, even Christian therapists occasionally leave their clients little better off than they found them. One lady we prayed with spent more than $10,000 on an allegedly Christian therapist and ended up much worse than before.

In some cases, it is the fault of the therapist. There are good and bad (and competent and incompetent) therapists, both Christian and non-Christian. However, I believe that some of the problem rests with the methodology and the understanding of the MPD phenomenon. Even most Christian therapists do not give the cross of Calvary enough room to work. Let's talk about method for a moment.

Virtually all of these therapists, Christian or otherwise, are deeply invested into the concept that for a person who has been abused to become whole or well, *they must work through all the pain that they experienced and not keep it locked in their subconscious.* This is what takes up a great deal of the therapeutic time.

We have counseled with many people who have been "through the mill" with these therapists. Each week, the client is expected to go into the bowels of her unconscious and emerge with some new nugget of pain. This new painful episode is then relived—with as much EMOTION as possible. If the client doesn't achieve this, then they are blocking the pain, and are not being a "good" client.

Sometimes, these cathartic episodes are extremely emotional and dramatic, with the client (often under hypnosis) weeping, screaming and even falling on the floor or fainting, as well as *re-experiencing all the pain* of the initial abuse episode. This usually leaves both client and therapist feeling like wrung out dish rags.[7] I have to ask, where is the Cross in all this?

Assuming the client is a Christian (and the therapist also), what **BIBLICAL** precept demands that they re-experience all the pain of a past injury to facilitate healing? Here's the scenario:

1) The initial abuse inflicted upon the client as a child.

2) The Lord Jesus Christ takes, on the cross, every scintilla of that abuse upon Himself for the woman when she gets saved (Isaiah 53:4-5).

3) The woman, as an adult, re-appropriates (takes it back) and relives the abuse afflicted upon her in #1.

The question is: If Jesus took the pain for the woman, why does she need to take it back? Isn't the experience of Calvary all-sufficient? Look at these precious promises from God's Word:

> **"The Spirit of the Lord is upon me [Jesus], because he hath anointed me to preach the gospel to the poor; he hath sent me to heal the brokenhearted, to preach deliverance to**

> the captives, and recovering of sight to the blind, *to set at liberty them that are bruised,"*
> Luke 4:18

> "For Christ also hath once suffered for sins, the just for the unjust, that he might bring us to God, *being put to death in the flesh, but quickened by the Spirit:"*   1 Pet. 3:18

> "For the zeal of thine house hath eaten me up; *and the reproaches of them that reproached thee [the Christian] are fallen upon me [Jesus]."*   Ps. 69:9

> "For he hath made him to be sin for us, who knew no sin; that we might be made the righteousness of God in him".   2 Cor. 5:21

> "Christ hath redeemed us from the curse of the law, *being made a curse for us:* for it is written, Cursed is every one that hangeth on a tree:"   Gal. 3:13

If Christ took all of the pain, humiliation and cursing upon Himself on the cross for the Christian survivor, can it be Godly therapy to wrest the pain back from Jesus and make the person suffer it again?

BEATING A DEAD HORSE?

This kind of therapy—no matter how many elaborate phrases are used—is based upon a Freudian understanding of human nature and human emotion. This "model" of therapy cannot take into account the finished work of the cross because *it does not believe in it or accept it.* It adopts a "hydraulic" view of human pain and emotion which is not supported by either scientific research or the Bible.

This "hydraulic model" claims that all your pain and negative emotions which are not immediately reacted upon are repressed down into your unconscious, like an emotional trash compactor. Now, there is no scientific or Biblical evidence that we even HAVE an unconscious, but let's not get into that. The Freudian concept underlying this type of therapy is the idea of a psychic hydraulic system.

With real hydraulics, water is forced into chambers. The force of the moving water can push a piston up and move great weights.

This concept postulates that any emotion or pain that is not immediately responded to is pushed down into the wells of the human psyche, which makes something else get **PUSHED UP.** This is why, we are told, people with MPD end up with substance abuse problems. Their compacted (repressed) anger, rage and pain pushes up as a need to drink, take dope, or some other dysfunctional (sinful) behavior.

This is why you have therapies with people screaming at their pillows or pounding their sofas and pretending they are "venting" their anger toward their parents. This may help for unregenerate people (although there is little good science to indicate that it does), but for a Christian victim of abuse, what good does it do to resurrect old hurts and pains when they have already been done away with at the cross? What about Paul's advice?

> "...but this one thing I do, *forgetting those things which are behind,* and reaching forth unto those things which are before, I press

> toward the mark for the prize of the high
> calling of God in Christ Jesus. Let us
> therefore, *as many as be perfect, be thus
> minded:* and if in any thing ye be otherwise
> minded, God shall reveal even this unto
> you."   Phil. 3:13-15

Paul is saying that Christians who wish to walk
closely with the Lord should forget their past and
press on toward the prize of the high calling Jesus
has for them.

Some therapists say that these things are
repressed so deeply, they become "body memories,"
and are part of the person's own body and muscular
system! Paul, again, has the answer:

> "*I am crucified* with Christ: nevertheless I
> live; *yet not I, but Christ liveth in me:* and
> the life which I now live in the flesh I live
> by the faith of the Son of God, who loved
> me, and gave himself for me."   Gal. 2:20

You see that? If the person is Born Again, her old
self is crucified with Christ. That includes the little
girl who was so horribly traumatized! That little girl
lives no more, she is "dead in Christ." Remember,
when a person becomes Born Again, the Holy Spirit
performs a spiritual "operation" on them:

> "In whom also ye are circumcised with the
> circumcision made without hands, *in
> putting off the body of the sins of the flesh by
> the circumcision of Christ:* Buried with him
> in baptism, wherein also ye are risen with
> him through the faith of the operation of
> God, who hath raised him from the dead.
> And you, *being dead in your sins and the*

> uncircumcision of your flesh, hath he
> quickened together with him, having
> forgiven you all trespasses;"   Col. 2:11-13

Your old self is dead! Why else would Paul tell
us, "Likewise reckon ye also yourselves to be *dead*"
(Rom. 6:11). The problem is that all of these therapies
focus the Christian back on the self (which is dead
anyway) and try to "resurrect" those old memories
and experiences. Talk about beating a dead horse!

> "Knowing this, that *our old man is crucified
> with him,* that the body of sin might be
> *destroyed,* that henceforth we should not
> serve sin."   Rom. 6:6

> "Wherefore *if ye be dead with Christ* from
> the rudiments of the world, why, as though
> living in the world, are ye subject to
> ordinances (or the laws of psychoanalysis—
> author),"   Col. 2:20

> "For *ye are dead,* and your life is hid with
> Christ in God."   Col. 3:3

> "For we are the circumcision, which worship
> God in the spirit, and rejoice in Christ
> Jesus, and *have no confidence in the flesh.*"
>   Phil. 3:3

If we are to have no confidence in the flesh, then
why dig down into it to bring back memories of
things now crucified? The rules and principles of
psychoanalysis are fleshly, carnal rules which do not
appear to have any Biblical support.

> "Therefore, brethren, we are debtors, *not to
> the flesh,* to live after the flesh."   Rom. 8:12

Living after the flesh means trying to live after

the rules and limitations that the carnal man makes. The carnal man does not understand that we are spiritually circumcised and cut away from our old nature by the Sword of the Spirit (Heb. 4:12). You cannot make a dead man (or woman) obey laws. He or she is dead and buried!

> "But put ye on the Lord Jesus Christ, and *make not provision for the flesh*, to fulfil the lusts thereof." Rom. 13:14

You see, the "flesh" is the old woman, the one who died when the SRA survivor was Born Again. When you make provision for it, it's like you are trying to feed it, to resurrect it. There is a part of every person's "flesh" that enjoys nursing and talking about painful experiences—especially because such things make them feel special—like a kind of martyr. Indeed, many of these people ARE martyrs, but why dwell on things that are dead (crucified with Christ) and (should be) buried? What profit can there be?

When people are made to re-suffer things they suffered as children, it's as if the therapist is saying, "What Jesus did wasn't enough—you must suffer, too." I'm certain that they don't think it through in that fashion, but they are still doing it. They have bought into the world's lies, and are taking the very shine and glory out of the salvation process.

People often ask me why we bear so few scars from our evil days as Witches, Satanists, drug users, etc. The answer is that "Satanists Bill and Sharon Schnoebelen are **DEAD!**" Jesus now lives in us! Praise His mighty Name! *Every* Christian died the moment they were regenerated. But many Christians are running around like chickens with their heads cut off because no one ever explained this to them.

Therapists who expect people to relive their sufferings are like Dr. Frankenstein, trying to revive dead bodies by sending jolts of emotional lightning through them. They go through incredible torment, sacrifices on the altar of *"science falsely so-called."*

Most of the people we pray for have never heard this wonderful, Biblical reality. I spoke on this topic once at a seminar, and heard several audible sighs of relief from members of the congregation. IT IS ABSOLUTELY AND DIVINELY WONDERFUL! They find it so liberating that *they have permission to forget the things which are behind!* It is so precious to know that those old hurts cannot reach up through the veil of this spiritual circumcision, *unless we invite them to do so.*

Many ask us why their counselors or pastors made them go through such intense suffering when a simple prayer could have resolved the problem.

God doesn't expect His children to regurgitate every awful thing which was ever done to them. *The power of the blood of the Lord Jesus Christ is so much greater than that.* To be certain, if it helps a person to talk about their past, we are delighted to listen, but we explain to them that they can be delivered, healed and made whole by the Lord without having to go through all that.

There can be REAL POWER in letting people tell you their story. James 5:16 tells us to:

"Confess your faults one to another, and pray one for another, that ye may be healed. The effectual fervent prayer of a righteous man availeth much."

Most of these survivors have not so much sinned as been sinned against, but if they WANT to discuss some of their experiences, that is fine. Just so they understand that they don't HAVE to do it, or that they are being a "bad client" if they don't divulge every awful detail.

Jesus doesn't need details! He has the very hairs of our head numbered (Matt. 10:30). He just needs us to invite Him to come into our hearts and souls and set us free. Having established that, in a couple of chapters we will discuss what we believe is really happening with the MPD survivor, and how the Lord can help.

4

Learning to Loose the Bonds

> **"And ye shall know the truth, and the truth shall make you free."** John 8:32

After the run-in Sharon and I had with the demonic at our former pupil's apartment, we decided to stay away from that whole area. We were content to attend church, pray, study the Bible and grow in the Lord.

We already felt the hand of the Lord on our lives, calling us into ministry, but we knew that we needed to grow and mature in His love and wisdom. We were not expecting things to happen so fast!

The pastor who gladly received my huge collection of occult books and bric-a-brac for destruction by fire was still our pastor.[1] I had become a Sunday School superintendent in the church and began to study for ministerial credentials. However, some procedural problems with the by-laws of the organization necessitated that we seek a different fellowship.

The hand of the Lord was in that change, even though the church we began attending was sixty miles from our home in Dubuque! Pastor Don Allen, the pastor at our new church, and his wife, LaVena, were older and more seasoned in the Lord. They had been in ministry almost as long as we had been alive!

They took it upon themselves to truly disciple their new members, spending many Sunday afternoons with us and helping us understand how to study the Bible, pray and grow in Jesus. Much of our early growth in ministry we owe to them.

As months progressed, they asked us if we had ever had prayer ministry for deliverance. We said no, other than praying the prayer in the back of Johanna Michaelsen's excellent book, *The Beautiful Side of Evil* to renounce occultism. Don and LaVena said they were discerning some possible demonic oppression in us.

They had heard all the "gory" details of our lives as Catholics, witches, Masons, Satanists, Trance channelers and even Mormons. In retrospect, it is easy to see that if anyone would have demonic problems—we would!

The church we were in before had an official doctrinal position that a Born Again Christian could not be demonized. The term "demonized" may be new to some Christians. It is actually an Angli-cization of the Greek word frequently used in the New Testament, *daimonizomai*.[2] It is normally used to express a point on the continuum of demonic oppression somewhere between "no demons" and full-blown demon possession.

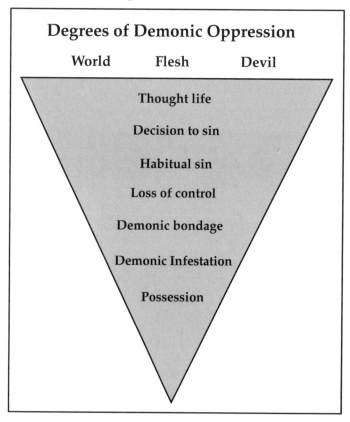

Degrees of Demonic Oppression

World   Flesh   Devil

Thought life

Decision to sin

Habitual sin

Loss of control

Demonic bondage

Demonic Infestation

Possession

Our old fellowship allowed that Christians might be attacked, or severely oppressed, from the outside by fiery darts (Eph. 6:16). But they could not be demonized (i.e. have a demon with them). We were told that the Holy Spirit lives within us! How could a demon live in the same place as the Holy Spirit?

Don and LaVena pointed out that nowhere does the Bible clearly state whether Christians can or cannot be demonized. They also mentioned that the Holy Spirit is everywhere in the universe. Would this mean that there are no demons anywhere in the universe? Obviously not.

Dr. Ed Murphy, a seasoned prayer warrior and missionary who has done years of ministry in this area points out this additional insight.[3]

> **"How is it possible that the flesh still has such a strong pull on the believer's life? How can the Holy Spirit cohabit the same body with the unholy flesh? ...the Scriptures teach that the true believer is no longer in the flesh but in the Spirit (Rom. 8:1-9). How then does the flesh continue to operate in the believer's life alongside the Spirit? This is just as much an apparent contradiction as the cohabitation of the Spirit with a demon in the believer's body. How can all this be possible?"**

Don and LaVena taught that our "flesh" is not any less evil or unclean than is a demon. Both the flesh and demons are in sinful rebellion against a holy God. Yet, if the Holy Spirit can indwell a saved sinner who still has the flesh, why can He not remain in a believer who has a demon?

Certainly, the demon being there would not "hurt" God the Holy Spirit. The thought is absurd.

On the other hand, many Christians feel that being near God might "hurt" the demon and cause it to flee automatically. Unfortunately, this premise is based more on the "Hollywood school of spiritual warfare" (vampires fly from crosses, werewolves flee from wolfbane and silver bullets, etc.) than on any Bible verse.

We asked about 1 John 5:18, which says, "...that wicked one (Satan) toucheth him (the Born Again Christian) not."

Don explained that it depends on how you define those words. Obviously, Ephesians 6:16 shows us clearly that Satan can 'touch' a Christian's body or soul with fiery darts. The issue becomes what part of a Christian CAN'T Satan touch!

He explained to us that we are temples of the Holy Spirit (1 Cor. 3:16). Just like the ancient temple of the Lord in the Old Testament, we have three basic constituents—body, soul, and spirit (1 Thess. 5:23). The temple had the outer court, the Holy Place and the Most Holy Place.

He showed us that just as the Shekinah glory of God resided in the Most Holy Place, and nothing unclean could enter without being consumed with divine fire, so the Holy Spirit dwells in our spirits and keeps them pure. This is the part of our spiritual "anatomy" that the wicked one cannot touch.

However, just as sinful men and objects were brought into the Holy Place and the outer court (Ezek. 8), so in our soul and body, sinful practices—before or after salvation—can cause demonization.

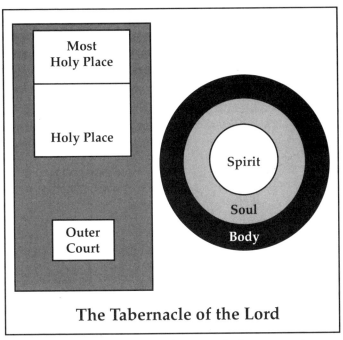

The Tabernacle of the Lord

"You guys must understand that anytime a Christian has not surrendered a part of themselves—however small—to Jesus' Lordship, that part becomes fair game for the devil to come in and take a seat. A lot of Christians still have small areas of their life—anger, bitterness, sinful habits, and such—that they are still clinging to sins. Hopefully, these aren't major, or frequent. But as long as they are there, the devil has an inroad."

He asked us to go to John 11—the story of Jesus raising Lazarus from the dead. Don and LaVena had us read the passage.

"See, kids, what Jesus did with Lazarus is a

perfect picture of what happens to a person when they get saved. You're DEAD in trespasses and sins. Jesus raises you up and gets you spiritually alive without help from any human agency. But look at verse 44:

> **"And he that was dead came forth, bound hand and foot with graveclothes: and his face was bound about with a napkin. Jesus saith unto them,** *Loose him and let him go.*"
> **John 11:44**

The pastor explained, "Many folks with your kind of background get "raised up" from the deadness of sin, but still have on some graveclothes which the Lord wants His servants to remove. That's what we would like to do for you."

We had come to love and trust this couple, so we agreed. The following week, they came to our apartment. Sharon's sister, a "fellow-traveler" on the byways of the occult and Witchcraft, was also there. She was going to go through the same ministry, since our backgrounds were so similar.

They patiently and quietly led us through prayers of renunciation for generational sin (Exodus 20:4-5) from our ancestors, prayers of renunciation of all the many cults we had been in and of our "spirit guides," which were actually familiar spirits or demons. We renounced any "ungodly ties" that were created by sexual sin and asked God to cut those ties.

They also had us command any demons within us to leave—and they did—effortlessly—because that is the kind of good God that Jesus is!

We felt measurably lighter (both physically and spiritually) after that, and our Christian walk took on a new power and vitality. We were blessed by how easy and dignified the entire process was. It was nothing like one would expect from the movies, or even from some Christian books on the subject. But it made sense. God does not want to embarrass His children or give any glory to the adversary.

Deliverance sessions which send people writhing about on the floor, shrieking, vomiting or cursing only serve to demoralize Christians and give the devil a side-show. Praise the Lord that the pastor and his wife who prayed for us were willing to be Biblical, gentle—and most of all, willing to stand aside and let Jesus Christ do His work.

That—we have learned over and over again—is the secret to effectiveness in this kind of ministry!

5

"... My name is Legion: for we are many."

"A double minded man is unstable in all his ways."   **James 1:8**

We have seen how unscriptural it is to make Born Again Christians relive traumatic and often forgotten experiences. However, the dilemma remains. There are people within the Body of Christ who have symptoms of what some psychiatrists call MPD. How are they to be helped, or should they be left to the tender mercies of Dr. Sigmund Frankenstein and his emotional electrodes?

If we are not to probe deeply and painfully into long-buried memories of childhood trauma and abuse (since such things are already crucified with Christ), then *how are we to proceed?* Is MPD a genuine affliction, or can it be safely ignored as a psychological conceit like the Oedipus complex? These are important questions which face pastors and Christian workers—some of them quite frequently.

In Chapter 3, we explained how the prevailing psychiatric theory accounts for the Multiple Personality phenomenon. We need to see if there is room within the BIBLICAL view of the human person for that kind of situation to develop.

In my opinion, disassociation is a real phenomenon. I believe psychologists are right—we all do a little bit of it. I also believe that creative people do it more than others. Getting "lost" in a good book is like disassociating. We all have experienced this. This is a mysterious process within the human soul, and I certainly don't understand it. The question is—can this kind of mild disassociation be extrapolated into MPD validly?

Also, *disassociation and even insanity are the very essence of magic.* No one can be a skilled magician without being able to disassociate in a powerful way. The point of having a "magickal identity," a "witch name," and a "Magick circle" to do your rituals in is that you leave the mundane world behind and "dissociate" yourself into an alternate "reality."

As witches and later Satanists, we held a series of fairly mundane jobs. Yet, when we entered our "sacred space" and put on our robes and our magic names, we ceased to be "Bill the teacher" or "Sharon the phlebotomist" and became something _entirely Other_. In fact, we practiced assiduously at being something entirely other—so much so that we often believed it ourselves. That's the essence of magic. But it's also the essence of madness and/or demonization.

Thus, it is not difficult to imagine that a child raised around Satanists might be conditioned to do such things. Some people who work with SRA survivors believe that the multiple personality phenomenon is either _deliberately created or exploited_ by the coven leaders to ensure secrecy. They feel that MPD might be a way that Satanists make sure the child never talks because the truth is buried in a rat's nest of split identities and alters.

These people aren't certain whether the MPD is a natural defense mechanism of the child's mind which the Satanists have discovered and exploited, or an artificial creation of the Satanists.

TWISTED TOOLS AND TWISTED MINDS?

So little is understood about MPD that almost anything is possible. We must bear in mind that the building blocks of MPD—dissociated personalities— are necessary tools of shamans, witches, Satanists and even psychics and trance channelers. This also means that they are the _tools demons use to make such people function in an apparently supernatural fashion._

Almost all witches and Satanists are trained to go into meditation or relaxation, to achieve a state of no-thought or "stilling the mind." It is one of the first lessons in Witchcraft. This means basically vacating the mind so that someone or something else can use it. Most low-level witches never consider it a possibility that something evil might take them over.

They are under the delusion that if they do their meditation or "quieting the mind" in a protective magic circle, they will be safe from harm. Actually, the magic circle is about as much protection as a screen-door in a submarine.

Through this kind of exercise, witches hope to contact a familiar or spirit teacher (terms vary but the idea is the same). This is believed to be an evolved being who no longer needs a body but hangs around the earth plane like a spiritual tutor, helping witches and psychics develop magically and spiritually.

For example, the first entity I contacted, around 1971, called himself "Ambrosius," and claimed to be a 15th century monk. Ambrosius stayed with me until a Christian pastor commanded it to depart in the name of Jesus in 1985. "Ambrosius" *was a demon!* I invited him (or it) into my body hundreds, if not thousands of times, and he created quite a stronghold for himself (see 2 Cor. 10:4).

A very similar phenomenon happens with SRA victims and the resulting splitting of personalities. But, instead of the child being taught meditation, *she is ritually abused!*

Something so horrifying is done to the child that she either leaves her body behind and lets it occur—like abandoning ship—OR she blanks out and retreats into a tiny part of her soul and "buries her head in the sand," metaphorically speaking.

Whether or not human beings have the ability to leave their body, either at will, or in times of extreme stress (called astral projection or out-of-body experiences—OOBE's) is a matter of controversy among sincere Christians. From my experience in the occult and my subsequent study of the Bible, I can find *nothing* that would lead me to believe that people cannot be drawn out of their bodies, either by the Lord, or by Satan.

Willfully leaving your body is a dangerous OPEN DOOR to Satanic infestation. It can normally only be done through the agency of Satan or his demons. **Rarely**, God causes this to happen to His children for His own sovereign purposes (Rev. 1:10). Then it is not sinful, because the Lord is doing it.

In any event, whether the child retreats within herself or out of the body during the abuse, the effect is the same. Once her body is left unprotected, for whatever reason, it is open to demonic invasion. This is especially true if the child is being sexually violated, since any sort of illicit relations are a key channel through which demons can pass—called an UNGODLY SOUL TIE (See Mark 10:8, 1 Cor. 6:15-18).

Once the demon strongman has taken residence in the child, repeats of the abuse will cause its hold to grow deeper and deeper. This becomes a strong hold. The order is not always clear here. In older people, who are more capable of willful, repeated sins, sinful acts create a strong hold, then a strongman will inhabit. In either case, the effect is the same on the child's soul. The stronghold becomes like a "boil" or a "tumor" on the child's soul, and leaves its mark.

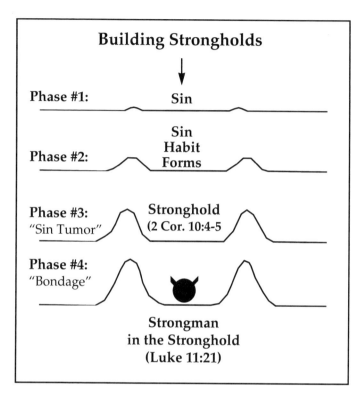

Unfortunately, because of the nature of ritual abuse, it usually creates a multitude of strongholds. For example, children who are abused are extremely frightened. This kind of terror is an invitation to the Spirit of Fear (2 Tim. 1:7). Being sexually defiled can be an open door for the Spirit of Jealousy (Numbers 5:14). Thus, the child's psyche takes MULTIPLE DEEP PENETRATION "HITS," from Satan's minions through the abuse.

Each time the abuse is afflicted, the "boil" gets

deeper and the stronghold gets more firmly entrenched. Thus, the child's soul (if it could be seen) begins to look like the craters of the moon—pockmarked with deep spiritual strongholds created by multiple abuse.

THE DIABOLICAL DIAMOND-CUTTER

The Bible does not precisely speak on the subject of MPD. It does talk about being "double-minded" (James 1:8). One Christian therapist whom I love and respect said that if you can have a double-minded person, why can't you have a *twenty-minded person?* I think this is *possible,* but we need to look at other explanations—explanations which are more in line with the Biblical view of human nature, and are less inclined to be influenced by Freud, et.al.

The root of the word which we translate as "diabolical" comes from the Greek, *Diabolos.* Oddly enough, the exact denotative *opposite* of diabolic is "symbolic." Just as a "SYM-BOL" draws two different things together—such as saying that the flag (a piece of cloth) is a symbol of *America* (a huge piece of land), so DIA-BOL splits things in two which should be together. Thus, the essence of the diabolic is to cause division, drive wedges and force things apart.

We see this in other areas of the devil's work. He splits up friendships, marriages, churches and even entire fellowships! So why shouldn't he do it within the human soul, if given the opportunity?

After praying for many people the Lord has shown us that there is an MPD-like phenomenon.

But the spiritual/emotional mechanics of it are *vastly different* than what is supposed among the psychiatric community. Needless to say, the "treatment" is also different.

Let's return to strongholds. Biblically, each stronghold, if skillfully constructed through Satan's demons and human slaves, contains a demonic strongman. All it takes is two such deep strongholds to create this sort of wedge in the human soul:

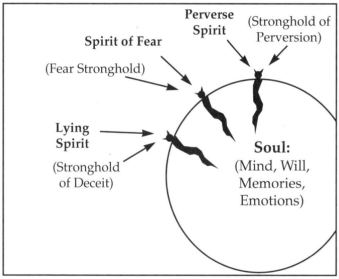

As these strongholds drive deeper with each incident of abuse, a fragment of the soul is separated from the rest. *It is still a part of the girl's soul, it is not demonic.* However, it is demonically created *and sustained*, and that is the BIG DIFFERENCE.

Over time, Satan drives these wedges into more and more areas of the child's soul until she has a fractured pile of emotional rubble—like what is hypothesized in MPD. Each fracture develops a personality around the core experience of the strongman/stronghold which sustains it. After awhile, it is difficult for anyone to tell where human personality fragments end and demons begin.

Often, the therapeutic community chastises Christian workers and pastors for trying to cast out "alters" which are not demons at all. This does get confusing, especially when some "alters" take (or are given) names like "Demon" or "Satan." However, the therapists are doing something far more dangerous by using hypnosis to try and help these different "alters" interact and integrate. The end result of SRA could well be a soul that looks like this:

Personality "Fragments" or "Alters" are the "flesh" or "old man" (Rom. 7:5, 18; 8:9) You cannot "cast out" the flesh, you can only crucify it (Rom. 6:6, Gal. 5:24).

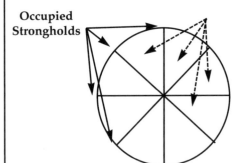

Occupied Strongholds

Portrait of a soul fragmented by severe multiple "hits" of abuse, and deliberate, scientific creation of many demonic strongholds. Only Jesus can tear down the walls (Eph. 2:14)!

The pie "wedges" are the human personality fragments, and the black stilettos are the demonic strongholds which keep them apart. Another metaphor which might help explain this situation is to think of the SRA survivor's soul as a brick wall. The bricks are part of the human personality, and the mortar—which both separates them and keeps them from completely flying apart—is the demonic strongholds.

No matter how you look at it, it's a multi-dimensional problem. You are dealing both with the human soul and demonic infestation. There is one more factor to consider.

THE SPIRIT OF LEGION

Legion is a variety of the Unclean Spirit. The very name often strikes fear into people's hearts because they assume it is some big, mean dude of a demon that was SO BA-AD that Jesus had to send it into an entire herd of pigs. Nothing less could contain it. Actually, Legion is just another "punk" of a demon. Compared to the power of the blood of Jesus, he is less than a fly speck. However, because he is not well known or understood, he can cause some problems.

It has been our experience that Legion is usually present as a strongman when the person suffered a sexual abuse or defilement as a child. This means that virtually all SRA survivors have a "Legion problem." This is where things can get confusing.

It is Legion's nature to be many different "genres" of demons rolled into one. In other words, although Legion has some distinctive traits, he can manifest as any other strongman in the Bible! This means he can put out a multitude of different "faces" to obscure and cloud the prayer session.

Legion can produce some very paradoxical behavior in the person he inhabits. These two facts can often create a purely demonic problem which is a precise "look—alike" for MPD. People who are afflicted with Legion tend to be either:

• Extremely compulsive in their behavior, very neat, tidy, totally into cleanliness, concerned with logic and precision in every aspect of life, and are perfectionistic. They often suffer from Anorexia or Bulimia, tend to write in an uncharacteristic blocky, precise almost machine-like hand and are excessively fearful of germs, infections... OR

• They are obsessed with decay and like to be around the smell of garbage or decayed flesh (i.e. cemeteries). They often feel compelled to perform bathroom duties outside in nature and may even wallow in or consume animal or human waste.

They may manifest both of these extremes at different times, or only one. Similarly, Legion can cause people to be:

• Flagrant in their nudity, exhibitionism and pre-occupation with sex, homosexuality, sex perversions and adultery. Often, if they are attractive enough, adults with Legion end up full-time in the pornography industry, ... OR

• Modest and prudish in the extreme. They are

reclusive, rigid and very controlled, fearful to shower in front of members of their own sex (as in physical education or health clubs), unable to enjoy sex even with their spouse and often will not even undress in front of their partner.

Legion also manifests often in these ways:

• Serious insomnia.

• Superhuman strength.

• Self-destructive behaviors (as with a deaf and dumb spirit), mutilation of self, suicide.

• Hearing many different voices in their head.

These are extreme cases, and if the person is a Christian, obviously Legion's power to draw them into many of these "less acceptable" behaviors is curtailed by the presence of the Holy Spirit. In such cases, usually the more perfectionistic and prudish side of Legion is allowed to manifest by the person, since such behavior is tolerated—even appreciated— within Christian circles. The person will fight, with the Holy Spirit's powerful help, their compulsions toward either sexual sin or scatological behavior.

Because of the chameleon-like nature of Legion, it is wiser to *assume* that Legion is present if the person alleges to have been sexually or ritually abused. It is important to be gentle in discussing the demonic with any person who comes for prayer, but it is especially true when bringing up Legion, because his "reputation" as a "major league" imp precedes him, and we need to reassure the person that Jesus is more than able to deal with Legion.

Thus, depending on the history of the person and their reported symptoms, it is possible that an SRA survivor who brings MPD symptoms to the prayer session may well have both Legion and numerous other strongmen infesting them.

FIRST THINGS FIRST!

As you may have noticed, it is the essence of Satan and his workers (either human or inhuman) to make things complicated. That is why he loves psychology, because it makes everything—especially getting free—quite complex. The Bible gives us no warrant to deal with each "alter" individually and get each saved and delivered in a process that could take months or even years, though many well-meaning Christian counselors try.

We know of one alleged SRA survivor who went to a Christian therapist three times a week (at well over $100 a session) for a year and a half, trying to untangle the psychological ball of twine which this MPD hypothesis had created. Sadly, she ended up worse at the end of the process. And hers is not an isolated case.

Obviously, Jesus did not sit down with the Gadarene demoniac and deal individually with the hundreds (or thousands) of demons within him. Although we do not have the same "full measure" of the Holy Spirit that Jesus did, we can simplify the process a bit toward that direction.

Our hypothesis, working from the assumptions outlined above, is that the ***primary cause*** of the perceived disintegration of the person's personality structure is the demonic infestation. Please note, it is not the ONLY cause, but we proceed on the assumption that it is the primary cause.

We have learned from experience that most child abuse victims (ritual or not) are infested with Legion, and probably other demonic strongmen. Unlike some other Godly and well-meaning prayer counselors, we believe that the FIRST step on the road to spiritual recovery is to be cleansed by the power of Jesus Christ from any possible demonic oppression.

Why should deliverance be first? Because our Biblical warrant of authority is *absolutely clean-cut* there. We are on very firm ground. If the survivor is a Christian, then the Bible is clear about the believer's authority. The devil's lackeys are squatters on "ground" that rightfully belongs to the Lord Jesus Christ! They are only there on "legal technicalities" that a few prayers can almost always clear up.

The Bible is *absolutely straight-forward* about this. If you as a Christian cover in the blood of Jesus any "legal ground" the devil has in your life, then the demons have to scoot (Mark 16:17). They cannot argue, they cannot sass you, they cannot hang on, and they cannot make you vomit. They have to leave and they do leave! Praise the mighty name of Jesus! Often, people are astonished at *how beautiful and simple the process is.*

Hollywood—and the media generally—have done everything in their power to destroy people's faith in the process of deliverance ("exorcism"). They have most people (even most Christians!) believing it is some weird, exotic ritual with people's heads spinning around or the client levitating or crawling on the ceiling or spewing fire out of her mouth. What sane person, Christian or otherwise, would wish to be subjected to all that—PLUS have some idiot in a black robe and a purple stole hollering at them and sloshing salt ("holy") water in their face?

That's why we do not even call it exorcism. It is not a scriptural term, since exorcism is actually a magical ceremony done by Jewish priests (and later Roman Catholic priests) who had no authority from the Lord. They got their clocks cleaned by the demon-possessed man and had to flee the residence naked and wounded (Acts 19:13-16). Usually, we just call it "prayer" (or more rarely, deliverance) because that is what it is!

We do the prayer for spiritual liberation first because we feel it is a lot easier to take a "fort" once the enemy has been removed from it. Remember our diagram a couple of pages back? You have strongholds driving deep into the person's soul and cracking wedges in it. Once those demons are removed, those strongholds are empty! *Nothing* remains to hold them apart but the person herself!

LET'S KEEP IT SIMPLE!

That's why it can be so simple, because once the strongmen (especially Legion) have been cast out, legally—juridically—the woman's soul is one again. The only thing keeping the "wedges" or "alters" from coming back together are the strongholds that have already been stripped of the demonic power which energized them. The strongholds themselves are constructed out of what Paul calls "the flesh" or the sin nature. Thus, through simple and prevailing prayer therapy, they begin to dissolve.

An easy way to understand a stronghold is that it was originally a bad habit, sin or mental or emotional way of viewing oneself which was outside the will of God. Obviously, many of the strongholds of an abuse survivor were created through no fault of her own. However, because some of her responses were sinful, they were still "ground" which Satan could claim.

Thus, to a term from a long-standing expert in this area, Dr. Ed Murphy, we have a "Continuum of Sin."[1] The strong hold is created by there being:

1) Sinful thought: Caused either by our flesh, the environment or Satan's servants (1 John 2:16). If not resisted, it leads to...

2) Sinful choice: To actually sin, in thought, word or deed. If this is repeated often enough, it leads to...

3) Sinful habit: This is where the stronghold begins to be constructed out of "the flesh" or sin nature. It is like a behavioral "groove" or "rut" which is easier to move into than to climb out of. If not resisted, this habit leads to...

4) Loss of control: Here is where the person no longer has a clear choice whether to sin or not, and this is where the demonic element begins to really take hold. If not stopped, this leads to...

5) Bondage: Here the strongman has taken residence in the stronghold and the person is demonically bound. If there is no spiritual intervention, we then have…

6) Total control: This is rare—if not virtually impossible—for a Christian to experience. In a non-Christian this would be demon possession. In a Christian, it would be the most serious form of demon oppression imaginable. We have only encountered a few like this.

That is how a stronghold is built, and it can be dismantled by:

1) Confessing and renouncing the sinful behavior to God.

2) Casting out the strongman through the power of Jesus.

3) In prayer, ask the Lord to dismantle the stronghold.

4) Surrender to God's Lordship of those areas of your emotional and thought life which Satan had prior control over.

5) Have prayer for healing of any emotional scars caused by the stronghold.

6) In prayer, ask the Lord to help you forsake the sinful habits which caused the stronghold (if any), then make your best effort to forsake the habit.[2]

That is how simple it can be. No agonized hypnotic catharsis—no trying to save and deliver twenty or thirty alter personalities. Just pray and cast out the demons that caused the fragmentation and then invite the Holy Spirit to come in and knit the fragile parts back together the way HE wants them. After all, He knows a whole lot more about the human personality of the person than you or me—or Sigmund Freud.

The wonderful thing about this approach is that it does not require that the person being prayed for reject the MPD hypothesis. It will work even if the person holds onto the MPD concept, although the healing may take a bit longer because of the person's expectation. Thus, this kind of prayer ministry can meet the person "where she is," and transform her without shattering any cherished beliefs.

If MPD is really a valid concept as described by secular psychiatrists, then this sort of prayer ministry can do no harm to the treatment. We are not trying to "cast out" the "alters," only those demon strongmen which exist in the interstices between the alters. Thus, no psychic violence is done. The only problems that can arise is if the psychiatrist continues to use hypnosis after the prayers. That can, as we shall see, often open doors for further oppression.

That is why we are now going to take a careful, scriptural look at hypnosis.

6

Stabs in the Darkness

> "Not by might, nor by power, but by my spirit, saith the Lord of Hosts."
>
> **Zechariah 4:6**

The lady was shrieking at the top of her lungs! I sat forward in my chair, inwardly thanking God that my office was out in the middle of the country where no one could hear. I was afraid someone would call the police.

"In the name of Jesus, I command you to be silent," my partner in prayer said in a low, firm voice.

But the lady kept on—her ululating wails were almost deafening in the small office. She was a large woman, and began shaking in her chair. On one side of her a female Christian friend was trying to hold her hand and comfort her. On the other side was the fellow who had asked me to sit in on this prayer session—an extremely intense young evangelist named James.

James claimed to have been a victim of multi-generational sexual abuse himself, and part of a major New Age-type cult. He also claimed to have prayed for hundreds of people to be set free from demonic bondage. This woman was one of his "clients," and was definitely challenging his ability to control the deliverance session.

Multi-generational Satanists are those who were born into families which have been Satanists for centuries. This is similar to Christian families that have been Baptists or Lutherans for generations. But instead of a heritage of salvation and Christian love, they get Satan's twisted catechism of pain and agony.

Many SRA survivors claim to be from multi-generational families. This makes sense, if their memories are to be believed, because they are often abused from before they can even talk or walk. James, for example, claimed he was indoctrinated and tortured into being a trance medium (or channeler) before he was three!

These multi-generational covens also produce what has come to be known in the field as "breeders." Breeders are women or young pubescent girls who have babies in Satanic ritual contexts. They are often impregnated with ritual rape. The baby is born, but not registered. Many witches, including Sharon and I, were trained to be midwives and encouraged to oversee the birth of their own children without hospital or any other official intervention.

Thus, when the baby is born, it is officially non-existent. The government doesn't know it is out there. Then, it is usually sacrificed. Often, the mother is forced to do the ritual murder herself, although some of them have become so callused and demonized that they do it willingly.

The screaming woman—call her Mamie—claimed to have been a breeder who was forced to kill two of her own babies in satanic rituals. Now, she was saved, but was still oppressed by demon spirits. James asked me to sit in because I had more first-hand knowledge of hard-core satanic practice.

When the woman's screams got louder, we began to sing Christian hymns and worship choruses about the blood of Jesus. The more volume to her screams, the more we sang out. It was a deafening encounter.

Finally, the woman wore herself out. Her screams subsided to hoarse croaks. James demanded to know the name of the demon spirit that was controlling her. It was not a good idea. Instantly, Mamie began to growl—a deep, basso-profundo growl that sounded like a cougar stuck in a storm drain.

"I discern it is a spirit of anger," James declared. He put his hand on her head and raised his voice over the snarling. "Spirit of anger, I command you to be gone in Jesus' name."

We all said "Amen," but the lady kept growling and James yanked his hand back as if he had touched a hot stove. The roars were getting louder, and I was beginning to despair of getting out of this prayer session with my eardrums intact.

"Why aren't you leaving?" I asked the spirit.

"I don't have to go," came the hoarse reply. "She sins! She sins all the time!"

"Satan, you are a liar," announced James. "You have no legal right to remain here."

Mamie (or something within Mamie) swore fluently at them. I wished Sharon was there, but she was at her secular job. I wasn't certain if any of us knew what we were doing—especially me!

This back and forth argument with the entities inside Mamie went on for another two hours. In total, the session was crowding five hours! This was only about the fourth deliverance prayer session I had been involved in, and it was definitely the worst.

Finally, James commanded the spirits of anger and bitterness to leave in Jesus' name. The screeching and growling stopped. Mamie burped and coughed a few times, and James said he discerned the spirits were cast out, but nothing seemed any different to me, other than the decrease in sound effects.

Poor Mamie was wrung out like a dishrag, and we were surprised she had any voice left. She wanly admitted she felt a little better, and she and her friend staggered out to the car.

James was also exhausted. "That was a tough one!" he admitted.

"Why was it so difficult?" I asked.

"Most of them are like that," James said. "The demons really resist coming out."

"But in the Bible, Jesus just tells them to go and they go. There's none of this arguing or screaming— at least not for mόre than a few seconds."

James smiled a tired smile. "We're not Jesus."

I gave him a slightly exasperated look. "I KNOW that, but He gave us His authority. What are we doing wrong?"

"Nothing," James insisted. "That's just the way it's done."

I asked myself under my breath: "But is it Biblical?"

A LESSON IN DOORWAYS

The next day, I sat down with an older minister named Hank. Hank had been doing this sort of ministry for many years. In fact, he was the resident "deliverance minister" in the area. I asked him why there was such a struggle? Hank asked if I knew about access points. I shook my head, no.

"Some people call them doorways or open doors. They can make all the difference in the world."

Hank proceeded to tell me about a prayer session that he had been involved in just a few days earlier, along with a local pastor and a lady prayer warrior.

The candidate for deliverance was a girl whose mother was a former witch. Her father was a former Freemason. The girl, around 11-12 years of age, had severe epilepsy which was not amenable to medication. Her illness had reduced her mental abilities to such a state that she functioned at about the level of an eight or nine year old.

Hank explained that a key thing he did in cases like that was have the parents—if Christians—pray to renounce generational curses. These, he explained, were especially common in people with backgrounds in any kind of idolatry—i.e., Wicca or Freemasonry! Right in the Ten Commandments, it clearly teaches:

> **"Thou shalt not make unto thee any graven image, or any likeness of any thing that is in heaven above, or that is in the earth beneath, or that is in the water under the earth. Thou shalt not bow down thyself to them, nor serve them: for I the Lord thy God am a jealous God, visiting the iniquity of the fathers upon the children unto the third and fourth generation of them that hate me: And showing mercy unto thousands of them that love me and keep my commandments."** **Exodus 20:4-6**

I couldn't recall James doing that with any of the people he prayed with. Hank explained that if there is idolatry (being in any cult or worshipping any false god) or other serious sin (drunkenness, suicide, sexual immorality, etc.) in the parents, then it could be an "open doorway," an access point through which Satan still might have legal right to come and trouble the person or their children.

"That might be why James had such trouble casting the demons out of this person," Hank suggested. He went on to say that the prayer sessions for this girl were grueling and tiresome even so. Finally, only one spirit was left. Hank and his prayer team—including the parents of the child— were seated in their living room. The girl herself was sprawled in the middle of the floor—exhausted.

Hank admitted that he was bewildered by the resistance they were experiencing. As they all took a breather for a moment, the girl looked up at him. Her young eyes suddenly blazed with the cold fires of disdain. A voice within the child spoke: "You cannot make me leave. I have a right to stay."

Hank sat forward and noted the girl's eyes dart briefly to the dining room. Prompted by the Holy Spirit, he walked casually into the dining room. He could feel the alien eyes of the thing within the girl upon him. He followed the direction of the girl's glance and saw a wooden rack filled with small collectible antique spoons.

Carefully, Hank ran his eyes over the extensive collection. Then something caught his attention. One of the tiny spoons had a little devil face or gargoyle on it, carved in bas-relief. It was scarcely more than a quarter-inch in size. He plucked out the spoon, pled the blood of Jesus over it and threw it out the open window.

Instantly, with a whimpering sigh, the demon left the girl! That devil-faced spoon, something the mother had bought years ago, was a tiny idol! With it gone from the house, the demon had no right to remain in the child. After that, the girl's epilepsy improved dramatically. Hank said to me:

"Understand, Bill. There are many different access points which Satan can use to make his claim to leave his demons within a person. It can be sin in the person's life, or sin in the life of the person doing the praying. That is why the Lord said that often certain spirits only come out through prayer and fasting (Matt. 17:21). Those practices draw us closer to Him, sharpen our discernment, and help us discern our own sinful nature more clearly."

A KEY TO THE PUZZLE

Later that night, I discussed the matter with Sharon. We prayed and sought the Lord for what the problem could have been with Mamie's deliverance. Eventually, the Lord took us to a passage in 1 Samuel 28 which concerned the woman with a familiar spirit in Endor whom King Saul consulted.

We noted that the sin of consulting a familiar spirit was so serious that it cost Saul his life (1 Samuel 28:19)! We understood that a familiar spirit was actually a demon masquerading as a departed loved one or family member.

It hit us like a thunderbolt. Seeking information from a demon was actually CONSULTING A SPIRIT. It was a kind of mediumship or channeling! Thus, for ministers to demand to know the name of a demon or how it came into a person was actually committing the sin of divination or necromancy![1]

Not only that, but the demonized person was committing the sin of mediumship or channeling.

Why, then, did ministers of the gospel do it? It was a very popular technique, especially in circles of "deliverance ministry" to have conversations with the demon—inquiring various things of it: how it came into the person, its name, etc. We began an exhaustive study of the Bible, trying to find any example of people doing that with demons.

The only place we found information being solicited from a demon was the single incident (reported in two gospels) of the Gadarene demoniac. Jesus asked the demon's name—Legion (Mark 5:9-10, Luke 8:38).

We knew enough about Bible hermeneutics to know that building a doctrine upon one isolated incident in scripture was tricky at best. That was how cults like the Jehovah's Witnesses and Mormons began—as we knew all too well!

PUTTING IT ALL TOGETHER

For the rest of the year, we did an exhaustive study of this subject. We found no indication that Christians could force demons to tell us the truth. We heard of some deliverance teachers claiming that they commanded demons to go before the throne of God, where they would be forced to tell the truth.

However, nowhere in the Bible does it say that we have the right to: a.) Command demons to go to the throne of God—or: b.) That such a trip would force them to be truthful. The Bible only indicates that we can do two simple things which Jesus did:

1) Command them to shut up.

2) Command them to get out of the person.

We watched a couple of friends who were involved in this ministry begin to get a bit "weird" doctrinally. We were quite afraid of the same thing happening to us. Therefore, we determined not to do anything in our prayer sessions with people for which we could not find specific reasons in the Bible.

We quickly realized that it was ludicrous and even dangerous to rely upon information provided by demons when all Christians have the Spirit of the living God within them. The Holy Spirit—if asked—will surely tell His children what they need to know to fight the forces of darkness. Why should we rely upon enemy spirits when the all-knowing Holy Spirit is willing to tell us anything we need to know.

It seemed clear that there was little difference between mediumship and seeking information from demon spirits—except that the practitioners of the former are unsaved New Agers and Spiritists and the practitioners of the latter are Christians. Thus, we asked the Lord to help us rely only on Him and not on any "enemy intelligence."

Interestingly enough, the next prayer session which came along, took a lot less time and effort— and the person was gloriously set free by our precious Lord Jesus Christ!

7

The Sleep of the Serpent

> "...a certain damsel possessed with a spirit of divination met us, which brought her masters much gain by soothsaying."
>
> **Acts 16:16b**

What is so dangerous about using hypnosis to help a person who thinks they suffer from MPD?

After being used by clinicians for more than a century, there is *no conclusive scientific explanation for what it is or why it works*—only a multitude of conflicting hypotheses.[1] Even the doctors must admit that hypnosis has a very spotty past.

The *(comparatively)* modern inventor of hypnosis is the **occult** healer Franz Anton Mesmer (1734-1815), who used "animal magnetism" in his healings. The concept of animal magnetism itself is based upon the doctrines of magnetic fluid developed by what a "Christian" encyclopedia of psychology euphemistically calls a "controversial doctor,"[2] Paracelsus. Calling Paracelsus a controversial doctor is like calling Anton LaVey a "moderately liberal theological scholar!"

Aurælus Philippus Theophrastus Paracelsus Bombast von Hohenheim (1493-1541) was the premier occultist and sorcerer of his century.[3] He was also probably the greatest alchemist who ever lived.[4] Paracelsus was one of *our* greatest heroes when we were into Witchcraft and Satanism!

Alchemy (the attempt to create an elixir of life which would enable one to live forever—among other things), sorcery and astrology were his fortés, including attempting to create tiny, artificial people, called homunculi, human children in miniature![5]

This is all the blackest sort of magick imaginable, and he was hounded from his home in Basle. The man was regarded as a satanic genius. History indicates that he was *poisoned to death by his own medical faculty* from that noted university in Basle. So much for finding the elixir of life.

Paracelsus' theories were picked up a bit later by a German mathematician, Athanasius Kircher (c.1646) who proposed that this magnetic fluid was a force in nature which caused disease. Mesmer popularized animal magnetism and used it to put people in trances so they could supposedly be healed.[6] This is why hypnosis used to be called "mesmerism." Mesmer, not surprisingly, was frequently accused of quackery and fraud.

The magnetic fluid theory was later discarded, and replaced by the psychological theories of a professor named Bernheim in the mid 1800's. Freud popularized its use in psychoanalysis. Please understand that NONE of the theories about hypnosis are any more provable than the old magnetic fluid theory. They are, for the most part, rooted in Freud's theories of the unconscious—again, *unproven.*

None of these people really invented hypnosis. Its use dates back to the dawn of history, when witches and shamans used it to facilitate healing. To this very day, most witch priestesses and priests (including ourselves) were well trained in the use of hypnosis.

In our counseling, with virtually all Christians, we have observed that in many cases hypnosis is a key **"doorway"** for demonic access—whether it's done on a stage by a performing clown, or in an office by a psychiatrist.

As witches and as Christians, we have observed that there doesn't seem to be any quicker way for a person to get demonized *than to be hypnotized.*

In fact, in the higher levels of Satanism, where we and our colleagues actually *sought* to be demon possessed, we often found that hypnosis aided the process considerably and made it easier for the demon spirits to assume complete control of our bodies, souls and spirits. This was (and is) because hypnosis produces a passive mental state.

WHAT SAITH THE SCRIPTURE?

Let's see what the Bible says about enchantments, charming and trances (these are the words used in the Bible for the hypnosis phenomenon).

Trances can be dealt with fairly easily because the term is only applied to two people in the Bible, Balaam, a heathen prophet in Numbers 24, and Peter in Acts 10-11. In BOTH cases, the trance fell on them *from God*. In Peter's case, it is was entirely unsolicited and unexpected. And Balaam got a trance he wasn't anticipating.

That is an important distinction because one thing that most Bible students agree upon is that the Holy Spirit occasionally induces phenomena in people that, *if not Spirit-led, would be deeply sinful.* Examples of this abound, and include:

1) Astral vision or clairvoyance (2 Kgs. 6:17).

2) Foretelling death for people (Acts 5:1-10).

3) Astral projection (Acts 8:39).

4) Cursing people (2 Kgs. 1:10 ff, 2 Kgs. 2:24).

5) Preternatural strength (Jgs 14:6).

However, the distinction is: we *must not seek these things out!* Peter was not on his roof praying for God to give him a vision. Nor did someone put him in a trance (as happens with hypnosis in the doctor's office). It just came to him out of the blue as a sovereign move of God.

Thus, you can search the Bible from stem to stern to find a Godly person hypnotizing someone for therapeutic (healing) purposes, but you won't find it.

Yet, the Bible DOES speak about hypnosis quite clearly, but you have to understand the terms in which it is phrased. As mentioned, two key words to look for in the Old Testament are "charmers" (Deut. 18:11, Isa. 19:3) and "enchantments" (Isa. 47:9, 12). In these passages, such practices are *soundly condemned* by the Lord as sinful, and mentioned in the same breath with wizards, familiar spirits (2 Kgs. 21:6), and even child sacrifice (2 Kgs. 17:17).

The first term, "charmers," invariably refers to sorcerers who used primitive forms of hypnosis to achieve their ends. Today, the word "to charm" or "charming" carries the idea of a hypnotic fascination, although they are usually applied to beautiful women or handsome men. This actually means to "cast a spell" over someone to make them think that someone is something they are not. Female witches sometimes did this to make themselves more glamorous.

From the realm of pagan legends, there is the account of Merlin the magician "charming" a woman so she would think that the man who came to her bed was her husband when actually it was his enemy, Uther Pendragon. The child fathered that night was the celebrated King Arthur. This is not much different from the stage hypnotist who hypnotizes some poor unfortunate into thinking they are a chicken.

The term, "enchantments," can also be applied to hypnotic techniques, as well as other occult practices. Again, today the term has a connotation of being beguiling or overwhelming in one's ability to influence another. It's important to remember that the origins of hypnosis are firmly rooted in shamanism (witch doctoring). That does not in-and-of-itself make them evil. Shamans used herbs for healing, and many of those herbs are still widely used today.

However, unlike herbal medicine, these hypnotic techniques are designed to impact not the body (except in cases of somatization[7]), but the soul or the spirit. This makes it pretty tricky from a spiritual perspective. The whole point of hypnosis is the creation of an altered state of consciousness in which the mind is more suggestible. In most cases it results in passivity.

Virtually EVERY person who ministers in the area of deliverance agrees that passivity is one of the most dangerous and vulnerable states for a person to be in—especially if they are at risk for demonic attack. Since most Christians who seek hypnotherapy are likely to be spiritually or emotionally out of balance, they would probably be more at risk than usual. Thus, you have a prime candidate for demonic attack sitting in a therapist's office and (without knowing it) begging demons to come in by allowing their therapist to hypnotize them.

CHARMED BY THE SERPENT

An even more alarming scriptural problem with hypnosis is found in the New Testament during the ministry of Paul. In the book of Acts, we find this:

> "And it came to pass, as we went to prayer, a certain damsel possessed with *a spirit of divination* met us, which brought her masters much gain by soothsaying: The same followed Paul and us, and cried, saying, These men are the servants of the most high God, which show unto us the way of salvation. And this did she many days. But Paul, being grieved, turned and said to the spirit, I command thee in the name of Jesus Christ to come out of her. And he came out the same hour"
>
> Acts 16:16-18

Here is one of the most powerful and dangerous demons encountered in sorcery, commonly called the "spirit of divination." However—and this is critical—the Greek words there are *pneuma Puthonos,* literally meaning "spirit of Python." What does this have to do with hypnosis?

We need to get back into the cultural context. This young lady was actually called a "Pythoness." This gets into a *vital and dangerous point of demonic access.* The dictionary explains that a Pythoness was a priestess of Apollo at Delphi. The broader context refers to any woman soothsayer or prophetess.[8] The best example was the Delphic Oracle—the most celebrated citadel of prophecy in the pagan world of the Mediterranean.

Here's how Pythoness worked. She was said to need certain occult stimulation to attain the altered state of consciousness needed to speak her "oracles" (prophecies). This involved her being charmed or hypnotized by a large *serpent* kept at the oracular temple. This supposedly placed her in an altered state of consciousness where the spirit of the Python (which the god Apollo had slain) came in and *possessed her* so she could speak the oracles. Hence, the Pythoness Spirit.

This relates to the common but incorrect idea that snakes can hypnotize people with their unblinking gaze. However, there is no doubt that these sooth-sayers acquired their skills from being hypnotized.

Because of this two thousand-plus year association, a tremendous amount of occult momentum has been built into hypnosis. It is a major doorway for one of the more dangerous spirits in the Bible, THE SPIRIT OF DIVINATION.

We have found that almost all the people we have ministered to who have been hypnotized have a spirit of divination. *This is a strong and difficult spirit to get rid of,* and this is why we counsel against hypnosis. Too many fine people have ended up demonized through being subjected to it, even from clinical practitioners.

The Nobel Laureate, Sir John Eccles remarked that the mind is essentially a machine which a ghost operates. That is an incomplete but theologically correct analysis of what happens in the BODY-SOUL-SPIRIT triad of the Bible. If your "ghost" is put to sleep, or placed in a state of passivity by hypnosis, then who—or *what*—is left to run the machine?

This PASSIVE state is the last thing which any

Christian needs to cultivate. It is what Spiritist mediums, mystics, witches and shamans try to achieve—it leads easily to an altered state of consciousness. Though not all altered states are bad, certainly the ones in which the mind is brought into a blank state are an open invitation to Satan to come in and take over the controls.

THE POWER OF SUGGESTION

The other difficulty is more "down to earth," but daunting none the less. It is the increasing danger of what is called *iatrogenic abuse* or iatrogenic psychopathology.[9] Sorry for the big words, but these terms simply mean that the doctor or therapist caused the problem. It's like when you go to the hospital to have your appendix out and catch AIDS. That is an iatrogenic disease.

Here is what *sometimes* happens with the therapist who uses hypnosis on a person who comes with a complaint of SRA.

Hypnosis, as most people realize, makes a person extremely suggestible. So a woman or adolescent girl who is a victim of sexual abuse is taken to a therapist or psychiatrist because that is what society (and often the law) expects. The therapist uses hypnosis to extract "memories" of the abuse, supposedly to discharge the pain and bring healing. (We have already seen that this is unnecessary for a Christian.)

Unfortunately, therapists are just as prone to fads and "bandwagons" as anyone else, including Christians. Thus, if the therapist is "hot" on the subject of

SRA, he or she may contaminate the woman's mind with concepts not originally there. It's like the old proverb, "When you're a hammer, everything looks like a nail."

Because of certain subtle (often unintentional) verbal cues given while the client is in a highly passive and suggestible state—and VERY eager to please—the client gets the idea in her head that her abuse was not just sexual, but satanic.

A clear example of this was shown on a major news documentary.[10] A lady was shown on a clinical videotape being hypnotized and asked about memories supposedly being unearthed through the hypnotic process. She began to list the names of people present for the abuse. As the number edged up to twelve, the therapist asked her if there were thirteen because if there were, it would be like a coven. She said that there might be thirteen, and the therapist dogmatically announced that it was a coven! That is pretty lame!

Another example from our own experience is a lady who brought forth a memory of two or three men doing a sex perversion best left undescribed. The therapist told her that this practice was done as a satanic ritual. (In our experience and study, it is not—ever!) But this one memory, now framed in the context of Satanism, became the grounds for the woman to accuse her father of being a Satanist. It has unnecessarily torn the family apart.

This is NOT to say that real SRA cases don't exist. They do! In fact, in the vast majority of our cases, we are completely satisfied that the abuse is both genuine and ritually motivated. However, when these things are said or suggested to a client under hypnosis, the statements acquire a force all out of proportion to what they would have in normal consciousness. The client is extremely vulnerable and suggestible.

Since they trust the therapist as an "expert," this brings even more weight to the assessment. They begin to believe, and even have visual memories of events which never happened.

In consequence, we have some cases where "normal" abuse cases have escalated into SRA accusations, and even cases where the client came for some other reason (depression, eating problems) and was diagnosed falsely as being an SRA survivor.

This is two scores for Satan—one point for making the real SRA victims (and the Christian workers, pastors and counselors who work with them) seem less credible, and a second point for causing pain and heartache in homes and tearing families (and sometimes churches) apart with false accusations of SRA.

False positive diagnoses of SRA make it that much more difficult for the true victims of satanic abuse to be heard, and to get the ministry they so desperately need.

The bottom line is that these false diagnoses make it harder for real survivors of SRA to put their lives back together, and make the job of Christian workers more difficult as well. The power of these (usually) unintentional deceptions is made all the more dangerous through the use of hypnosis. This makes it even more risky as a therapy alternative.

BUT IT WORKS!

In many cases, the Holy Spirit, through His sheer graciousness, may protect the Christian from demonic access through being hypnotized, but we are not to tempt the Lord our God. If hypnosis has been used to help people, praise the Lord. However, I believe that people who use hypnosis are playing the spiritual equivalent of Russian roulette.

The cry I often hear from counselors I know who use hypnosis is "But it works... it really helps MPD people!" That might be true. I know that we, as witches, often cured people with our spells. I know some people are helped by psychic surgeons that open up your tummy with rusty knives and remove ovarian tumors with the help of "spirit doctors." The point cannot be—does it work! The point should be—*is it of God?*

Pragmatism—the end justifying the means—is not smiled upon by God. The Bible is full of people who were "pragmatic failures." Abraham sired Ishmael through a pragmatic decision to conceive with a woman besides Sarah. The result? He got a son alright, but it was a son which was cast out. And that son's descendants have been the bitter enemies of Abraham's promised seed, Isaac, to this day.

King Saul was pragmatic. Samuel was late, and he knew he needed a sacrifice which normally only

Samuel could offer (1 Sam. 13). Pragmatically, it seemed the right thing to do, but it was the beginning of Saul's slide into apostasy.

The cross is the ultimate answer to pragmatism, because it was the most "un-pragmatic" method possible of creating the most incredible victory in the history of the world. Had God been a pragmatist, He could have simply taken away our free will and forced us all to be perfect. But He chose a harder way, both for Himself and for us. The message of Calvary is— among other things—that pragmatism is a lie.

For God, the "recovery" of a patient may not justify the means used to achieve that recovery. It is our belief that God will bless those ministers who do **NOT** use the tools of witches and sorcerers, but rely upon the Holy Spirit and His anointing. We have *never* used hypnosis since being Born Again. We never will. Yet, the Lord has chosen to use our poor broken selves to help many people struggling with these problems.

Are the people using hypnosis sinning? That is between them and the Lord. We believe the Bible says it is sin, and we have seen the poisonous fruit it bears. Beyond that, it must be a matter of careful prayer for any counselor or psychiatrist who calls himself a servant of Jesus.

They need to ask themselves if they have bought into the cultural world-view around them? Do they assume that there are constructs within the mind like the unconscious and the subconscious, just because these terms are used all the time by the world and the medical profession? Do they believe in them, even though there is *no Biblical or scientific evidence* that they are anything more than the fevered imaginings of a God-denying, cocaine-addicted fool—Sigmund Freud? (See Psalm 14:1.)

Have they chosen to take for granted something our culture has contaminated us with, just because "men of science (falsely so-called)" say it is so? I realize that the whole issue of the unconscious and the subconscious is another can of worms... beyond the range of this book.

However, do be aware that both of these are theoretical constructs made popular by Freud and his followers. *They have never been proven in a laboratory,* they have never been isolated in neuro-psychiatry, and *few psychotherapeutic models of treatment have been more discredited than the Freudian and Neo-Freudian models.* However, even though many Christian counselors have discarded "St. Sigmund," they have retained his constructs, though there is no Biblical or scientific reason to do so.

How many "cultural values" have we Christians absorbed without critically analyzing them? How many things do we take for granted as true because the culture around us assumes they are true, without bothering to check them out. The theory of evolution is an excellent example.

My friend, Jim Spencer, has an excellent illus-tration of this kind of thinking. When he speaks in churches, he starts talking about the cosmos and the secularist mindset. He then asks for a show of hands on how many people have seen pictures of the Milky Way galaxy—like the popular poster/t-shirts which have a photo of the spiral galaxy and a little arrow pointing to a place on one of the pinwheel arms of the galaxy saying "You are here."

He then points out that NO ONE has ever seen a picture of the Milky Way! Why? Because we are IN IT! The pictures we have all been seeing in grade school textbooks and on posters are actually pictures of the next nearest galaxy, the Andromeda galaxy! To get a picture of our galaxy, we would have to send a Galileo-like probe out hundreds of light years beyond the rim of the galaxy to get the "snapshot." Even our great-great-great-great grandchildren wouldn't live to see it!

Actually, we don't know what the Milky Way looks like! Astronomers have taken some educated guesses, but we only assume that it looks like Andromeda! It might look different. Most people— both in and out of the church—assumed that it was a picture of our galaxy. *We assumed wrong!* This shows how insidious culture can be!

Similarly, today everyone "assumes" that we have unconsciouses and subconsciouses. You hear the word thrown about every day on talk shows. Is everyone assuming this because it provides a way to avoid human responsibility and that ugly "s" word—**SIN?**

Obviously, the human mind is wonderfully complex. However, the Bible, which was written by the greatest Psychiatrist in human history, says nothing about these subconscious elements. These are elements of the human soul and the human spirit. If they were real, surely God would have told us about them! It goes without saying that if there is no subconscious, then we need to find a new model for why hypnosis works. It is our honest belief that it works because it is demonically fueled.

Jim Spencer told me back in the beginning of my Christian walk that the true Christian should camp as far away from the "borders of Egypt" and as far into "Canaanland" as possible.

The best you can say about hypnosis is that you are camping extremely close to the border of "Egypt," spiritually speaking. The faith and strength of will of a Christian therapist may keep him or her safe, but what about other, less mature Christians whose "weak consciences" might well be wounded by seeing them practice or recommend hypnosis (Rom. 14:13-23, 1 Cor. 8:7-13). The true Christian attitude would be that of Paul:

> **"Wherefore, if meat make my brother to offend, I will eat no flesh while the world standeth, lest I make my brother to offend."**
> **1 Cor. 8:13**

That has been our stand, and we pray it will be yours.

8

The Curse of Molech

**"Thou shalt not be afraid for the terror by
night; nor for the arrow that flieth by day."**
Psalm 91:5

More and more people began contacting us for
deliverance. Usually we tried to minister together.
However, sometimes the wishes of the person being
prayed for precluded that.

Rachel was such a case. I was finishing up my
Master's degree and doing an internship with a
major Christian counseling center in northern
Seattle. One of the cases I assisted in was with Dr.
Walters, an esteemed psychotherapist with a PhD.
who specialized in survivors of child abuse.

I had been brought in as part of my internship and sat in on perhaps a half-dozen sessions with Rachel. She lived almost three hundred miles away, and had to come this far for a decent Christian counselor. Thus, her sessions were twice as long, but only every two weeks—so she wouldn't have to drive every week.

Rachel was quite an extraordinary woman! She was a mom on her second marriage, going to nursing school, raising six kids—some hers, some his and some theirs. She was an active Christian in her church but carried a dark well of inner pain. She had been both neglected and sexually abused by her father when young. Additionally, she had been nearly raped by her best male friend while a teenager. Her first husband, a less than satisfactory husband, was killed in a road accident.

In spite of all this, she usually managed to be bright and effervescent, though the tears frequently flowed during the sessions.

After my internship was over, the therapist called me back. Rachel, it seemed, was manifesting symptoms of demonic infestation! Dr. Walters felt out of his depth with this part of the healing process and hoped that I could assist in the deliverance.

I asked if Sharon could come also—explaining that we worked as a team. The doctor said no, that Rachel felt comfortable with me since I had been with her through hours of counseling. She didn't feel emotionally strong enough to let a stranger into her inmost boundaries.

A BATTLE ROYAL

Feeling more than a little anxious, I arrived at the counseling center one afternoon. I was apprehensive at first because I didn't like doing this kind of demanding ministry without Sharon. It felt like fighting with one arm tied behind my back. Also, I wasn't sure how much free rein I would have. Dr. Walters, a man of international renown and reputation, intimidated me. Still, I prayed silently that the Lord would make up for all my deficits. In my heart, I knew He would.

Rachel looked little different from when we had last seen her some months before. Her long, brown hair was loose, and she was dressed in light, cheerful colors. She had brought with her a friend—a missionary wife from her home church—as prayer support. That made me feel a bit better. Usually missionaries from the foreign fields had a LOT of experience with this sort of ministry.

To his credit, Dr. Walters assured me that I would be given wide latitude, and that I would lead the session. As normal in all our sessions, I opened with a prayer asking for the Lord's guidance and for His protection from satanic interference. Then, as with all of our cases, I asked Rachel to affirm who Jesus was to her.

We do this partially because it infuriates Satan. He knows we overcome him by the blood of the Lamb, and by the word of their testimony (Rev. 12:11). It also asserts the authority of the person being prayed for, to stand in Jesus' name against the dark forces that might be oppressing her, and to cast them out. Finally, it assures us that the person is indeed a Bible-believing Christian. We have found it to be a grave mistake to pray for the deliverance of someone who is not a Christian, unless an extraordinary leading from the Lord explicitly prompts us to do so.

In this case, however, we almost immediately ran into a snag. Rachel could barely get the word, "Jesus," out of her mouth. She attempted to say that Jesus was her Lord and Savior, but a dramatic change took place in her countenance almost immediately. Before she could finish one word, her face became hard and expressionless.

Though this woman had professed Christ numerous times, and even led people to a saving knowledge of Him, now she could not even say "Jesus is Lord!"

I rebuked the spirits which were inhibiting her from speaking, but they were adamant.

"I don't have to leave!" said a voice out of Rachel's lips. It was her voice, and her vocal cords producing the voice, but the tone and inflection were utterly alien to her.

By now, the missionary lady and Dr. Walters were praying furiously. I declared, "In the name of the Lord Jesus Christ, I command you to leave Rachel!"

Her eyes, which had been closed, now opened. They were like stainless steel ball-bearings in their merciless cruelty! The eyes bored into me. "She is mine. She is not His!" spat out the voice.

"Satan is a liar and the father of lies. Rachel has confessed Christ. She belongs to Jesus," I insisted.

"But she LIKES belonging to me," sneered the voice.

"In the name of the Lord Jesus Christ, I command all enemy spirits to be silent immediately," I commanded.

"I don't have to be silent. She WANTS me." The woman took on a sexually provocative position.

I began leading the two others in singing choruses about the blood of Jesus Christ. After a few minutes, Rachel became more subdued and almost silent, except for small moans of protest. I was bewildered by the incredible level of resistance in this case. It was more than I had encountered before.

It took almost the entire two hours of the session just to get Rachel to the place where she could wearily croak out "Jesus...is...Lord." We had to alternate between praying against the spirits, singing hymns and reading Bible passages aloud to achieve that. Unfortunately, by then the next person's appointment was upon us.

It would be another two weeks before Rachel could be there again. Everyone in the room, even Dr. Walters, felt drained and exhausted by the encounter. I assured Rachel that we would be praying and fasting for her in the time between, and that I would be back with her in two weeks.

Over the next fourteen days, Sharon and I used every free moment to pray, study and try to determine the source of the incredible resistance we experienced. No answers were immediately forthcoming.

ONCE MORE INTO THE RING

The next session went only slightly better than the first one. This time, Dr. Walters had blocked out a three hour span in his schedule so that we would have a little more time. Once again, it took about three-fourths of that time to elicit a statement from Rachel that Jesus was the Lord of her life.

Most of the prayer time preceding that declaration involved me and the stalwart missionary lady interceding for Rachel, and declaring that Satan had no right to afflict her in such a manner. Nevertheless, it was still a battle.

The demons in her were firm in their refusal to depart, but a tremendous amount of standing in for Rachel in prayer finally silenced them. We were all getting increasingly worn out.

Once Rachel's affirmation of the Lordship of Christ was out, things moved a bit more easily. We had become accustomed to praying first against any possible generational sin in the family line. This was because usually there was less emotional and spiritual resistance to doing that first, and such prayers often remove a substantial portion of the "ground" upon which the evil spirits make their stand.

In Rachel's case, it was a terrible process. We literally had to fight to get every word out of her mouth. We normally have the person being set free repeat the prayers of liberation after us. In this way, they know that THEY have the authority—through Jesus Christ—to cast the demons out themselves. This empowers them and helps them to rely on the Lord rather than on us.

Rachel was one of the extremely few cases who was not able to do that—at least for a very long time. I had to pray over her, at times literally on my knees, for nearly an hour—breaking generational curses. Finally, toward the end, she was able to trudge through the prayer herself.

Though utterly exhausted, she was heartened by her victories of the afternoon. However, once again the clock was our enemy, and we had to bring the session to a close. In two weeks she would be back.

LONG DISTANCE DELIVERANCE

Halloween fell the day before her next scheduled appointment. I was scheduled to fly to Virginia to appear on *The 700 Club* for their Halloween broadcast. I was supposed to discuss Satanism and promote my newest book, **Wicca: Satan's Little White Lie.**

I made certain that I would be back in time to meet with Rachel, but was beginning to dread these grueling sessions. I was still praying and periodically fasting for her, and I could not understand what was taking so long.

About the time I was preparing to fly to Virginia Beach, another client brought something to my attention. The fellow had long since been set free, but still called to check in every now and then. This time he brought with him a prayer sheet produced by Brad and Darlene Huckins, another couple in the greater Seattle area that did this sort of ministry. It was called "Binding Evil Before a Meeting."

We were intrigued with it because it embodied in one, concise prayer many of the spiritual warfare tactics we had employed. It was evidently designed to be prayed before a church service, but could just as easily be used before a prayer session. The key and valuable concepts it embodied were:

• Affirming the Lordship of Jesus Christ over the place.

• Binding—in advance—all spirits, principalities and powers which were identified by the Lord as His enemies anywhere around the place.

• Asking the Lord to break down all lines of communication between any spirits and their "higher ups."[1]

• Purifying with the blood of Christ all four of the elements (fire, air, water and ground) and cutting off any enemy routes of entrance or exit.

• Binding—in advance—the spirit world from attacking anyone involved in the meeting or any member of their family or their property—either now or in the future.

• Binding—in advance—any spirits brought into the place of the ministry by those entering, and cutting off their lines of communication as well.

• Praying to seal off completely the place of ministry with the blood of Jesus.

• Inviting the Holy Spirit to come and work through the Christians laboring in ministry.

Both of us really liked this prayer, and we began using it before every prayer session. Although we have fine tuned it in the past few years and added some things here and there, it is substantially the same prayer we use to this very day.

It had never occurred to us to take authority over demons in advance of the prayer session. Obviously, we prayed in advance for the person—asking the Lord to set her free. However, this was a subtly different tactical approach. It was like a pre-emptive surgical strike in advance—taking out Satan's troops and lines of communication before they could gather—and binding his ability to influence the elemental forces around the building.

Still, Rachel was on my mind a lot as I flew back east and even as I did the show. It went very well. I was on with Bob Larson and we both gave a firm testimony of the dangers of Halloween and of practicing Witchcraft.

The staff from *The 700 Club* got me back on a plane by late afternoon. As I was flying back to Seattle, I was really seeking God about what to do concerning this challenging case.

I felt the Lord speak to me and say, "I am not limited by space or by time as you are. Pray now for Rachel, that she might be set free."

I had been praying in a general way for Rachel's liberation. Both of us had been doing so for weeks. However, this was something quite different. It was taking the concept of the prayer before a meeting one step further. Naturally, I was excited.

As the huge jet rocketed across the Midwest, I prayed the deliverance prayers for Rachel, just as if she were sitting in the seat beside me. Fortunately, the seat was first class and there was no one sitting near me. For though I prayed under my breath, I still had to pray in an audible voice. I thanked the Lord for the pervasive noise of the jet engines.

I spent the better part of the five-hour flight praying that demons might be bound and cast out of Rachel. I saw that hundreds—or even thousands of miles would make no difference to the power of God. I felt a little crazy doing it, but it was certainly worth a try.

By the time the plane landed and Sharon met me, I felt drained—but full of a wonderful anointing from the Lord.

The next day, I was exhausted but excited. For the first time, I was almost looking forward to the prayer session with Rachel. As I arrived in the early afternoon, the same "team" was there. Rachel looked normal, but then she always looked normal until we starting trying to throw demons out of her. However, there were some subtle improvements which I discerned in her spirit. My hope grew stronger.

Feeling a bit silly, I had stashed the "Prayer Before a Meeting" inside my Bible. After the beginning pleasantries and some initial assessments were done with, I used it to open the session. There was no discernible response from Rachel.

We began as before, with Rachel attempting to affirm her acceptance of Jesus as her Lord. She smiled uneasily and declared, "Jesus Christ is my Lord and my Savior." She looked pleasantly startled at how easy it was!

The team and I responded with cries of "Praise the Lord!" and "Hallelujah!" Rachel beamed like a little girl who had just won the spelling bee.

To reassert ground that was already gained, I led Rachel through the prayers to break any generational curses from her ancestry. Again, things went remarkably smooth. There was almost no resistance.

Fighting back a sense of apprehension, I progressed into spiritual "terra incognita,"—going boldly where Rachel had never gone before. I had her make a list of "religious" sins which she had committed. This proved to be a relatively short list— primarily things like the childhood use of a Ouija Board. However, I knew from experience how powerful and dangerous the Ouija Board was as an access point.

However, it was only marginally difficult for Rachel to declare her repentance for using the Board and the other occultic practices and then to command any spirits which may have gained access to her through its use to depart. When she commanded them to "GO" where Jesus wished them to go, there was new strength and fire in her voice.

Once again, we all stopped and praised and thanked the Lord, who was giving Rachel her new and precious victory.

Moving on to the next point, I asked her to make a general list of any serious non-religious sins (i.e., sins which did not involve practicing false religions or occultism, such as unforgiveness, anger, lust, drug abuse, etc.).

Rachel began to look nervous, but she complied. As we began the prayers of repentance, I could sense in my spirit that something was amiss. Suddenly, Rachel stopped. Her eyes flashed at us, and they were filled with cold, sulfurous fire. "You cannot make her do this!" hissed a voice from within her.

Instantly, I knelt and prayed. "Lord Jesus, I ask you to bind this Lying Spirit and loose the Spirit of Truth in Rachel's heart."

The hatred roaring out of Rachel's eyes was almost palpable. The room seemed to grow colder. "She doesn't want us to leave. We are her friends and she belongs to us."

The missionary lady and I both knelt beside Rachel as she sat, twisting and writhing under the weight of some unseen burden. I felt led to do something that we normally never do. I took Rachel's hand in my own and began praying.

> **"Father, in the name of the Lord Jesus Christ, I petition you on behalf of Rachel. You know she wants to be free. We now stand in prayerful agreement with her for**

> **You to grant her that freedom. Please, Lord,
> empower her to say whatever she needs to
> say to break the hold of this foul thing
> upon her. In Jesus' name. Amen."**

Suddenly, the frozen tension in the room snapped like a sonic boom. Rachel began weeping, and she let out a keening wail. "Forgive me, Lord Jesus! I had an abortion!"

For a brief second, a truly disgusting odor filled the counseling room. Then with a howling rush it was gone. Quickly, I rose and placed my hands on her shoulders. With the strongest possible prayer, I came against the strongmen of Molech and Lilith, then led Rachel in a prayer in which she was finally able to command them to leave her forever.

The peace that pervaded the room was glorious. The few remaining prayers came easily. At the end, I was not surprised to learn that Rachel had never renounced that abortion before in a formal way.

We knew, from our own past in Satanism and Witchcraft, that two extremely ancient and powerful principalities reign over abortion. They were Molech, the god of child sacrifice in the Old Testament (see Lev. 18:21, 20:2-4, 1 Kings 11:7, 2 Kings 23:10) and Lilith, not mentioned by name in the Bible, but regarded by rabbinical sources as the terror which flies by night. Lilith is actually a corruption of an ancient Sumerian goddess, Lilitu, and she (it?) is believed to be the "patron saint" of infanticide and what we call today "Sudden Infant Death Syndrome."

As the Bible tells us, all these "gods" and

"goddesses" which the pagans worship are actually demons (Lev. 17:7, Deut. 32:17, 2 Chron. 11:15, Psalm 106:7). The curses which come onto unsuspecting women from abortions because of these strongmen are both powerful and awful to contemplate. It is a tragedy that the media and contemporary culture have tried to trivialize the crime of child murder and make it a "woman's right to choose."

More recently, we have also learned that the IUD, a birth-control device popular in the sixties and seventies, was actually a tool for causing abortions. Thus, if a woman used one of these, she may have the same oppression which comes from knowingly having an abortion.

Rachel's shame and unwillingness to confess her abortion was possibly the single major stumbling block towards her full liberation. But much of that shame was a lie that Satan had placed in her mind:

> **"There is therefore now no condemnation to them which are in Christ Jesus, who walk not after the flesh, but after the Spirit."**
> **Romans 8:1**

She needn't have been so ashamed. Her sin was under the blood of Jesus! She was completely forgiven. However, the Deceiver was using it as a club to beat her down. She only needed to renounce the sin as an access point to break Satan's power over her.

Praise God that He is so gracious as to supply our needs so wonderfully!

9

Meditations before the Battle

"Blessed be the Lord my strength, which teacheth my hands to war, and my fingers to fight."   Psalm 144:1

As should be clear from the preceding material, a great deal of sensitivity is required in ministering to people coming out of Satanism, either survivors of SRA or those who joined the cult in adolescence or adulthood.

On one hand, it is important not to diminish the pain these people feel. On the other hand, we must not allow them to lose sight of Jesus by focusing on their pain.

This tendency to wallow in past hurts is an unfortunate legacy of the psychological smog bank in the atmosphere of our churches. It is vital that prayer and communication with the Lord be paramount in the minds of any Christian who wishes to work with these people.

If you are not spending a LOT of time in prayer and Bible study daily, then it will be difficult for you to be sensitive to the Holy Spirit's promptings concerning when to move the person along and when to allow them to spend time grappling with their emotions.

A Christian who moves into this ministry must be willing to acknowledge the nearly infinite complexity and multi-dimensional (body-soul-spirit) nature of the human person. This makes it essential that we be humble before the Spirit and transparent to His leading and will in every situation.

We must be willing to set any of our models, world-views or theories on the shelf according to His wishes. **HE** must be the Counselor. All we can do is prayerfully try and stay out of His way and let Him work through our frail human vessels.

When these people come to you, you must receive them as Jesus Christ would. Meet them "where they are," and allow the Holy Spirit to draw them to the level of divine Truth which they need to access. Listen to them openly and empathetically, whether you are immediately willing to accept the account of their story or not.

These people often surprise us. Sometimes those

you think are deluded turn out to have amazingly accurate and consistent histories. And some who seem quite together turn out to be misguided. This is why you must not pre-judge anyone.

Be aware that once they see that you will listen patiently, they may say things they think you wish to hear. They may have been conditioned into doing that by prior therapists. Most of these people are very eager to please. Some have even been hypnotized into being more eager to please. This is why you should not ask leading questions or give them ideas about where YOU would like the account to go. If they get an idea about your expectations, they will often seek to fulfill those expectations.

An example of a leading question is: "Were the people who abused you wearing black robes?" That leads the person to think that you expect her to say that they were wearing robes and that if she wants to keep in your good graces, she had better say "Yes." This is how those "false positives" show up.

As a general rule, it is better to ask open-ended questions, which cannot be answered "Yes" or "No." A better question to extract the same information would be: "Describe how the people who abused you were dressed." This allows the survivor to tell her own story in her own way.

Be patient and keep a poker face. Some SRA victims take a long time to warm up and trust you. Also, many will shy away if they perceive horror, disgust or disbelief on your face. They are used to those sorts of receptions and will be disappointed.

It sometimes helps to reassure them that you have heard many strange and bizarre things (or in our case, even that we had DONE many strange and bizarre things) if that is, in fact, the case. These people are torn between wanting to be accepted and "normal," and wanting to exult in their pain and strangeness. Again, empathy and sensitivity to the Spirit's promptings are essential.

With this sort of ministry, legal issues often surface. Felonies are frequently involved (murder, child abuse, etc.). If there is a possibility of arrests, it would be wise to have an experienced interviewer present (with the woman's permission, of course). Taping the sessions might be in order, although we have avoided that. It often inhibits the survivor. If they are taped, it MUST be with her permission.

Most experts in this field feel that at least 60-65% of the people who claim to be SRA survivors actually have been satanically abused. Of the remaining 35%, a very small number are being deliberately and cleverly deceitful. Psychologists refer to them as suffering from Munchausen Syndrome. But frankly, they are just clever liars who enjoy the attention they get from being part of the latest therapeutic trend. The vast majority who were not abused sincerely believe that they were. They are telling you the truth—as they see it, at least.

THEY STILL NEED MINISTRY!

Whether or not the person is a genuine SRA survivor, they almost certainly BELIEVE they are (or have been led to believe that they are)! We have found that either way, it is better to meet them where they are and pray for them. Prayers for liberation, done in a sensitive manner, seldom hurt anyone. This sort of person obviously needs some kind of prayer.

Because of the way the psychiatric establishment works, women come to us having been repeatedly hypnotized, which lays them open to any demonic infestation Satan wishes to throw into them.

Also, there is a near epidemic of women being sexually abused or harassed by their therapists. We counselled one woman who was hypnotized then raped while under trance. The therapist of another woman made lewd advances to her in the name of "therapy."

Even so-called "Christian" therapists are not immune to this abomination. An ordained Methodist minister and a founder of the School of Psychology at Fuller Theological Seminary in Pasadena, CA, who was highly esteemed among the Christian therapeutic community, was recently fined in our state for engaging in "nude therapy" and having sex with six of his female clients. The 78-year-old therapist had his license revoked for twenty years![1]

Some counselors and psychotherapists (hopefully not many) are little more than secular witch-doctors. All sorts of occult and New Age healing techniques are now popular within the therapeutic community. Thus, some people come to us "satanically abused" by their own therapist!

When we pray with these unfortunate women, we frequently find it necessary to have them pray for release from demonic oppression for a constellation of reasons. They are always better for it.

BEWARE OF "SOME NEW THING" (Acts 17:21)

Both with psychotherapy and spiritual warfare counseling, there is often a tendency to run after something new and different. One example is this pagan, astrological "Four temperament" nonsense.

Another is a lot of the "Inner Healing" material. These are like fads which run through the Body of Christ with great frequency, and because they are promoted by "Great Men (or Women) of God," or "Great Men (or Women) of Science," they are often received uncritically by Believers. There is some excellent advice in the Word about this tendency:

> **"Thus saith the Lord Stand ye in the ways,
> and see, and ask for the old paths, where is
> the good way, and walk therein, and ye
> shall find rest for your souls. But they said,
> We will not walk therein."   Jeremiah 6:16**

Can you imagine Paul the apostle testing the Corinthian church to see if their temperaments were melancholic, sanguine, choleric or phlegmatic—then telling them which spiritual gifts they had on that basis? He would probably have ripped his robe and poured ashes on his head at the thought!

A minor thing, which has become major, started showing up in our prayer sessions a few years ago. This was the use of "special" anointing oil. We have encountered two versions of this anomaly, both equally unfortunate from a Biblical perspective.

The first variety of "special" anointing oil was from a trained counselor who went to a charismatic church known for being on the cutting edge of ecumenism and quasi-occultic weirdness. He was enterprising enough to go to a friend who was a Roman Catholic priest and persuade him to share some of the special anointing oil used in the Catholic priesthood, called "holy chrism." This is the oil they use to anoint the sick—to anoint baptismal and confirmation candidates—and for the priesthood.

He was even anointing people on their hands in the same manner as the Catholic priests used to have their hands anointed to receive the "power" to celebrate the Eucharistic liturgy. Whatever the Catholic hierarchy might think of this ecumenical cooperation, it is important to understand that such oil has NO special efficacy in the sight of God.

To the contrary, because it is blessed by the Catholic priesthood, it is actually a carrier of the spirit of priestcraft and should be avoided at all costs! Things it's supposed to bless would actually be cursed!

The other, more common variety of "special" oil is frequently sold through Christian bookstores. It is supposedly made from the same special, "sacred" recipe used by Moses (see Exodus 30). At least this sounds more Biblical. It is even from the Bible. However, these people, in their enthusiasm, are neither rightly dividing the Word of Truth, NOR are they reading the entire passage. While Exodus 30:23-25 gives the recipe for the oil, a further study in the chapter shows this:

> "And thou shalt speak unto the children of Israel, saying, This shall be an holy anointing oil unto me throughout your generations. Upon man's flesh shall it not be poured, neither shall ye make any other like it, after the composition of it: it is holy, and it shall be holy unto you. Whosoever compoundeth any like it, or whosoever putteth any of it upon a stranger, shall even be cut off from his people." Exod. 30:31-33

Note, please, that this is a special anointing oil ONLY to be used on the house of Aaron of the tribe of Levi. There was a death penalty for anyone else using it. Now, praise the Lord, we are under grace— not law. This doesn't mean that anyone using this oil is going to be struck dead! But it DOES mean that such oil obviously has no efficacy, unless you were under the Law. And if you WERE under the Law—it would curse you. It is like a "Catch-22."

We had one case where a person had to renounce and repent specifically of having this oil used, so you never know when Satan—the old accuser—might use something against you. Just use regular old olive oil. It's only a symbol for the anointing of the Holy Spirit and the protection of the blood of Jesus. We have even had success using 10W40 motor oil in a pinch. God is gracious!

STOPPING THE SIDESHOW

Probably the single most helpful thing we have learned over the years is that we must pray initially in the name of Jesus Christ and bind any demons from manifestation. Although some ministers believe in "calling demons out" (like gun slingers on Main Street in the Old West) into manifestation, we believe this can easily get out of control.

Demons are great "hams" and egotists, just like their boss. They love to create a scene and frighten and humiliate the person and terrify those praying for her. We heard one deliverance minister brag about how one woman ran around his office on all fours, barking like a dog—as if this was something to be desired. This just glorifies Satan, not God!

Our advice is to "nip the problem in the bud" by praying up front, before any counseling or prayer begins—and binding any manifestations that are not of the Holy Spirit of God.

Since we began doing that, we have never had any problems with unfortunate scenes or barn-yard imitations. If you forget to do this, or if demons attempt to manifest (this can be seen by voice changes, changes in the eyes, growling, shrieking, etc.) command them to be silent in Jesus' name. They must obey, and they do! Praise God!

Understand this please: if you bind demons from manifesting and you get manifestations anyway, then they may not be demons. They could be the person's flesh—their own human nature. Remember, many people have been "trained" by movies, books or other ministers to think that unless there is growling and vomiting or people crawling around on the ceiling, it really isn't a good deliverance.

Sometimes, without even realizing it, they act up out of their own flesh, either through a desire for more attention, or out of misunderstanding. If this happens, we pray and sing hymns to Jesus until it subsides, then go forward without comment.

It is a grave mistake to try and get feedback, history, theology or other information from demons manifesting in the person. This often involves asking the demon its name, how it got into the person, who its "boss" is, etc. Some ministers actually ask demons for information about Satan's command structure and his plans! We cannot understand how they think this is justified!

First of all, demons lie! That ought to be obvious, but some ministers believe that they can "bring demons before the throne of God" and force them to tell the truth. Chapter and verse on that, please?

Actually, there is no Biblical evidence that we can force (even in the name of Jesus) demons to tell the truth. Nor is there any evidence that we can force them before God's throne, or that they would be forced to tell the truth even if we could. Satan comes before the throne and lies about Christians all the time. (See Rev. 12:10 and Job 1-2). Why should his demons be any different?

Some ministers believe in commanding the demons to speak to them or use them to draw information about how they came into the person. This is even worse than what is mentioned above. Aside from the fact that they lie, by commanding the demons to speak you are forcing the person for whom you are praying to be a trance medium!

Think about it. That is what a trance medium

does—they have demons speak through them and impart information to human beings. The only difference is that with the medium (often called a "trance channeler") the demons pretend to be dead people. This is the very serious sin of sorcery or necromancy (conjuring up the dead to talk to them) and it is forbidden in the Bible (Deut. 18:10, 1 Sam. 28:11, 2 Kgs. 17:17, 2 Kgs. 21:6, Is. 8:19-20, Isa. 47:9, Mal. 3:5, Rev. 18:23, Rev. 21:8, etc.).

It is evident that you cannot shut sin "doorways" and cast out demons if you are in the middle of serious sin yourself, since both the minister and the person being delivered would be sinning in this matter. Therefore, we recommend that you rely upon the person's own feedback, their emotions, and physical sensations. But above all else, rely upon the Holy Spirit and His gifts of discernment (1 Cor. 12:10).

Some Christians will mention the case of Legion, the only place in the entire New Testament where anyone ever asked information from a demon.

> **"And he asked him, What is thy name? And he answered, saying, My name is Legion: for we are many."** **Mark 5:9**
>
> **(See also Matt. 8:28 ff and Luke 8:30 ff)**

Most Bible students agree that these three accounts describe the same incident, just like many other narratives in the synoptic gospels. The point is that it is always dicey to build a theology or practice out of a case which appears only once.

Nowhere do we see anyone else ever asking a

demon its name or demanding information from it. Paul didn't do it with the girl possessed of a spirit of divination in Acts 16:16. Apparently he didn't NEED to do it. Jesus never did it in the many other cases where he cast demons out of people.

To the contrary, He did just the opposite! He commanded them to shut up! (See Mark 1:25, Mark 1:34, Luke 4:35, Luke 4:41.)

In sound Bible interpretation, you never build theology out of one verse—especially if there are other verses which move in a different direction. This is called the "Law of Two or Three Witnesses" (Deut. 19:15). Most cultic doctrines are built upon a single verse without other verses to support it.

For example, the Mormon doctrine of baptism for the dead is based on 1 Cor. 15:29, with no other basis. The doctrine of baptismal regeneration is based only on Acts 2:38. Thus, we need to be careful about making the incident with Legion normative.

Besides, we all understand that Jesus sometimes did things that He would not wish His disciples to do—because He was God Almighty! When we cannot find any instance of apostles (or even the Lord) doing it again, we steer clear—especially in the light of the clear teaching of the Bible against conversing with "the dead" (i.e. demons).

Please, if you don't pick up anything else from this chapter, please remember NOT to permit the demons to talk to you, nor command them to speak.

10

The Case of the Needle in the Haystack

> "Many of them also which used curious arts brought their books together and burned them before all men: and they counted the price of them and found it to be fifty thousand pieces of silver." **Acts 19:19**

Early on in praying for people, we learned the importance of making certain that your home is free of occult or cultic objects. Sometimes, though not often, the presence of such objects can be a reason why a prayer session is not successful.

There are many ways in which "cursed things" in a home can have an impact. Sometimes they are things brought in by the person without knowledge of their occult meaning, and sometimes they are things brought in by OTHER persons who know their meaning all too well. And sometimes they are part of a person's cultural heritage.

"NEEDLE" CRAFT?

A serious situation developed with a couple we counseled named Will and Cheryl. As the prayer counseling developed, revelations came to the surface that at least one, and possibly both spouses, had been ritually abused when children.

(It is not uncommon for SRA survivors to marry one another without knowing of each others' past. They are often magically-arranged weddings. This doesn't mean that the marriages cannot be sanctified by the blood of Jesus if both partners surrender to Him! It happens all the time. Satan meant it for evil, but God turned it into good! Praise His Name!)

Will's parents were trying to maintain their occult influence over the family. The couple had cut off all possible contact with them but the prayer sessions were not fully successful. Will, especially, was having trouble getting victory.

Over the weeks, we prayed for them and they also sought the Lord's guidance. Then Cheryl recalled (or the Spirit brought to her mind) a set of pins and needles which had been left by the parents. She examined them and found they all had an odd bluish discoloration on the ends. They brought them to us and we told them of certain occult potions (possibly even poisons) which would produce such an odd stain. We took the needles and pins and disposed of them. Once they were out of their house, 90% of the oppression lifted like a cloud!

We explained to them how object links work. This is an occult term which means that something physical is used to established a link through which magic (demonic) power can travel. It can be something from the person being cursed (a lock of hair, nail clippings or clothing) which is in the possession of the magician...

OR it can be something from the magician which has been magically charged (i.e. worshipped or chanted over in a magic circle) and then placed on the person or property to be accessed. In the case of the couple above, the pins were probably charged in a magic circle and perhaps even coated with occult tinctures or poisons.

Technically, (remember Satan is the accuser of the brethren and thrives on legalism) that makes these little needles into idolatrous objects—cursed things. Thus, no matter how carefully Will and Cheryl tried to cleanse their home of occult or cultic objects, as long as those pins were there, they provided an access point for demonic invasion.

Great spiritual strides had been made in that family in the past year. There was no way spirit intruders could access the home. Then, unexpectedly, Will's parents showed up at the door—from halfway across the country! He was at work, and Cheryl did not even want to let them in the house. When she went to call him, their littlest boy innocently let "grandma and grandpa" into the living room. As soon as Cheryl came back she got them to leave.

Though they were only in the living room minutes, the Holy Spirit prompted Cheryl to give the room a thorough once-over. Sure enough, she found many of those same discolored bluish pins in various seldom-seen parts of the room—despite the fact that she had thoroughly cleaned the house the night before and found nothing!

It was obvious that the parents (who were believed to be Satanists) had exhausted every means to invade and attack the home once it had been cleaned out and Will and Cheryl had been liberated by the Lord Jesus Christ. They were desperate enough to travel 2,000 miles and scatter more object links into the home, just to reopen their access to the family's life and health. Praise the Lord, Cheryl was responsive to the Spirit's prompting and searched the place thoroughly!

THE CASE OF THE "GOLDEN BIBLE"

A different kind of illustration happened to us as we were finishing this book. In addition to the many other cults we were involved in, for almost five years we were Mormons (Church of Jesus Christ of Latter-day Saints).[1] Because of this, we have a special burden to win Mormons to Christ.

So when Sharon answered the door one day, and saw two Mormon missionaries standing there, it was a rare opportunity. She talked with them for about an hour and a half. The dialog was powerful, and she cast several doubts into their minds. As they left, they insisted on leaving a copy of the *Book of Mormon* for Sharon to read and "pray about."

Mormons believe that the *Book of Mormon* was translated by their founder, Joseph Smith, from gold plates dug out of a hillside in upstate New York in the 1820's. Hence, some people call it the "Mormon Bible" or even the "Golden Bible." Actually, it is a badly written example of false scripture.

Sharon reluctantly accepted the book but refused to promise to read it, since she had already studied the *Book of Mormon* when she was a Mormon. She immediately prayed over it and pled the blood of Jesus over it. Mormons are taught that the *Book of Mormon* actually has a "familiar spirit," which they do not understand is a demonic power.

Just to be on the safe side, Sharon put the book out on the back porch. Even so, within a couple of hours, Sharon and I got into a real serious argument over nothing important. (Normally, we only have about one argument a year, praise the Lord!)

We didn't know whether the spiritual attack was from the *Book of Mormon* or from the spirits of false priesthood (priestcraft) which the Mormon "elders" bring with them into peoples' homes. We immediately prayed over the home, invoked the power of the cross and the blood of Jesus. We took authority over any lying and deceitful spirits of the Church of Jesus Christ of Latter-day Saints and cast them out. The atmosphere lightened instantly and we haven't had an argument since! Hallelujah!

THE CASE OF THE HAUNTED LAND

Another woman who came to us for prayer had several areas of spiritual oppression, including involvement in a cult-like church.

In addition to her other problems, Joannie and her husband had just purchased an exotic, beautiful country home in the northern suburbs of Seattle. Soon after moving in, they learned that a very high level warlock had built the home and lived in it for several years. The spiritual oppression in the house was overpowering, and even the property seemed haunted by evil and malignancy. Both the children and adults suffered from an overwhelming sense of fear, plus nightmares and insomnia.

After settling in, they noticed odd stains in the dark, vaulted cathedral ceilings. Exploration with a powerful flashlight showed that the wood paneling was smeared with blood! They had been "prayed for" by a supposed expert in deliverance from their neck of the woods who was—himself—seriously demonized! His "ministry" had added another layer of occult bondage to their problems. The more they investigated the house, the worse it seemed.

They noticed tiny nails driven into the walls in the shape of pentagrams (see Chapter 11). With a metal detector, they found odd masses of metal behind the walls in the bedroom.

The stream on their property seemed foul and polluted. It ran through their property from a tract of land owned by witches. They also found evidence of past (and reasonably present) Satanic rituals being done in the woods to the rear of their land! Finally, their cellar became mysteriously infested with huge numbers of rats. That was when Joannie came to us.

First, we prayed for Joannie to be set free. Then, we offered her advice on "cleaning up" her property. Sharon told her it was possible that the former owner, the "warlock," had deliberately filled the house with occult booby-traps. His plan might have been to sell them the house for a very handsome price because of its striking architecture and its beautiful, secluded setting.

After they moved in, the house would be so over-powering and oppressive that they would be literally driven out after a few weeks. They would sell it, perhaps for much less than they paid and take the loss. One of the warlock's witch friends (who would LOVE the "vibes" in the house) would pick it up as "a steal," and the original owner would still have the huge sum he originally got for the house.

However, we told Joannie that we believed Jesus had OTHER plans for their house. We explained that in the occult, both iron and the number five are sacred to Mars. Therefore iron nails would make excellent Mars talismans.[2] Plus, the Nail is one of the code words for Satan himself within the Brotherhood.[3] It would be impossible for them to remove all the nails in the house—or to determine which of the thousands of nails were in an occult pattern.

Nor could they rip out all the walls and floor-boards to find possible (but by no means certain) occult trinkets buried beneath. We suggested that they do a major spiritual house dedication and anoint every room with olive oil. (See appendices for full instructions.)

We told them to firmly declare that everything in this room is now consecrated to the Lord Jesus Christ, and ask Him to remove any occult defilement from the room. We instructed them to do this in each and every room in the house— and in the basement.

We also suggested that they prayerfully walk the entire property line and place a periodic drip of oil on the line. We told them to plead the blood of Jesus Christ over the property, and ask the Lord to forgive the sin of shedding any innocent blood on the land by anyone at any time (See Deut. 19:10, and 21:1-9. Finally we told them to claim Joshua 14:9:

> **"Surely the land whereon thy feet have trodden shall be thine inheritance, and thy children's for ever, because thou hast wholly followed the Lord my God."**

Concerning the stream, we drew on the experience of Elisha in 2 Kings 2:19-22, where he healed the foul waters by praying and casting a cruse of salt into them. That strategy had worked for us on at least two other occasions.

Joannie returned home and did as we suggested. The results were a blessing! An incredible amount of spiritual oppression in the home lifted! The stream miraculously became crystal clear, and no longer smelled. The rats instantly fled and never returned. Praise the Lord, for His mercy endures forever!

THE CASE OF THE CREEPING SLIME

Finally, an example of how innocent-looking objects may be used by covens as access points. A lady named Shannon called us from Texas. She and her husband had run afoul of a coven full of Satanists. It seems their business was next to a business that the coven operated. The coven discerned that they were Christians and immediately began to curse them.

Before Shannon figured out what was happening, two coven members came to her home for a visit. Now she was experiencing bizarre manifestations in her home. First, towering, ghostly figures were appearing in their bedroom at night—waking her up while her husband snoozed peacefully. Then she'd hear low, sinister-sounding chanting reverberate through the house during the night.

She would rebuke these things in the name of Jesus, but it would take an unusually large amount of prayer for the frightening visions to dissipate.

The final straw which led her to call us occurred as she rested on her bed in broad daylight after a particularly awful night. First, she heard the chanting and smelled an incredibly foul odor. Looking around, she saw a pus-like ichor oozing by the cupfuls out of the wall behind the her bed! She had trouble keeping herself from nausea and panic!

She ran into the bathroom and began praying furiously to Jesus for help. It took more than an hour for the phenomenon to disappear, and the stench lingered for a couple of days.

On the phone, I explained to her about Spiritual Hygiene (see Chapter 11). Shannon assured us that she had gotten every conceivable occult or cultic object or book out of their house. I asked if any cult members had gotten access to her home. She recalled that a couple of them had visited her, and had asked if they could use her bathroom.

I explained how relatively innocent objects can be "loaded" with demonic energy and deliberately left somewhere in the home as an object-link or access point. I suggested that she pray and ask the Lord's guidance in finding the thing, since it could be a safety pin, a glove, a scarf, or almost anything! I suggested that she start with her bedroom since that was where the manifestations centered.

Shannon prayed, and felt led by the Spirit to move the bed and look behind the headboard. Sure enough, barely visible on the floor was a tiny glass vial with some clear white-ish liquid in it. She called me back and I advised her to plead the blood of Jesus over it and command any spirits, fetches or familiars to go immediately where the Lord Jesus Christ tells them to go. Then, I told her to throw it into the fire. Shannon carried out the instructions, and their home was freed of further occult attacks. Praise God for His faithfulness!

11

"Spiritual Hygiene"

> "Neither shalt thou bring an abomination into thine house, lest thou be a cursed thing like it: but thou shalt utterly detest it, and thou shalt utterly abhor it; for it is a cursed thing."
>
> **Deut. 7:26**

A big consideration in doing spiritual warfare is keeping your own "armed camp" (your home) clean spiritually. Many Christians don't understand that if they are doing anything for the Lord, their homes are going to become battlegrounds.

We all would like to think of our homes and churches as safe refuges and citadels of holiness and sanctity. Oftentimes, that is the case. However, Satan will fight back if you are making inroads into his domain. If you pray for souls, witness, work hard in your church—he will come after you.

It is amazing how Hollywood has corrupted our understanding of spiritual realities. We counselled a good Christian family a few days ago. The husband is a great guy, but was under the impression that Satan couldn't get inside a church building. Perhaps he got the idea from a vampire movie—that crosses or something could keep the devil out. Unfortunately, Satan often works his hardest in churches.

We don't know how Satan spreads his "troops," but we doubt he sends a lot of additional demons to porno shops, bars or crack houses. Since he has finite power and energy, and a limited (though large) number of demonic foot-soldiers, he isn't going to take ground which is already his. Like any wise general, he only leaves a skeleton force at such "dens of iniquity" just to maintain a military "presence."

His most aggressive activity is directed at Christians and churches that are doing a work for God. This is true of homes, families, and churches. Unless you are a "Couch-potato Christian," you can bet that Satan is attacking (or plotting to attack) your family!

BEING A SOLDIER OF THE CROSS

Therefore, your home should be spiritually spic-and-span because it is a camp of the Lord's army! Both the passage quoted at the beginning of the chapter and the following verses speak of conduct within the camps of Israel's armed forces:

> "Thou shalt have a place also without the camp, whither thou shalt go forth abroad: And thou shalt have a paddle upon thy weapon; and it shall be, when thou wilt ease thyself abroad, thou shalt dig therewith, and shalt turn back and cover that which cometh from thee: For the Lord thy God walketh in the midst of thy camp, to deliver thee, and to give up thine enemies before thee; therefore shall thy camp be holy: that he see no unclean thing in thee, and turn away from thee."   Deut. 23:12

Obviously, there were good hygienic reasons why one would wish to follow these instructions, but the larger issue is that if the Lord, who is our general, is fighting for us, then He has every right to inspect the camp!

These passages demonstrate that He may well move through our home like an Inspector General and give us a "white-glove inspection." He does this for much the same reasons that earthly officers insist upon "spit and polish" in their men, but also because He knows that spiritual sloppiness can lead to open doorways that Satan can move in through and attack.

> "Thou therefore endure hardness, as a good soldier of Jesus Christ. No man that warreth entangleth himself with the affairs of this life; that he may please him who hath chosen him to be a soldier. And if a man also strive for masteries, yet is he not crowned, except he strive lawfully."
> 2 Tim. 2:3-5

The application of Deut. 7:26 to Joshua's later

battles in the Promised Land is very instructive. The account of Achan of the tribe of Judah bringing a "cursed thing" into his tent, and the Hebrew army's subsequent demoralizing defeat at the battle of Ai in Joshua 7 shows that even one forbidden object can open up all sorts of reasons for spiritual catastrophe.

> **"Be not deceived; God is not mocked: for whatsoever a man soweth, that shall he also reap."** Gal. 6:7

Praise the Lord, we are in the age of grace! We can rejoice that since Jesus Christ has nailed the law to the cross (Col. 2:14), our "sowing and reaping" has nothing to do with our eternal destiny, as long as we have received Him as Lord and Saviour. However, since we still live in a fallen world, in fallen bodies, we can sow and reap in terms of our lives, our health, our children, our finances, etc.

Just as parents are careful to keep their home free from putrefying or decaying garbage, and teach their children to wash their hands before meals, so a Christian parent should be concerned about the spiritual "germs," their family members come in contact with.

As in the world of health, bacteria and viruses, children are often more vulnerable to unwholesome spiritual influences. But it is not just children we should be concerned about. The following suggestions are measures that we urge every Christian to undertake—especially if they feel called into a prayer, intercession or other ministry in which they will be stealing souls from Satan's realm.

CLEANING YOUR HOUSEHOLD

First of all, some of these things might be controversial. But after praying for and counseling with hundreds of people who have been under various forms of spiritual affliction, we have found these things to be problematic—sometimes severely so. If some Believers disagree, that is up to them.

Other Christians may go in the opposite direction and think that we have not included enough items which need to be purged. A couple of examples are in order.

Some Christian teachers have urged people to get rid of all statues or pictures (paintings, needlepoint renderings, etc.) of owls, cats, frogs, pigs, etc. on the grounds that these animals are either associated with Witchcraft or are unclean in the Old Testament laws.

We respectfully disagree, unless the owner of the statuettes, etc. is bowing down and worshipping them. God DID make owls, cats, etc. They are wonderful parts of His creation. They are good and to be received with thanksgiving (1 Tim. 4:3-4). Of course, there needs to be balance. If a woman has a knick-knack shelf with 600 little toad statuettes on it, you might wonder a bit. However, because these animals are true creatures of God, we don't think that an occasional picture or ceramic statuette is going to bring down curses.

Another area is concerning pictures. One woman wrote us about my book, ***Masonry: Beyond the Light.*** She loved it, but was distressed by the cover and felt led to rip it off before putting it on her bookshelf. The cover shows the Masonic square and compass with a shadowy goats' head (Baphomet) lurking in the background. She burnt the cover, feeling it would attract demons. Obviously, if we felt that putting an occult picture on a book would draw demons, we would never do it.

Through our experience, in most cases, three-dimensional objects are most problematic. With one exception (see Ezek. 8:10), which may or may not be talking about painted pictures (it may be talking about bas-reliefs), there is no condemnation of two-dimensional images, only 3-D things, like statues. Most Christians who minister in this area agree that pictures are not nearly as problematic as statues and graven images.

The intent and use of the picture make a difference as well. Many Bible study books and encyclopedias have pictures of ancient idols from Nineveh or Babylon in them. Like in my book, those pictures were designed to instruct and inform, not to elicit worship. Yet we would not counsel Christians to destroy those books or tear the pictures from them.

On the other hand, a two-dimensional talisman drawn in ink on a piece of parchment by a sorcerer might have incredibly evil power because it was energized deliberately to draw evil spirits. Hopefully, Christians who produce books about the cults and occult, or about ancient civilizations, are not energizing or worshipping the pictures in their books. Thus, there should not be any problem.

Here then are some broad categories of things

(and practices) which we have found to be open doorways for Satan to access and attack your home:

I. PAGAN ART OBJECTS:

These are artifacts which are often quite intricate and beautiful from countries steeped in paganism (i.e., Africa, China, India) which are also religious icons that are worshipped. Please note that not everything produced in a pagan nation qualifies. One evangelist recommended casting Buddhist or Shinto demons out of Japanese cars. That probably isn't necessary. Here are a few suggestions:

1) Statues of the Buddha, Kwan Yin, Fo Hi, Foo dogs and some other Oriental sculptures.

2) Native American sand-paintings, Kachina dolls, totem art, etc.

3) African statues: Especially when they are overtly sexual in nature.

4) African Obeah wands or staffs: Often sold as canes, they can be noted by their intricate carvings.

5) Dragons: A common symbol in the East, the dragon is venerated and worshipped in most Oriental faiths. It is also a symbol of Satan in the Bible.

6) The Tai Chi symbol: This is a circle divided in half by an S-shaped line. One half is black, the other half white. It is the sacred symbol of Taoism and is used extensively in the Martial arts (and also featured on the Korean flag).

Tai Chi Symbol (Yin and Yang)

II. OCCULT IDOLS:

These are objects more associated with the occult or Witchcraft subculture than a particular culture. Some have been venerated for centuries as sources of dark power:

1) Unicorns: Though marketed today as symbols of fantasy, freedom and purity, the unicorn is worshipped in the occult as a symbol to invoke sexual lust and is believed by Satanists to be the "white horse" upon which the anti-Christ will ride (See Rev. 6:2 and Dan. 8:21-24).

2) Crystals: Not so much crystals as they appear in nature, but crystals which have been "charged," "loaded" or prayed over by New Age practitioners or witches. This means they have attempted to put spirit power or "life force" (i.e. demons) into them.

There is an incredibly complex science of occult gemology and crystalomancy. Our advice is that if you have crystals you are uncertain about, pray over them and plead the blood of Jesus over them. Then enjoy them as the beautiful creations that they are—unless they have been shaped into occult artifacts.

3) Hex Signs: Pennsylvania Dutch. Also called "painted prayers," these circular and colorful designs seen on farms and barns in Pennsylvania and elsewhere are actually occult talismans. Their foundational symbols are drawn from occult workbooks.

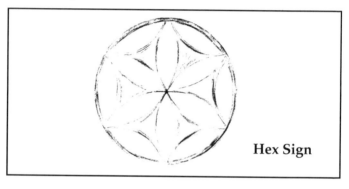

Hex Sign

4) The "Italian Horn" Jewelry: This is said to represent a Unicorn horn and is often worn by men to increase their sexual power. It is a talisman to provoke lust, and should not be worn by Christians.

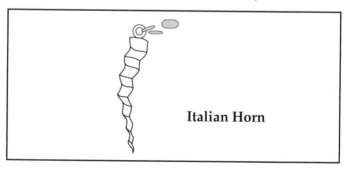

Italian Horn

5) Pegasus: The winged horse. Like the Unicorn, this is another mythical beast. Remember, what we call myths today were the very serious religions Paul denounced among the ancient Greeks and Romans (see Acts 17:16-23). These are not to be trifled with!

6) Occult toys: Some of these are a bit older or dated, some still popular, but they illustrate what parents should be on the look-out for.

a) Dungeons and Dragons games and figurines. Also many other fantasy role-playing games and their pieces.[1]

b) Masters of the Universe (He-man and She-Ra, etc.)

c) Smurfs

d) Some "My Little Pony" type figurines (Unicorns, Pegasus, etc.).

e) Care Bears

f) Ouija Boards—extremely bad.

g) Teenage Mutant Ninja Turtles (because of the ninja elements[2]).

h) Halloween-oriented toys.

i) Some video games (Nintendo, Sega, etc.) have high occult content, some do not. These need to be examined on a case-by-case basis.

j) Cabbage Patch Dolls: Though apparently innocent, we have had several children who were oppressed by these.[3]

7) Heavy Metal Rock posters or albums (secular or "Christian"). Heavy Metal music cannot be Christian, anymore than one could have "Christian topless dancing" or "Christian gambling." Virtually all artifacts surrounding Heavy Metal music are either occult, satanic or associated with the dark world of sado-masochism and perverted sexual dominance and bondage of women.

8) Occult jewelry:

a) Pentagrams: 5-pointed stars, either inverted (two points up, the symbol of Satanism) or upright (one point up, the symbol of "white" witchcraft.)

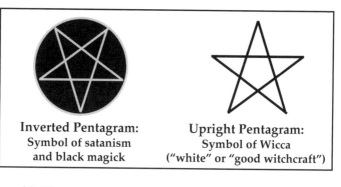

Inverted Pentagram:
Symbol of satanism
and black magick

Upright Pentagram:
Symbol of Wicca
("white" or "good witchcraft")

b) Hexagrams: 6-pointed stars, symbol of the anti-Christ in Satanism (6 points, 6 angles, 6 planes = 666), especially if the star is circumscribed by a circle.

c) Ankh: (Crux ansanta or looped cross) Egyptian symbol of eternal love and lust. Now has been adapted into the symbol of feminism from the astro-logical symbol for the planet Venus.

Ankh
(Crux Ansanta)

d) SS runes (Nazi & ancient Norse): Looks like twin stylized lightning bolts. These are the disguised initials of the Horned God of Witchcraft.

Twin Sowelus
or "SS Runes

e) Skull and crossbones: Another symbol of the Horned God of Witchcraft.

f) Birthstone jewelry: Borderline—you need to pray about it. Birthstones are rooted in astrology.

9) Crucifixes, statues of Mary, other Catholic statuary: All of these are three-dimensional symbols

of the dead. Even the "Jesus" on the crucifix is a dead Jesus. They are used in Catholic piety to direct prayers to dead "saints." Talking to the dead is strictly forbidden by the Bible. Thus, these items constitute idols, just as much as Buddhas, etc.

10) Rosaries are also a problem because they are rooted in the Hindu concept of the mantra and the mala. Mantra is the continued repetition of certain "sacred" names or prayers. This is what a rosary is, and the Lord forbids it (Matt. 6:7).

The mala is a string of beads originally used by Hindus to keep track of prayers. It was later used by devout Muslims. The mala is a symbol of bondage to the deity to whom the prayers are directed. Since rosaries are primarily (10:1 ratio) prayed to Mary, this is placing oneself in bondage to a dead woman— actually a demon masquerading as the real Mary.

The technical theological term in Catholicism for their veneration of Mary is Hyperdulia—which is Greek, translated as "super-bondage" or "super-slavery." These things need to be disposed of!

11) Masonic regalia:

    a) Aprons, sashes, jewels of office.

    b) Rings and other personal jewelry.

    c) Shriner fezzes and regalia.

    d) Books, ritual monitors.

12) Occult or cultic books:

    a) Magic, New Age, Witchcraft or astrology books.

b) Book of Mormon, other Mormon books.

c) Jehovah's Witness literature, their "Bible," the New World Translation.

d) Catholic missals, Bibles, hymnals, prayer-books, etc.

e) Literature from any other cult group.[4]

III. PORNOGRAPHY:

There is another reason, beyond the issue of sexual morality, that no Christians should have this in their home. Careful study shows us that the oldest "idols" or objects of worship in human history were the human sexual organs. This is probably natural, since they produced life and pleasure.

Since most pornography (at least of the photographic variety) focuses on primary or secondary sexual characteristics, indulgence in it becomes—both literally and spiritually—a kind of idolatry or Ba'al worship. This, we believe, is why pornography is so terribly addictive. Its use opens doorways and brings spirits of lust and whoredoms.

IV. ILLEGAL DRUGS:

Like the previous classification, reasons for this may be self-evident. However, it is not well known that many "natural" drugs (cocaine, marijuana, heroin, hashish, peyote) were once worshipped as gods by the indigenous peoples that used them. Thus, their use CAN open doorways for spiritual attack from these "gods" which are actually demons.

Even liquor, which is legal in America, has ancient demonic strongholds that can hold one in bondage. This is (partially, at least) why such drugs are so addictive.

V. OCCULT PRACTICES:

While these are not "things" that can be present in a home, it is our opinion that the Bible shows that practicing them can open doorways for demonic attack in the home.

1) Astrology: Beware! Some highly regarded Christian writers now promote forms of astrology. The most obvious example is the teaching on the "Four Temperaments" (Sanguine, Choleric, Melancholic and Phlegmatic) and their use in counseling and determination of supposed spiritual gifts.

It is based on the teachings of Galen, a pagan philosopher from hundreds of years ago. There is as much scientific basis for this model of thinking as there is for swinging a dead cat around a graveyard at midnight on the full-moon to get rid of a wart.

2) Other Forms of Divination: These are various ways of foretelling the future. Among the most commonly used are:

a) Tarot cards or regular playing card-reading (cartomancy).

b) Palmistry: Reading palms.

c) Tea-leaf reading.

d) Ouija Boards.

e) I Ching (coin or yarrow stalk method).

3) Spiritism, channeling, mediumship. Following various "channeled entities," including, but not limited to:

a) J. Z. Knight (Ramtha)

b) Jane Roberts (Seth)

c) Kevin Ryerson

d) J. Pursell (Lazaris)

e) Penny Torrence (Mafu)

f) Various Marian apparitions. Most recently, Our Lady of Medjugorie.[5]

4) Visualization, and some practices of "Inner Healing," especially where an abuse victim is told to visualize a "Jesus" coming to them in their childhood trauma and comforting them. This is occult based and is not supported by the Bible. Beware!

5) Jungian analysis and dream interpretation. Carl Jung's methods are based on mysticism, astrology and alchemy. They are occult and highly dangerous.

6) Martial Arts, especially the "internal styles:"[6]

a) Tai Chi Chuan

b) Hsing I

c) Pa Kua

d) Kung Fu

e) Aikido

7) Yoga (Hatha, Gnana, Raja, Bhakti, Tantric, etc.)

8) Some practices of alternative or "Holistic" healing, including:

a) Hypnosis (see Chapter 7 for details)

b) Acupuncture, acupressure, Touch for Health.

c) Polarity Therapy

d) Shiatsu and Reflexology

e) Homeopathy[7]

f) Bach Flower Remedies

g) Reichian Therapy (Wilhelm Reich)—orgone boxes, etc.

h) Rolfing (Ada Rolf)

9) Motivational and Self-Improvement Cults: These groups normally don't claim to be religious, but rather offer themselves as psychological or motivational therapeutic strategies. They are springing up like crabgrass, so be careful. Just because something isn't listed, doesn't mean it is Biblical. Check it out!

a) The Forum (formerly called est)—Werner Erhard.

b) Kroning

c) Pacific Institute (Lou Tice)

d) Transcendental Mediation (TM). Also called "The Science of Creative Intelligence."

e) Other Eastern Meditation systems and/or gurus:

- Siddhi Yoga (Swami Muktananda)
- Sri Chimnoy
- Gopi Krishna
- Swami Rama

- Ananda Marga Yoga Society
- Bhagwhan Shree Rajneesh (now dead, but still has disciples).

f) Silva Mind control

g) Scientology (Dianetics)

h) Lifestream

i) Napoleon Hill (Think and Grow Rich)

j) Possibility Thinking (Robert Schuller)

k) Roy Masters: Foundation for Human Understanding.

10) Some "Stress Reduction" Techniques:

a) Emptying the mind.

b) The visualization of "wise persons" or "counselors" to help you in decision making.

If you have any of these artifacts, books, albums, etc. in your home, we recommend that you destroy them by fire (Acts 19:19). If you have practiced any of the things itemized (or something similar), you need to repent of the practice, renounce it, and see if you have any demonic oppression because of it.

Pictured on the following three pages are various other occult symbols and their meanings.

"CORNU"

Sign of the Horns. The universally recognized salute for Satanism. It stands for the horns of the goat being exalted.

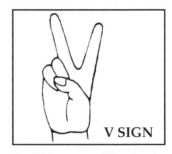

V SIGN

An 18th century Illuminati symbol that represents the fulfillment of Illuminist founder Adam Weishaupt's satanic Law of Fives.

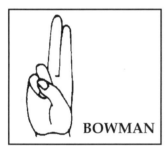

BOWMAN

Exalts the horns of Satan over the 3 fingers of the Trinity. "The Sign of Nimrod" or "Sign of the Bowman" (the position of one's fingers to draw back the string on a bow). In the Bible, the bow symbolizes wicked men, lost people, etc. (Gen. 10:8-9, 21:20, 27:3, Ps. 11:2, Ps. 37:14, Jer. 51:1-3ff, Ezek. 39:3, Rev. 6:2).

Disguised 666

A disguised interlocked trio of sixes, symbolic of the anti-christ. Also symbolizes the triple goddess of Wicca (three interlocked vesica pisces together). Commonly used in Catholic liturgical iconography, and has recently found its way into the logo of the New King James Bible.

666 - Mark of Anti-Christ
FFF (6th letter) is a coded
way of writing the same
thing.

"A" symbol stands for
nihilism and anarchy.

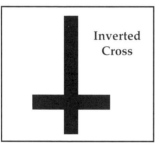

**Inverted
Cross**

Often used over satanic altars.
Symbolizes the inversion of
Christian values.

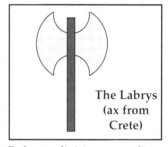

**The Labrys
(ax from
Crete)**

Refers to division or rending
asunder. Used by many
feminist witches and satanists
as a symbol of Matriarchy.

Peace Sign

Known in satanism as "The
Witches' Foot." Based on
ancient rune eolh-secg.

Pontifical Cross of Lucifer

Used in *The Satanic Bible*.

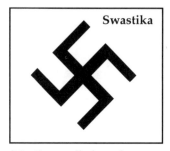

(Nazi) actually based on
ancient Hindu idol and
ancient Norse Sunwheel.

Symbol of a Thelemic Group
(followers of Aleister
Crowley).

12

The Christian's Manual of Arms

> "Put on the whole armour of God, that ye may be able to stand against the wiles of the devil."   Eph. 6:11

You can't go into war without your battle armour on! We need to spend some time discussing this armour, and how it works.

There are several excellent books already out which discuss the battle armour Christians are to wear when they come against the enemies of Jesus. William Gurnall's books[1] are certainly the best of the lot. They contain a tremendous amount of "meaty" and challenging material.

Of course, the warfare manual for the Believer is the Bible, and especially the Book of Ephesians. Most Christians concerned enough to have gotten this far into this book probably know that the principle text for the armour of God is found in Ephesians 6:10-18.

This is a spiritual armour which Christians are to put on to protect themselves from the attacks of Satan (called "fiery darts"). Anyone who is going to engage in intercession, and/or praying for people who are coming out of the darkness of Satanism needs to know how to put their armour on!

In the 1970's, a phenomenon called "streaking" swept the nation. During sporting events, some oddball (usually male) would run naked across the playing field, often wearing just a ski mask. It was an ungodly and cheap thrill-seeking sort of activity.

However, many Christians are spiritual "streakers." The only piece of the Armour of God they have on is the Helmet of Salvation (they know they are saved). Otherwise they are spiritually naked as a jaybird! All Christians should appropriate the Armour of God daily, especially those feeling called into the ministry.

We will run through the commonly known and understood pieces of Armour. In the next chapter, we will share a few others which many do not know about, including our only defensive weapon, the Sword of the Spirit—the Word of God!

PREPARING TO DEAL WITH THE DEVIL

Before talking about the Armour, we need to discuss something so basic, yet so often neglected by people who feel called into spiritual warfare. Though it is the last thing mentioned in the Ephesians passage, we think it needs to come first. We need to Pray! This is absolutely vital!

We need to get on our faces every day and seriously seek the face of God. Approach Him in prayer, and thereby anchor your soul in the depths of His unfailing Love. Talk to Him and reaffirm Him as your personal source of power and safety! Get your marching orders for the day! Remember that we are in an army, and Jesus Christ is our Captain! A troop needs to keep its line of communication to the commander open at all times, and prayer is our line of communication.

Sometimes that prayer will be simply a time of thanksgiving and praise to the Father for Who He is and what He has done for you. Other times, you'll have a large number of requests for yourself, loved ones, friends and fellow church members.

Also, it is wise to affirm, in prayer, who you are in Jesus Christ—and to claim your favorite scriptural promises. Tell Satan to take a long walk off a short pier, and remind him that Jesus is your Great High Priest, standing in before the throne of God and interceding for you.

If you are anticipating a specific encounter with the enemy (witnessing, prayer for deliverance, etc.) in the coming hours (or even days), begin praying for it and about it—incessantly! Fasting can also be a great strengthener of the spirit, although it needs to be done prudently, and under the guidance of the

Holy Spirit. Additionally, there are some items of business you need to be certain you have dealt with:

1) Repent: In your prayer time, be certain to confess and receive cleansing from all sin (1 John 1:9). Keep "short accounts" with the Lord. You must be free of Satan's power to accuse (cf. Revelations 12:10-11), especially if you are going into a prayer session for demonic oppression.

We have heard of the devil actually bringing up—through the demonized person—unconfessed sins of a minister right in the middle of a deliverance session. That can be very embarrassing and demoralizing, to say the least. Once a sin is under the blood, Satan cannot use to it get under your skin. As Thomas White, another author[2] in the field of spiritual warfare, puts it: "Holiness removes sin handles!"

Obviously no one is perfect, but if all your sins are under the blood, then Satan has no "handles" to seize and attack you with in the midst of the struggle. Keep your life as holy as possible, repent quickly with a truly broken heart, and continually seek the guidance of the Holy Spirit to help improve yourself. Ask the Spirit (and mean it) to show you areas of your life that need improvement. He will!

2) Ask: Continually make yourself transparent to God's wisdom. Ask Him for it (James 1:5-6). Also be sure to request a sharpening of discernment (1 John 2:20, 27) to be empowered to see the situation as God sees it! Ask Him for a fresh infilling of the Holy Spirit and a fresh anointing to accomplish the ministry He has before you for that day.

3) Be certain to beckon the Holy Spirit to take full control of each situation you face! Whether you are ministering, witnessing or praying for a person with demonic affliction, the more of yourself you open to the anointing and power of the Spirit of the Lord, the more effective you will be.

The Holy Spirit is always a Gentleman, and will not come where He is not invited. But if you make clear to Him that you are surrendering the time to Him, He can and will do amazing things.

None of us can have the Holy Spirit beyond measure, as the Lord Jesus Christ did. However, through daily (or even more frequent) "soaking" with prayer, your soul and spirit become "softer" clay with which the Spirit can work. The more time you spend with Him, the more time He will spend with you.

A "DOGFACE" IN THE ARMY OF THE LORD!

Next, you need to put on the Full Armour of God (Eph. 6:10-17, 1 Thess 5:8). Suit up and prepare for battle! Carefully and prayerfully "put on" each piece of your divinely provided protection and "take up" your divine weapons. Be aware that this armour is plainly the armour of a first century Roman foot-soldier—an infantryman!

Why is that significant? Basically all wars are over real estate.Thus, all wars are ultimately settled by this "pawn," the foot-soldier or (as they used to be called "dogface.") In physical war, you cannot run a country unless you rule it, and you cannot rule it unless you possess it, and you cannot possess it unless you are on it, and you cannot get ON it without fighting on your feet.)

This is even more true in the spiritual arena. Though the battle is ultimately fought and won by the Lord (the killer blow was dealt on Calvary), He uses us as infantrymen (and women) to claim individual areas of spiritual "real estate." First of all, this is done by a house-to-house battle within our own souls and bodies, as we reclaim areas of our lives and place them under the Lordship of Jesus. Ultimately, THAT is the most important form of spiritual warfare.

As any combat veteran will tell you, that kind of "house-to-house" foot-by-foot fighting can be the most difficult and challenging. It's usually where the most casualties occur. In the war of the heavenlies, a larger dimension of this kind of fighting occurs. Once you have staked out your own "house," it's time to go forth, one person at a time, and claim precious souls for the Kingdom of God.

Remember, demons think of the people they reside in as their "houses" (Mt. 12:29, 44). Thus, soul-winning is also a house-to-house battle, as you send the Sword of the Spirit probing into an unsaved person's heart and soul, that is another way you will begin to claim territory for your Commander.

Nowadays, it sometimes seems that there aren't enough Christian soldiers in this country to form one good regiment. You can't get a choir to sing "Onward Christian Soldiers" because there are too many spiritual pacifists in the choir! They won't sing "Power in the Blood" because it sounds "gory."

Either that or the troops want to be captains or generals instead of non-coms! They want to take on fights which are "over their heads!" The newest rage sweeping some churches is the idea of Christians attacking "territorial spirits" or principalities over communities or states. We cannot find any Biblical precedent for that. We believe it is like an infantry-man moving into areas where his Commander has not ordered him to go.

We do not believe that the Bible gives us the authority to take on such high level demonic beings. We have seen a few sincere prayer warriors get "beaten up" badly because they tried to spiritually attack out from under the umbrella of the Commander's protection. We do not see Paul rebuking the Principality of Unbelief over Ephesus or Macedonia. Even he, the great apostle to the Gentiles, simply engaged in "house-to-house" combat, bringing souls into the Kingdom one by one.

If certain Christians are called and anointed by God to engage in this kind of cosmic warfare with the principalities and powers over cities or nations, praise the Lord. But we definitely advise caution before entering into this sort of prayer warfare.

The INDIVIDUAL dogface is the decisive element in combat. A fiercely contested piece of ground (i.e. Antietam, in the Civil War) can wreck the plans of the whole opposing army! Therefore, a true soldier of Jesus Christ needs to have guts! He (or she) should hold their ground and then dish it out to the enemy like a spiritual Rambo.

> **"Be sober, be vigilant; because your adversary the devil, as a roaring lion, walketh about, seeking whom he may devour: Whom resist stedfast in the faith,"**
> **1 Pet. 5:8-9**

To understand what Paul is discussing, we need to know that the historical Roman foot-soldier's armour normally came in seven pieces: loin girdle, breast plate, sandals, shield, helmet, sword and leg-guards (greaves).

One commentator points out that the last item is not mentioned in the text.[3] That is because the Christian soldier is kneeling (in prayer) to receive the cavalry charge and the flying arrows of the enemy artillery. His knees, therefore, are already covered (see vs.18).

There is not exactly a "backplate" to the armour because the soldier is supposed to "face up to the enemy" and not retreat. This carries two implications:

1. If he turns and runs, he'll get shot in the back.

2. If he presses the attack too far ahead of his Captain, (i.e. messing with supposed territorial strongmen) he may get hit with friendly fire!

BREAKING DOWN THE ARMOUR:

The Girdle of Truth: You must be convinced of the truth of God in His Word and His promises therein (John 8:31-32). Meditate and claim relevant portions of scripture. "…loins girt about with truth." A person's strength is in his loins, and a person girds his loins. Why? To serve (see John 13)!

This calls for an open, honest, sincere warrior who is girded about with dependability and integrity—and is confident of God's truth. He or she must be willing to serve, not just in spiritual battle, but sometimes in the less "glamourous" aspects of Christian service.

> **"For a day in thy courts is better than a thousand. I had rather be a doorkeeper in the house of my God, than to dwell in the tents of wickedness."** **Ps. 84:10**

The Breastplate of Righteousness: A conscience cleansed from sin (1 Cor. 1:30) "…having on the breastplate of righteousness;" This is personal righteousness and matches the practical admonition of Eph.4-5 to remember to put on something that God has already given! The Believer already HAS God's righteousness (Rom. 10:1-3, 1 Cor. 1-2), but he or she needs to KNOW it as a Bible-based fact. That enables him or her to wear it into battle.

Feet shod with the Gospel of Peace: Above all else, this means a readiness to reconcile broken or strained relationships (Rom. 12:18). The verse, "…your feet shod with the preparation of the gospel of peace;" tells the Christian to be prepared to proclaim the gospel wherever his feet take him, under the most mundane or extraordinary of circumstances. John Wesley witnessed to highwaymen while they stole money from his saddlebags!

The Shield of Faith: This is the unwavering confidence that God will perform what He has promised (Rom. 4:20-21).

> **"Above all, taking the shield of faith, wherewith ye shall be able to quench all the fiery darts of the wicked."** **Eph. 6:16**

Most historians say the Roman infantryman's shield was made out of heavily woven wicker, covered with pitch. This would stop just about any missile or arrow. However, the flaming arrows (beloved of the old cowboy and Indian movies) required a special kind of attention.

The soldier going into combat would wet down his shield with a good dose of water. That would keep the wicker supple (rather than brittle) and would prevent the wicker or pitch from catching fire.

That teaches the soldier in the Lord's infantry that he or she needs to go daily to the Living Water of Jesus Christ (John 4:14, 7:38) and soak their faith in that Water. That means daily praise, prayer and Bible study. Otherwise your faith becomes brittle and easily cracked, and it could "catch fire" with the wrong kind of flame!

Daily applications of Living Water will nourish and strengthen your faith in what God has already accomplished in Your life—and in what He will continue to do. You need that if you are experiencing "incoming fire" from the adversary. The Lord permits those fiery darts to hit because each time our "shield" is able to shrug one off, our faith becomes that much stronger.

Sharon and I both remember the first time we ministered to someone who was demonized. We were so frightened we could hardly talk. But our faith held, and God made it go easy for us.

The next time, our shields were a bit stronger. And the time after that, stronger still. It is almost like a muscle which you have to build up by putting resistance against it. God uses Satan to build up our spiritual muscles so we end up looking like Arnold Schwartzenegger in the spirit! Praise God!

Job knew something about that kind of testing by fiery darts. Jeremiah also had his share slung at him. Paul used to collect them (2 Cor. 11). In appropriating the shield of faith for ourselves, we Christians have to remember that the Lord Jesus Christ took the whole arsenal full in the chest for us (Is. 53, Col. 2) and recovered (Heb. 12:24) with nothing but a few minor scars. We can have that same victory if we keep Jesus between us and whatever the enemy throws against us.

Those Bible heroes teach us that sometimes the Lord allows the arrows of Satan to get through in spite of the best that we can do. At that point, we need to realize that the Lord is tempering us like fine steel and sharpening our edge for battles to come.

Once we have "put up" our shield of faith and strengthened it with daily devotions, we need to humbly and prayerfully receive any arrows which the Lord allows to penetrate our armour, and ask Him for the grace to grow and learn what He wishes us to accomplish.

Christians who think they are intercessors or prayer warriors and go into this kind of fray without their shield are asking for it!

The Helmet of Salvation: This means that in your mind you are certain that you belong to Jesus Christ and that nothing can separate you from His love (Rom. 8:37-39). All soldiers need a helmet of some kind. You can recover from an amputated leg or arm, but it is awfully hard to recover from an amputated head. Christians desperately need to know of their security in the Love of Jesus, and to guard their thought life if they wish to enter into this battle!

Satan can always find something to accuse the warrior about. This is especially true if you are in this kind of struggle. He'll whisper in your ear, "You can't be a Christian, you just hollered at your kids!" or something like that. He also loves to attack believers from occult or cultic backgrounds by telling them that Jesus couldn't save them because they were too evil. Keep that helmet on!

The Sword of the Spirit: This is the Word of God. Since this is the only offensive weapon we are equipped with by our Commander, we feel it deserves a chapter all by itself. Chapter 15 covers it.

Praying in the Spirit: Christians need to understand that their prayers, prompted precisely by the Holy Spirit, are like extremely accurate missiles that can fly right down hell's smokestacks and demolish enemy strongholds. "Pray without ceasing," Paul commands us (1 Thess. 5:17). That may seem like a tall order, but the more time you spend on your knees and in the Word of God, the more you'll find that the Holy Spirit's dynamism and influence in your own spirit grows geometrically!

Finally, His Spirit works and prays within you all the time, if you permit Him to (Romans 8:26-27). This lifestyle of prayer may seem almost impossible with our late 20th century "busy-ness," but with a little soldierly discipline, it can be accomplished.

Above all else, you need to ask the Lord to help you develop your prayer life. Ask Him for help everyday, and He will move in your life in ways that will truly astonish you. You will find yourself praying without even realizing that you had begun to intercede! Your thoughts will move through symphonies of prayer under the conducting baton of the Holy Spirit.

And when job or family demands take your mind completely off spiritual matters, that doesn't stop the Holy Spirit from interceding within you—nor does it stop our Great High Priest from interceding on our behalf before the Father's throne.

Open yourself up to the "College of the Holy Spirit" and major in prayer. If you invite Him to help you and work on you and in you, He will. Then you will really be "praying always" in the Spirit.

ENTHRONED WITH THE CAPTAIN!

Finally, it is important to realize that you truly are seated in heavenly places with Jesus Christ. Your battle is not a contest! Victory has been won, and the Victor has you seated spiritually beside Him (Eph. 2:6).

Also remember that you are to be strong in the Lord and in the power of HIS might! You are not fighting Satan with your strength. (If you are, it's a big mistake!) Instead, you are clothed with the supernatural power of the Father, and His resurrection power flows like molten gold through your veins! (Eph. 6:10, 1:19-21).

Another ally which we sometimes overlook is God's mighty angelic host (Heb. 1:14). While many things are not clear about angels, this much is clear. They are powerful beings and we can ask the Lord to send them to help us. In prayer ministry, and many times in our day-to-day lives, we have been astonished at the faithfulness of the angels of the Lord.

We are confident that we have only the tiniest idea how many times God has sent His angels to protect us, yet we were blissfully unaware of it. This is why whenever we pray for someone, we always ask the Lord for angelic protection—even a legion of angels to be around the property.

He is faithful to oblige, and we seldom have any unseemly outbreaks in our prayer sessions. We know it is nothing of us, but rather because there is a clash of supernatural steel in the heavenlies between the Lord's angels and Satan's imps—and guess who gets sent home limping every time!

This is a substantial part of the battle armour you need if you are going to go into the fray. A couple of additional pieces of armour which the Lord has shown us can also be a real help. They are covered in the next chapter.

13

Is Some of Your Armour Missing?

Though most well informed Believers know about the armour of God passage in Ephesians, not as many know that other pieces of the Lord's armour for us are found elsewhere in the Bible.

We feel that the Lord is bringing these other armaments to our attention because the Holy Spirit is awakening the Church of Jesus Christ to a new level of spiritual aggressiveness.

Satan has definitely stepped up his battle plan as the Second Advent draws nearer. Unfortunately, many Christian churches have been caught unawares by this new assault. So many Christians who come to us for prayer and counsel act like they've just been run over by a Mack truck and are totally bewildered. They are asking, "What hit me?"

In some cases, this is because they have not heard about the authority they have as Believers in the Lord, nor about the power of prevailing prayer. In other cases, it's because they do not know what it means to pray with violence and aggressive spiritual force.

Many other Believers give no heed to the dangers of the occult, cults and the supernatural realm. They are relatively ignorant of the wiles and tactics of Satan because these subjects are not preached about in most churches, even though the Bible warns us that Satan can get an advantage of us if we remain ignorant of his devices (2 Cor. 2:11).

Fortunately, this situation is improving. Due to the efforts of many pastors and teachers, the Body of Christ is becoming aware that they are in a war zone—even in areas as "normal" to church life as soul-winning efforts, missionary outreaches and marriage and family concerns.

Praise God, millions of Christians now know that there is such a thing as the "whole armour of God" (Eph. 6:10 ff) and are girding it on daily to do battle for their heavenly Captain... in the business world, the neighborhood, the living room and even within the church. As a result, we are seeing an incredible hemorrhage within Satan's kingdom.

People are coming out of the darkness of the devil's churches and into the light of Jesus at what appears to be an unprecedented rate! The evil of cults and false religions is being exposed now more than ever!

All this is the result of praying, "armored-up" Believers who are willing to intercede with assertive, forceful prayer for lost loved ones and friends. However, this kind of battle is not without its toll. Many prayer warriors are feeling the battle fatigue of fighting against an enemy that doesn't tire out.

We all know that God doesn't get tired, but His front-line soldiers do. This is because Satan isn't taking all these assaults lying down. He is counter-attacking with everything he can muster, and many Christians who have committed themselves to spiritual warfare are in a battle which sometimes seems overwhelming. Families are under attack, job and health problems rear up and praying churches get into splits.

THE GARMENT OF MESSIAH

It seems the Lord is telling us that we need to bring up everything in our arsenal. The armour of God is vital, but many saints have not considered a couple of vital pieces. In Isaiah 59:17, we read:

> **"For he put on righteousness as a breast-plate, and an helmet of salvation upon his head; and he put on the garments of ven-geance for clothing, and was clad with zeal as a cloak."**

This passage is talking about Messiah and His Second Advent, especially in the light of Jesus' role as Intercessor. The previous verse says:

"...he saw that there was no man, and wondered that there was no intercessor: therefore his arm brought salvation unto him; and his righteousness, it sustained him."

Interceding Christians must never feel that they are in the fray alone. Jesus is our great High Priest and chief Intercessor. Since we are—collectively—the Body of Christ, there are two key pieces of battle armour that we may be neglecting.

The "garments of vengeance" are probably disturbing to most Christians because we are normally taught not to take revenge. This is correct. Vengeance belongs to God, and Him alone (Rom. 12:19). But, this garment is actually Messiah's and we must remember that we are members of the Body of Christ. That is the only way we can appropriate ANY of the blessings of the armour!

To understand what this garment is and how the Lord gives it to us to use, it is helpful to apply the "Law of First-Mention." This means examining how a term is used the first time in the Bible for keys to its meaning later.

In Genesis 3:21, we find garments being created by God for Adam and Eve after they realized they were naked. The Bible calls them "coats of skin." They were evidently made through the shedding of some animal's blood.

Subsequent revelations show that this was to teach them the enormity of their sin, and that without the shedding of blood, there could be no remission of sins (Heb. 9:22). God rejected their self-made "aprons" of fig-leaves and clothed them by shedding innocent blood.

Aside from the main application of salvation by grace through the shedding of blood, this passage instructs us in putting on the garment of vengeance. We must do so with prayer and deliberation, making certain that it is indeed the Lord's garment, and not an "apron" we have whipped up ourselves. We must, as Jude puts it, hate the garment spotted by the flesh (Jude 23). Our garment of vengeance must have none of our "flesh" on it, none of our own human desire to "fix" someone, or set things "right" according to our opinion.

Also, the close link between shed blood and the garment is critical. Look at this passage, which talks about the coming of Jesus at the Second Advent:

> **"Who is this that cometh from Edom, with dyed garments from Bozrah? this that is glorious in his apparel, travelling in the greatness of his strength? I that speak in righteousness, mighty to save. Wherefore art thou red in thine apparel, and thy garments like him that treadeth in the winefat? I have trodden the winepress alone; and of the people there was none with me: for I will tread them in mine anger, and trample them in my fury; and their blood shall be sprinkled upon my garments, and I will stain all my raiment."**
> **Isa. 63:1-3**

This warfare is not for the faint-hearted, beloved.

When Jesus comes again, there will be great bloodshed:

> **"And he was clothed with a vesture dipped in blood: and his name is called The Word of God."** **Rev. 19:13**

I hate to say it, but the battle of Armageddon is going to be the ultimate "splatter movie" (Rev. 14:20). In all of our spiritual conflict, we overcome by the blood of the Lamb (Rev. 12:11). This makes sense when we see that these garments are also related to our own salvation (Isa. 61:10).

This is a wonderful thought, for it takes care of the problem we alluded to earlier. The Armour of God in Ephesians provides nothing to cover our "rear flank." A garment normally covers a person from neck to ankles. This means that as we appropriate this garment, we are covered—even from attacks from behind.

That can be very helpful, especially since lately a serious part of spiritual warfare has become attacks from fellow Christians who are supposed to be "behind us," yet are used by the devil (often without their knowledge) to "stab us in the back."

TAKING OFF THE KID GLOVES

However, there is a more important lesson to be learned about this garment, and how we use it. Jesus' version of the garment is stained with the blood of His enemies. Words like "fury" are used to describe His temperament, even though these blood-stained garments are also described as "glorious." This image of Jesus is not one immediately accessible to many Christians. They are used to seeing the classic paintings of a quiet, almost effeminate Jesus with a sheep in His arms leading a flock.

For many reasons, Christians have allowed the image of Jesus in the gospels as gentle, meek and mild to predominate their thinking. This is only natural, since the gospels provide the most thorough portrait of the incarnate Lord. Truly, there is a place for the "Suffering Servant" prophesied by Isaiah who would not even quench a smoking flax or break a bruised reed.

It is good for Christians to keep the gentle, merciful image of Jesus in our minds because that is the side of Jesus which we get to experience:

> **"For God hath not appointed us to wrath, but to obtain salvation by our Lord Jesus Christ."** 1 Thess. 5:9

We must remember that the entire Bible—Old and New Testaments—is the consummate revelation of the Lord Jesus Christ. The Book of Revelation and much of the Old Testament present another side of the Lord's personality—the side relating to His awesome sense of justice, His righteous and boiling anger over the sin and blasphemy of the world.

Praise God, we will never see His wrathful side! But the Lord is showing us that we can put on the garment of vengeance in our prayers and intercessory warfare. It's time to "take off the kid gloves!" Too many wonderful Christians are reeling from pillar to post, from one attack to the next. And the Lord is saying, "Clothe yourselves in my garments of vengeance." Anger against sin is not sin. It's time for Christians to take up the sword of the Spirit and battle aggressively—ever bearing in mind that our struggle is with a spiritual foe, not with deceived cultists or occultists who are Satan's victims.

> **"Ye have not yet resisted unto blood, striving against sin."**   **Heb. 12:4**

While this verse can mean resisting temptation, it can also mean actively STRIVING against sin! How does one strive against sin, and the wiles of Satan? God is saying here that the best defense is a good offense. It isn't enough to stand there and grit your teeth until the temptation is over. Christians often forget that Jesus' promise to the church is that:

> **"...the gates of hell shall not prevail against it."**   **Matt. 16:18**

Too many Christians see themselves in a citadel of righteousness (their family, home or church) with the door barred and Satan trying to break in. That's NOT what Jesus has in mind. This verse says that hell has tried to bar its gates against the onslaught of the Church, but the Church will smash through those gates like an M-1 Abrams tank going through a shower curtain.

It's time that, in our prayers and warfare, we begin to batter down hell's gates. Certainly, the Church has always done that through soul-winning, missionary work and the proclamation of the gospel. However, we need to don the garments of vengeance and, with their protection, begin to pull down:

> "…strong holds;) Casting down imagina-
> tions, and every high thing that exalteth
> itself against the knowledge of God, and
> bringing into captivity every thought to the
> obedience of Christ; And having in a readi-
> ness to revenge all disobedience, when your
> obedience is fulfilled."   2 Cor. 10:4-6

Many spiritual warriors stop before verse 6, but look what it says! We are to have a readiness to "revenge all disobedience" when we are obeying the Captain. That is critical! We must be certain that we are in the Lord's will, and are obeying Him. Then we will have the comprehensive covering of the garment of vengeance underneath all our other armour.

Then when Satan attacks us—our health, loved ones, finances, church—we can say NO MORE MR. NICE GUY! And we can know that we are standing completely swathed, enclosed and encapsulated in the blood-dipped righteousness of the Lamb of God, before whose face mountains and kingdoms will one day flee. Clothed in these garments, our praying will be fueled by the seething nuclear turbines of the boiling-over cauldron of God's righteous wrath and fury as He declares to Satan, "The Lord rebuke thee, Satan—take your hands off My children!"

THE CLOAK OF ZEAL

Applying the Law of first Mention to the cloak of zeal, we find that the Isaiah passage cited earlier is the first time a cloak is mentioned in the Word of God. We can deduce that it has to do with zeal.

When we check out the references for zeal, a

couple of passages seem to apply. The first contains one of the most famous messianic prophecies:

> "For every battle of the warrior is with confused noise, and garments rolled in blood; but this shall be with burning and fuel of fire. For unto us a child is born, unto us a son is given: and the government shall be upon his shoulder: and his name shall be called Wonderful, Counsellor, The mighty God, The everlasting Father, The Prince of Peace. Of the increase of his government and peace there shall be no end, upon the throne of David, and upon his kingdom, to order it, and to establish it with judgment and with justice from henceforth even for ever. The zeal of the LORD of hosts will perform this." Isa. 9:5-7

This is a critical passage because it deals with the Incarnation. It speaks both of Jesus' First and Second Advent, and the everlasting government of power and glory which will someday be the Lord's permanently on the earth. It is one of the few Old Testament passages that clearly identify the Messiah as "The mighty God." It concludes by saying that the zeal of the Lord will perform all of these things.

The concept of the zeal of the Lord accomplishing something is mentioned a couple of other places in the Old Testament:

> "For out of Jerusalem shall go forth a remnant, and they that escape out of mount Zion: the zeal of the LORD of hosts shall do this." Isa. 37:32
> (See also 2 Kgs. 19:31.)

Both of these passages have to do with the Lord delivering the holy remnant of Israel out of the hands of the Assyrian invaders. This is the incident in which the angel of the Lord smote 185,000 soldiers in one night! That's what we would call a deliverance!

Thus, we see that the cloak of zeal must involve zeal which the Lord provides. And it must be a divinely anointed zeal, not something we crank up out of our own emotionalism. It is also evident that this zeal provides the Incarnational/Resurrection power to effect deliverance from the power of the enemy (whomever he might be).

The quality of the oil makes the flame burn brighter and longer. Much is written in Christian psychological literature these days about "burnout." I believe this passage shows us that if we wrap ourselves in the cloak of the Lord's zeal and let His zeal be the flame which lightens us from within, it will be much more difficult to get "burnt out."

How can you burnout when you have wave after wave of Resurrection power flowing through your spirit? Burnout can only occur when you substitute your own strength and zeal for His. We all do that on occasion. It's part of being human. But if we daily wrap ourselves in His cloak, it can and will refresh us.

Like the "garment" discussed above, this cloak also covers our rear. It would normally be the last thing you put on as a soldier, with the possible exception of the helmet, shield and spear. It also would serve the additional function of keeping the soldier warm and dry in inclement weather.

AN ADMONITION FOR TODAY'S CHURCH

The other significant passage from which we might glean some insight is in Revelation 3, in the message from the Lord to the Laodicean church. Here we see it, given in context:

> "...These things saith the Amen, the faithful and true witness, the beginning of the creation of God; I know thy works, that thou art neither cold nor hot: I would thou wert cold or hot. So then because thou art lukewarm, and neither cold nor hot, I will spue thee out of my mouth. Because thou sayest, I am rich, and increased with goods, and have need of nothing; and knowest not that thou art wretched, and miserable, and poor, and blind, and naked:
>
> I counsel thee to buy of me gold tried in the fire, that thou mayest be rich; and white raiment, that thou mayest be clothed, and that the shame of thy nakedness do not appear; and anoint thine eyes with eyesalve, that thou mayest see. As many as I love, I rebuke and chasten: be zealous therefore, and repent."   Rev. 3:14-19

This message was written to the church of Laodicea by John, from the island of Patmos. It can also be applied prophetically to the last of the seven great church "periods."[1] In other words, the letter to the church of Ephesus (Rev. 2:1-7) spoke doctrinally and prophetically to the apostolic and post-apostolic church (c. 33-200 a.d.).

The letter to the Philadelphia church (Rev. 3:7-13)

speaks to the 6th period of c. 1500-1900 a.d. (Protestant Reformation). The message quoted above speaks to the 7th or Laodicean period of church history (1900 a.d. - Second Advent). Thus, it applies to the church today.

It is obviously a message to a lukewarm church sliding gradually into apostasy. It is a church that thinks it is rich and wonderful, but is actually naked and destitute.

This certainly applies to many churches today, even among evangelical Christians—where "health and wealth" gospels are lauded, while servanthood and discipleship are passed over. The very name "Laodicea" means "rights of the people" or "human rights."

Has there ever been a century (1900-present) in which more people were concerned with their "rights?" Minorities want their "rights." Homosexuals want their "rights." Over-weight and short people want their "rights." Wives and husbands want their "rights." Now even children are demanding the "right" to divorce from their parents! Truly, this is the Laodicean age!

It is instructive to see the counsel that the Lord gives this age. We are to buy gold from Him which has been tried in the fire. This obviously refers to the testing of the Believer through trials. We are actually to seek from the Lord trials that will refine us into the purest gold (see Job 23:10).

Also, we are to buy "white raiment" to cover our nakedness. Besides symbolizing holiness and purity, could this be the cloak of zeal? WHITE-hot zeal?

Then we are to buy "eyesalve" to anoint our eyes that we may see. Anointing is often the type of the Holy Spirit, thus we are to earnestly seek the Holy Spirit and the gift of discerning of spirits.

The final command to our church period is to be zealous and repent! To appropriate the cloak of zeal, we must be repentant. This needs to be emphasized. Unfortunately, in this century we have seen an over-emphasis in some churches on "sloppy agape" with little teaching on holiness, separated living and purity. Sadly, the further we get away from God, the less likely we are to be aware of our imperfections and laxity. Conversely, the closer we get to the Lord, the more aware we become of how vile we are in His sight.

This is why we must wrap ourselves in this cloak of zeal. It is like wrapping ourselves anew every day in the righteousness of Christ. You cannot be much closer to something than your clothing. If you really make an effort to be zealous and repent, you will find yourself in the challenging, but glorious position of Isaiah the prophet:

> "Then said I, Woe is me! for I am undone; because I am a man of unclean lips, and I dwell in the midst of a people of unclean lips: for mine eyes have seen the King, the Lord of hosts." **Isa. 6:5**

Consider that while Isaiah felt this way after SEEING the glory of God, we Believers have that glory dwelling within us! That is a wonderful thought, which we must endeavor to grasp. The cloak of zeal is the Incarnational-Resurrection power of God covering us and enflaming us with His zeal!

It is virtually impossible to have white-hot zeal and be a luke-warm Christian. You cannot have bland jalapeño peppers, and you cannot have a zealous, apathetic Christian. God warned us about the perils and temptations we will encounter in this period of church history, right before the coming of the Lord. We must equip ourselves with the cloak of zeal if we are to combat the creeping apathy which is spreading through so many churches today.

When you have that true zeal, which only comes from God, the labors of the Lord become effortless. It is like you are fueled on something from beyond earth. Today, our battle-weary warriors need to wrap themselves in the white-hot cloak of zeal and draw closer to their Captain—the better to hear and carry out their marching orders.

> **"He that hath an ear, let him hear what the Spirit saith unto the churches."** Rev. 3:22

14

Drugs and Doorways

> "Look not thou upon the wine when it is
> red, when it giveth his colour in the cup,
> when it moveth itself aright. At the last it
> biteth like a serpent, and stingeth like an
> adder."   Prov. 23:31-32

Drugs are obviously a plague upon our society.
However, even some of the most ardent foes of drug
abuse don't understand that they are fighting not just
a psychoactive or criminal foe, but a spiritual one as
well.

The two great popularizers of drug mysticism in
the last half of this century were Dr. Timothy Leary
and Carlos Castaneda. They "pushed" the use of

psychedelic drugs such as LSD, mushrooms, etc. as ways of accessing magical realms or expanding one's consciousness into new horizons. What many didn't realize is that Leary and Castaneda were building upon the foundations of earlier writers such as Alduous Huxley and— Aleister Crowley![1]

Crowley, who called himself "The Great Beast," was the most influential magician of this century and the first Westerner to introduce into popular consciousness the idea of using hallucinogenic drugs as Shamanistic tools for consciousness expansion.

Sharon and I were both very familiar with drugs, and with the theories of these writers. We both used virtually all the popular drugs of the day! We combined these drugs with the practice of Yoga and ceremonial magic to great effect.

A BURN HOLE IN THE FABRIC OF TIME

My first profound experience as a Witch with the Shamanistic side of drug use came in the summer of 1975. I was riding as a passenger from a weekend in the country and a marijuana "joint" was being passed around the car. As the joint was passed to me, I inhaled deeply. A marijuana seed popped out of the joint, propelled by the extreme heat. Those seeds were known to be extremely hot, and this one landed on my forearm, burning a small hole in my arm.

I cried out in pain and jumped, then passed the joint onto the next passenger. A very strange thing began to happen to my arm. As the sting of the burn subsided, I felt something growing on it. Slightly light-headed from the dope, I turned to look at my arm. It was growing leaves!

My entire arm stopped smarting and began turning a strange, brownish green. The arteries in my forearm turned into sinewy, vine-like tracings which pulsed up and down with a greenish light. At that point, I shut my eyes as wave after wave of strange, green, velvet fire washed over me—concentrating especially in the area occultists call the "Third Eye."[2] I may have passed out, for by the time I opened my eyes, the car had arrived in Milwaukee.

After that, I had an extraordinary ability. Virtually at will—or with at most a few moments' meditation—I found I could "evoke" the consciousness of a marijuana "high" without even smoking a puff!

Our spirit guides later told us that this was a result of my coming in contact with the "Deva" of marijuana. The Deva is rooted in the world view of pantheism or animism. It is not taught in the Bible. Pantheism is the belief that God is all, and all is God. Animism is the belief that everything (rocks, trees, people, etc.) has a soul and is alive.

The concept of the Deva is an occult doctrine. Devas are thought to be nature spirits in the occult discipline of Theosophy.[3] Theosophy itself is the fountainhead of the New Age, and was founded by a Russian psychic, Helena Blavatsky.[4] Virtually all key New Age doctrines, including the belief in Devas, can be found in Theosophical teachings.

Devas are felt to be the spirit rulers over the kingdom of plants. There is a Deva for garlic and another Deva for marijuana. It might be helpful to think of them as patron saints of various plants. The root of the word comes from the Sanskrit language, and means god or deity.[5]

In the Hindu religion, Devas are felt to be gods or good spirits of nature, but in Zoroastrian religion, they are felt to be demons.[6] We were told that by becoming "one" with the devas of various drugs, we could evoke the influence of those drugs at will, without having to take the drug.

We found this to be true, at least with "natural" drugs, such as cocaine, "magic" mushrooms and marijuana. It was not true of "synthetic" drugs such as LSD or PCP (angel dust). The spirit guides (demons) told us that this was because natural drugs were directly derived from the vegetable kingdom of the Devas, and that many of these drugs were worshipped as deities by indigenous peoples.

BREAKING ANCIENT CHAINS

Fortunately, the Lord Jesus Christ set us free from bondage to those drugs in a miraculous and complete way. Even highly addictive cocaine, which we both indulged in considerably, caved in before the power of the blood of the Lamb. Praise His wonderful Name!

However, in praying for many people in bondage to drugs or the occult, we have found the insights into the dark world of demons and drugs to be most helpful. Two essential principles need to be borne in mind when ministering to someone struggling with serious bondage to drugs:

1) Drugs, especially those of an hallucinogenic character (marijuana, LSD, mescaline, psilocybin, peyote, etc.) are powerful initiatic tools in Witchcraft. They are specially designed to "blow open" the so-called "Third Eye." So whether or not the drug user ever explicitly practiced Witchcraft, they have—de facto—been defiled by the occultic power of the drug. They have been initiated![7] If they've experienced strong hallucinations, out-of-the-body experiences, etc., they have probably acquired the Spirit of Divination and possibly the Familiar Spirit.

2) Drug abuse is idolatry. Especially with older "natural" drugs, people who are still struggling with bondage to drugs may need to renounce the Strongman over the particular drug which is holding them in thrall.

This is not to neglect the physiological and psychological strongholds which drug abuse can create. Not everyone will be set free as easily as we were. We cannot understand why some drug abusers struggle for awhile and some get immediate victory—either right after being saved, or right after being liberated from demonic power. It is lost in the mystery of the fresh and uniquely individual way God deals with each one of His children.

But in our experience, a Christian who wants to forsake the sin of drugs or liquor (liquor is one of the oldest and most dangerous drugs) will probably find it about 75% easier to keep their victory if they have been through prayers for liberation. An even higher percentage of the people we pray for with drug problems have been completely set free. Glory to God!

Here is a sample prayer for renouncing drugs
and a list of drug Strongmen. These prayers are only
to give you an idea—there is nothing "magical"
about saying these exact words. These prayers
normally should be done in the context of a broader
session of prayer for liberation in other areas, unless
specifically directed otherwise by the Holy Spirit:

> **"In the name of the Lord Jesus Christ,[8] I now
> repent of my involvement in the use of
> illegal and soul-destroying drugs and ask
> You, Abba Father, to forgive me for using
> them. I repent of the sin of using (liquor,
> marijuana, cocaine, crack, acid, speed,
> heroin, etc.) to dull and cripple my will, my
> mind and sensibilities. I only want to use
> my mind to serve and honor you, Lord.**
>
> **"I speak now in the authority of the name
> of the Lord Jesus Christ to all the strong-
> men and principalities over the drugs I took
> and declare that you have no power over me
> any more for I am bought and paid for by
> the blood of Jesus shed on Calvary. I es-
> pecially come against the Spirit of Divination
> and any other demonic spirits (_____)
> which came into me through my use of
> drugs. In the name of the Lord Jesus Christ,
> I bind you all present together. I command
> you to go where the Lord Jesus Christ tells
> you to go by the voice of His Holy Spirit."**

In some cases it may be necessary to rebuke some
specific spirits related to specific drugs. This is not
common, but with severe bondage, it can help. Here
is a brief list:

1. Liquor—Iacchus (Bacchus), Dionysos, or "John Barleycorn."

2. Marijuana—Sativa, "Mary Jane."

3. LSD and many "natural" hallucinogens (i.e., peyote, mushrooms, mescaline)—Peyote, Mescalito.

4. Tobacco—Gitchie Manitou (Native American "Great Spirit").

5. Cocaine (or crack) —Coca, Lilith, Vlad, "White Lady," "White Queen."

6. Hashish—Melek Taus or Allah.[9]

7. Heroin, opium, morphine—Lung (Chinese) or Morpheus (Graeco-Roman).

> **"Abba Father, in the name of Jesus Christ my Lord, I ask You to shut any doorways of demonic access which may have been opened by my abuse of drugs. I ask You, Father, to seal those doorways by the Blood of the Lamb, shed on the cross of Calvary, and I invite, with thanksgiving the full and manifest presence of the Holy Spirit of God to come in and dwell with me, filling the void places with the healing balm of His love and power."**

A WARNING

Drug addicts are frequently referred to "12-Step Programs" which are based, to a greater or lesser degree, on Alcoholics Anonymous. This is even true in Christian churches and counseling environments. In fact, many Christian churches have their own 12-Step meetings.

We felt obliged to caution you that many people have gotten in bondage to 12-Step programs! They used to be addicted to drugs, now they are addicted to 12-Step programs!

A.A. and its many "children" are not Christian in nature. They are more humanistic and New Age than anything else. They also buy into the "disease" model which views alcoholism and substance abuse (almost NEVER called drunkenness and drug addiction) as sicknesses, not sins.

Obviously, if alcoholism is a disease, it cannot be a sin. But the Bible clearly identifies drunkenness as a sin (Luke 21:34, Romans 13:13, Galatians 5:19-21). If drunkenness can keep a person out of heaven (Gal. 5:21), then it cannot be just a disease.

Additionally, many 12-Step programs refuse to acknowledge the Lordship of Jesus Christ or even the Biblical God. They promote calling upon a "Higher Power" or "God as you conceive him to be." That could be anyone—even Satan!

Therefore, we do not recommend involvement in 12-Step programs—even ones which have been given a coating of Christian terminology. Even those that attempt to cast a gospel message from Romans still buy into the disease model.

Let the buyer beware! Check these programs out carefully before you invest your time and yourself in them—make sure that they measure up to Biblical truth. We have found that—generally—they do not![10]

15

"As One Having Authority"

> "...Jesus I know, and Paul I know, but who are ye?"   Acts 19:15b

We had heard stories about this woman!

Her name was Chloe, and she had been prayed for by experts. Her last encounter with prayer warriors ended with one pastor seriously injured in the hospital, and another one badly beaten up.

These were true men of God, seasoned prayer warriors, who had fasted and prayed for Chloe for days at a time. Nevertheless, an entire room full of Christian workers could not keep her in line.

Chloe was an SRA survivor who claimed she had been a candidate to be a Bride of Satan. She had been prepared for this "high honor," since before birth and was subjected to a level of abuse unparalleled in most peoples' experience.

Supposedly, Satan raped her mother when she was carrying Chloe, and claimed Chloe while yet in the womb. She was now in her early twenties, and a Born Again Christian. But according to everyone who tried to minister to her, she was "hell on wheels!"

Her counselor was afraid to pray for her deliverance. When he heard about us, he referred her to us. Chloe came halfway across the state to meet with us and a couple of our prayer support team.

We knew of her reputation for savage manifestations. Even though she was small, she had broken the back of at least one Christian man twice her size who was trying to minister to her. Sometimes she growled with a volume that shook entire buildings.

Thus, we prayed and fasted extra-hard and long. We also called for "back-up" prayer from several of our key people. We assumed that the previous prayer teams had taken these precautions, yet they ended up on the Blue Cross rolls. Therefore, we felt like "High Noon" on the spiritual warfare plane.

BIG DEMONS COME IN LITTLE PACKAGES

When we finally met Chloe and her husband, Roy, at the church where we did our prayer sessions, we were surprised at how pleasant she was. But we also knew such things could be deceptive. As the sun set in the west, strange clouds were gathering on the horizon. The air smelled of electricity and ozone.

We sat down and prayed, and as usual, bound all manifestations which were not in God's will. No problem there.

Then we moved into the data-gathering phase. We allowed the couple to tell their story. It was all-too-familiar. Their marriage—though Christian—was being strained to the breaking point by her surfacing memories and their accompanying emotional turmoil.

Like many SRA survivors, Chloe believed that she suffered from MPD, and as is our custom, we met her where she was with that issue. Also, like many survivors, Chloe's "alter personalities" had produced some drawings which represented various images of her abuse and her inner torment.

Some of the material in the art showed us clear proof that Chloe had the dubious "honor" of having a very high Strongman as her personal "bodyguard."

In Satanic "theology" it is believed that certain high level members of the Brotherhood—or those marked for special "sexual favors" from Satan—had a special "Arch-duke of Hell" assigned to them to protect them from attack.[1]

My mentor from Chicago had such a bodyguard. It was supposedly powerful enough to once reduce an on-coming semi which threatened his life to literal shreds of metal the size of confetti in less than a second! If indeed Chloe was being "protected" by such an "Arch-duke," it was no wonder that people who tried to cast demons out of her were running into some powerful resistance.

Still, we knew that even an "Arch-duke of Hell" was less than a fly-speck next to Jesus! We quietly prayed and asked the Lord to bind the Strongman (Matt. 12:29). No resistance was manifested, praise the Lord. So we proceeded with the prayers.

THE CRACK OF DOOM

Midway through the generational prayers—usually our second step—Chloe began to "bog down." It took her minutes to get out a sentence. Finally, like an old gramophone running down, her attempts to follow our prayers ground to a painful halt. A reverberating growl came out of her.

"I am hers by heredity. You cannot make me leave," rumbled a totally alien voice from within her. It sounded like thunder coming up from the earth.

We began reading scripture out loud, especially passages from the end of Revelation. Chloe tried to rise out of her chair. "I will crush this building like a matchbox…" the voice within her roared.

Sharon cried out, "The Lord rebuke thee, Satan! You are bound and you have no place here. This is a House of God."

Chloe sat back down as if someone had punched her in the stomach. She was breathing heavily, but said nothing more. We continued our out-loud Bible reading until she was able to continue. She got through the generational prayers without a further hitch.

We worked through most of the prayers with her, and finally got to the "Ungodly Ties" part of the prayer ministry. This involves the severing of all soul-links created by sexual acts—either willing or unwilling. As Chloe began to pray, the resistance heated up. She began to slow down. Our prayer support team stepped up their prayers and she found herself able to continue.

About half-way through the prayer, suddenly there was a grinding roar. The entire church building shook as if someone had picked it up and shaken it. The windows rattled nastily and dust pattered down from the acoustic tiled ceiling. Thunderclaps smashed outside the windows and lightning could be seen arcing across the distant hills. The sky outside looked green-black.

Everyone managed to get their hearts out of their mouths, and I said, "It's alright. These are manifestations from outside the building. It can't get in because Jesus is protecting us. It's just trying to scare us."

Roy, Chloe's husband, was livid with terror. "It's doing a pretty good job."

We looked at Chloe and she nodded, ready to continue. We prayed again and asked the Lord to take control over the forces of nature. Then we settled down to continue. We finished, only an hour later than usual, and Chloe was gloriously set free. Praise the Lord!

THE MYSTERY

Why did we have such a relatively easy time, compared to all the other people who prayed for Chloe? It has absolutely NOTHING to do with us. There is NOTHING special about us! We are unworthy bond-slaves of our glorious Master Jesus Christ. We do not wish to imply that there was anything spiritually amiss in any of the other prayer teams which worked on her.

Nor should our peculiar (to say the least) past make any difference. Though we do possess a lot of first-hand occult information, anything a Christian prayer group needs to know they can be told by the Holy Spirit! They don't need "walking occult encyclopedias" to help them. Nor do we think that we fasted any "better" or prayed any "better" or had more faith than the other people. It is nothing of us.

There is, nevertheless, one well-kept secret which Satan is trying to keep the church from discovering, because he knows it is God's "secret weapon." As far as we can tell, it is one of the few distinctive differences between the way we minister and the way all these other prayer teams labored for the Lord.

We don't want it to be a secret any longer. So we will discuss this "secret weapon" in the next chapter:

> **"What new doctrine is this? for with authority commandeth he even the unclean spirits and they do obey him."   Mark 1:27b**

16

Putting Teeth Back into Your Church
The Issue of Authority in Spiritual Warfare

Please pay close attention to these scriptures:

> "…yea, let God be true, but every man a liar;" **Rom. 3:4**

> "When the even was come, they brought unto him many that were possessed with devils: and he cast out the spirits with his word, and healed all that were sick:"
> **Matt. 8:16**

> "Jesus answered and said unto them, Ye do err, not knowing the scriptures, nor the power of God." **Matt. 22:29**

In this chapter, we are going to discuss our only offensive weapon—God's secret weapon, the Sword of the Spirit, the Word of God. Since this is the only weapon with which we can fight back against Satan, it is important that we understand the underlying Biblical principles involved.

A key issue in any sort of spiritual warfare is spiritual authority. Most Christians understand that they have the authority of the Believer. But where does that authority come from, and upon what does it rest? Obviously, in the ultimate sense, it comes from Jesus. As the following scripture makes clear, there was something different in the way Jesus taught when He was on the earth:

> **"And it came to pass, when Jesus had ended these sayings, the people were astonished at his doctrine: For he taught them as one having authority, and not as the scribes."**
> **Matt. 7:28-29**
>
> **(See also Mark 1:27 and Luke 4:32.)**

In contrast to the religious leaders of His day, Jesus taught with an authority the people had never seen. He had this authority because He was the Incarnate Word of God. He had the assurance that He was walking in the authority of God's Word because He WAS God's Word (John 1:14). Incredible as it sounds, Jesus granted His disciples some of that authority:

> **"Then he called his twelve disciples together, and gave them power and authority over all devils, and to cure diseases."**
> **Luke 9:1**

That is a wonderful gift. The entire ministry of the church of Jesus Christ rests upon that basis. This is backed up by the Great Commission passages in Mark 16:15-18 and Matthew 28:18-20, and also by Luke 10:17. The last scripture is important because some Christians believe that only the apostles had the authority to do these things. But the passage in Luke states that seventy other disciples—who were never apostles—were also given this authority.

Now that Jesus—the Word made Flesh—has ascended and is seated at the right hand of the Father, the church derives its authority from the written Word of God, the Holy Bible. Christians should look to the Bible as our ultimate source of *all* truth. It should be our *only* guide when it comes to how we attain salvation, live our lives and serve our King.

This is why the Word of God is such a vital tool in spiritual warfare—and probably the most important part of the armour. Without it, we become like the Jewish exorcists, who heard the demons say:

> **"Jesus I know, and Paul I know; but who are ye?"**   **Acts 19:15**

This is partially because without the Bible, we wouldn't even know what authority we had. It's also because the Bible is the source of our faith:

> **"...faith cometh by hearing, and hearing by the word of God."**   **Rom. 10:17**

COSMIC COUNTERFEITS

Most Christians understand that part of Satan's strategy is to try to rob the authority and glory away from Jesus Christ and place it in various pseudo-scriptures, false gods or their human "apostles."

Any Christian who surveys the religious land-
scape today can see that it is littered with cults that
try to steal the glory away from the true Jesus and
place it in some human fraud, whether it is the
Mormon prophet Joseph Smith or some New Age
guru. All of these cults have "another Christ" (Matt.
24:24) and "another gospel" (Gal. 1:8).

We all know about the anti-Christ. The prefix
"anti-" can mean two things. It can mean that which
opposes OR it can mean a substitute for. Contrary to
Hollywood movies, the anti-Christ is not going to be
a supernatural ogre who will make Hitler look like
Mr. Rogers. No, the anti-Christ will be the most
perfect counterfeit for Jesus Christ yet seen on the
earth. He'll be the most "godly" man of his time. He
will be part of the greatest "church" in "Christendom,"
and a great ecumenical leader.

What is the essence of this anti-Christ spirit?
While there WILL be a supreme, ultimate anti-Christ
who is revealed during the Great Tribulation, he has
been preceded by other anti-Christs (plural—2 John
7), people who are possessed by the spirit of anti-
Christ to a greater or lesser degree. Here is what the
Bible tells us:

> **"Who is a liar but he that denieth that Jesus
> is the Christ? He is antichrist, that denieth
> the Father and the Son. Whosoever denieth
> the Son, the same hath not the Father: [but]
> he that acknowledgeth the Son hath the
> Father also.   1 John 2:22-23**

> **"Beloved, believe not every spirit, but try
> the spirits whether they are of God: because**

many false prophets are gone out into the world. Hereby know ye the Spirit of God: Every spirit that confesseth that Jesus Christ is come in the flesh is of God: And every spirit that confesseth not that Jesus Christ is come in the flesh is not of God: and this is that spirit of antichrist, whereof ye have heard that it should come; and even now already is it in the world." 1 John 4:1-3

FALSE TEETH ANYONE?

The key test is that the anti-Christ spirit will deny that Jesus is (note the present tense) come in the flesh, and/or will deny the deity of Jesus. We have spoken of anti-Christs and alluded to the fact that the devil has his "anti-churches." Paul confirms that he also has an "anti-gospel" or an "anti-Bible:"

"For if he that cometh preacheth another Jesus, whom we have not preached, or if ye receive another spirit, which ye have not received, or another gospel, which ye have not accepted, ye might well bear with him."
2 Cor. 11:4

Many cults are successful because they offer a nearly perfect counterfeit of Jesus, His salvation, His church and His gospel. Why are we surprised then when Satanism runs rampant, or when the majority of converts to cults like Mormonism come from supposedly historic Christian churches? What are we doing wrong?

Part of the reason the church of Jesus Christ is so reluctant to confront these warfare issues head-on is that many good people in leadership have been defanged, declawed—and dare we say it—spiritually gelded by an anti-Christ spirit which has pervaded the highest levels of Christian pulpits and academia.

Most "leaders" won't attack the devil and defend the faith once delivered unto the saints because Satan has stolen their "teeth"—their authority! If they are doing anything at all, they are trying to "gum" the devil to death, because they have lost their spiritual authority.

This issue of spiritual authority involves how to take back—through the Word of God—that ground which Satan has stolen.

A CASE STUDY IN RELIGIOUS "CASTRATION"

In an earlier chapter we spoke about the need for saved cultists to renounce their false scriptures like the *Book of Mormon*, and shut doorways for satanic access into their lives. Now we need to draw that principle a bit closer to home! We ask, how about a set of scriptures that deny the Virgin Birth?

> **"The child's father and mother marvelled at what was said about him."**

COMPARE TO:

> **"And Joseph and his mother marvelled at those things which were spoken of him."**
> **Luke 2:33**

Who was Jesus' father, Joseph or God? How about a set of scriptures that casts doubt on Jesus being the son of God?

> "Indeed, Herod and Pontius Pilate met together with the gentiles and the people of Israel in this city to conspire against your holy servant Jesus, whom you anointed."

COMPARE TO:

> "For of a truth against thy holy child Jesus, whom thou hast anointed, both Herod, and Pontius Pilate, with the Gentiles, and the people of Israel, were gathered together."
>
> **Acts 4:27**

"Child" more clearly declares Jesus as the Son of God. We are all God's servants.

How about a set of scriptures that throws out the clearest verse in the entire Bible on the Trinity? (1 John 5:7)

How about a set of scriptures that throw out the blood of Jesus?

> "...in whom we have redemption, the forgiveness of sins."

COMPARE TO:

> "In whom we have redemption through his blood, even the forgiveness of sins:"
>
> **Col. 1:14**

How about a set of scriptures that deliberately avoid confessing that Jesus Christ is God come in the flesh?

> "...He appeared in a body, was vindicated by the Spirit, was seen by angels, was preached among the nations, was believed on in the world and was taken up in glory."

COMPARE TO:

"And without controversy great is the mystery of godliness: God was manifest in the flesh, justified in the Spirit, seen of angels, preached unto the Gentiles, believed on in the world, received up into glory."
1 Tim. 3:16

Finally, how about a set of scriptures that attack the very verse (1 John 4:2) which gives the criteria for discerning an anti-Christ influence by placing it in the past tense?

"Every spirit that acknowledges that Jesus Christ has come in the flesh is from God..."

By now many of you have figured out what we are talking about. It is a set of scriptures drawn from the same corrupt manuscripts as the "New World Translation" of the Jehovah's Witnesses. It is a set of scriptures translated by men who deny that we hold the inerrant Word of God in our hands today. It is also one of the best-selling "bibles" in Christian bookstores, the New International Version, (NIV).

TRUSTING IN THE (ACADEMIC) ARM OF FLESH?

We are certain that at least a few readers feel like we are "messing with their heads." We may have even popped a few of your blood vessels. Isn't the NIV recommended by many great men of God? Isn't it a more modern, better and more readable translation? Does it really make any difference which Bible "version" you use, as long as it isn't some obviously flawed thing like the JW's "New World Translation" (NWT)?

Recall what we have established from the Bible— if anyone denies that Jesus Christ is God come in the flesh, then that is of the spirit of anti-Christ. We have just shown that, at least in one place, the NIV denies that Jesus Christ is God come in the flesh (1 Tim. 3:16). It also denies the Virgin Birth, the Blood of Jesus, etc. etc.

So does every other major, popular "modern Bible" on the market. There is only one Bible in English today which does not deny those things— the Authorized Version—1611 King James Bible.

Here is the question: If you use the NWT of the Jehovah's Witnesses, what do you have? A "Bible" which is perhaps 90% alright and 10% error. If you use the NAS (New American Standard), you have a "Bible" which is perhaps 94% okay and 6% error. If you use the NIV "Bible" you may have a book which is maybe 95% alright and 5% in error.[1]

But the trouble is—if it even has .0001% error in it, it cannot BE the Word of God! God's Word, HE SAYS, is perfect (Psalm 19:7). God, as the saying goes, does not make—or write—junk! If it isn't 100% perfect, then it isn't the Word of God.

The Bible tells us that there is the spirit of truth and the spirit of error (1 John 4:6). Obviously, the Holy Spirit is the Spirit of Truth. Who—or what— could be this "spirit of error?" Evidently, it is Satan, or one of his minions.

Following through, we see that Jesus is the "Living Word," (John 1:1) and the real Bible is the "Living Word" (Heb. 4:12). This is where the "rubber meets the road" in terms of spiritual warfare. The Spirit of Truth and the Incarnate Word are ALIVE in your Bible, *if* you have a real, God-breathed Bible (2 Tim. 3:16).

The problem is that the position of 99% of the "respectable" Christian scholars and pastors who are recommending the NIV or the NAS is that you do not have a perfect inspired Bible in your hands. They will tell you that only the "original autographs" written by the apostles are inspired.[2] Of course, the "original autographs" don't exist anymore, so therefore you have to trust these learned "men of God" with their vast erudition and understanding of the Greek to tell you what the text really means.

These scholars are telling us that we can't really access the true and perfect Word of God anymore, but with their intellectual prowess in Greek and Hebrew, THEY can dispense the truth of the Lord to us. Doesn't that sound too much like the Vatican's approach to the Bible? That should not surprise you because the texts upon which these modern translations are based are Roman Catholic. One of them, the most popular and highly regarded, is even called "Vaticanus" (from the Vatican) and can only be seen in the Vatican Library.

They are asking us to trust them—sinful, fallible, imperfect human beings—to interpret the Word of God for us. That is contrary to scripture (2 Pet. 1:20).

ANOTHER BIBLE, ANOTHER SPIRIT?

If your "Bible" has places where it denies or deletes the fundamentals, and if it isn't 100% perfect, can it really be the inerrant Word of God? Can it have the Spirit of God dwelling within it? Anything which tries to take away glory from Jesus is courting an anti-Christ spirit, to say the least!

Suppose you are doing your spiritual warfare using a Bible with an anti-Christ spirit in it? How effective a "Sword" would you think that would be? If you don't have a true Bible, then you don't have a true spirit IN your Bible. It's that simple. Here is how this works in practice:

When you read the Holy Bible—especially out-loud—you transfer the Holy Spirit into yourself in a new and vital way. This is like the fresh manna which God gives us anew every day. Reading the Bible silently is fine for communion with God, for strengthening the inner man and for building the temple of the Holy Spirit—but to have a spiritual impact in your home, and to get into serious spiritual warfare you have to read the Bible out loud because the devil can't read our minds.

What if there is a faulty Bible—an anti-Bible, or "other gospel" (Gal.1:8)—trying to get the glory as if it were the living Word of God? If we read THIS regularly, what sort of spirit would be coming into us when we read silently? When we read out loud, what spirit would come into our home and into our prayer closets? How would this effect our family? What spirit is transferred by all these modern

"Bibles" today? The Spirit of truth—OR the spirit of error (1 John 4:6)?

Many wonder why so much of the preaching today is lifeless and insipid, why the church is not smashing through the gates of hell like it used to. Others wonder why their prayers have less power than they used to possess. Might this not be traced to the proliferation of Bibles which may not be Bibles? What if Satan has managed to defang the Christian church by replacing its swords with butter-knives?

UNITED WE STAND?

Yet another point of view on this disturbing issue is the total disappearance of group, communal Bible-reading from our churches. If the pastor of most churches were to ask his congregation to open their Bibles and begin reading aloud together (which used to be common practice), there would be a babel of confusion. Words would be changed, phrase order would be different and sometimes entire verses would be missing. But let's look at some amazing prayer meetings in the Book of Acts:

> "These all continued with one accord in prayer and supplication, with the women, and Mary the mother of Jesus, and with his brethren." **Acts 1:14**

> "And when the day of Pentecost was fully come, they were all with one accord in one place. And suddenly there came a sound from heaven as of a rushing mighty wind, and it filled all the house where they were sitting. And there appeared unto them

cloven tongues like as of fire, and it sat
upon each of them. And they were all filled
with the Holy Ghost, and began to speak
with other tongues, as the Spirit gave them
utterance."   Acts 2:1-4

"And they, continuing daily with one
accord in the temple, and breaking bread
from house to house, did eat their meat
with gladness and singleness of heart,
Praising God, and having favour with all
the people. And the Lord added to the
church daily such as should be saved."
                                    Acts 2:46-47

"And when they heard that, they lifted up
their voice to God with one accord, and
said, Lord, thou art God, which hast made
heaven, and earth, and the sea, and all that
in them is:... And when they had prayed,
the place was shaken where they were
assembled together; and they were all filled
with the Holy Ghost, and they spake the
word of God with boldness."   Acts 4:24,31

(See also Acts 5:12, 8:6, 15:25.)

The power of the Holy Spirit is awesome when
there is true unity, not just ecumenical chumminess,
but true unity of doctrine—doctrine derived from
the perfect Word of God. People were being saved
and filled with the Holy Spirit. Entire buildings were
shaken! That's the power of being "with one accord."
But how can we have unity of true doctrine when we
cannot even agree on which Bible to use? See what a
trick the devil has pulled on many Christians?

I'll never forget the time I was teaching in a

church on how to witness to Jehovah's Witnesses. I was explaining how to teach a Witness about the Trinity (a doctrine the J.W.s deny). I had everyone turn to 1 John 5:7. One sweet lady raised her hand and said, "That's not in my Bible." She had an NIV.

Imagine coming up against a Jehovah's Witness (whom everyone agrees is a strong opponent) and finding that your "Sword of the Spirit" has the cutting power of a limp noodle! This happened because the woman trusted slick advertising, smooth Christian bookstore salespeople (who often get bonus points and prizes for shoving NIV Bibles down the throats of unsuspecting customers), or a pastor who should have known better.

If the Church of Jesus Christ cannot even pray one verse of the Bible together in unity, how can they stand shoulder-to-shoulder against Satan?

LET GOD BE TRUE, BUT EVERY MAN A LIAR

Before you dismiss all this as too bizarre for consideration, here are a couple of concepts for you. Jesus promises us:

> **"For verily I say unto you, Till heaven and earth pass, one jot or one tittle shall in no wise pass from the law, till all be fulfilled."**   **Matt. 5:18**

> **"Heaven and earth shall pass away, but my words shall not pass away."**   **Matt. 24:35**

> **(See also Mark 13:31 and Luke 21:33 for verbatim repetition of this verse.)**

Do you think maybe God is trying to tell us something here? Peter promised us:

> **"For all flesh is as grass, and all the glory of man as the flower of grass. The grass withereth, and the flower thereof falleth away: But the word of the Lord endureth for ever. And this is the word which by the gospel is preached unto you."** 1 Pet. 1:24-25

If this is true, then if even one verse in the Bible is wrong, then it cannot be God's Word. It doesn't matter what all the Bible scholars, pastors and teachers in the world say. If God said it, it's true. That is the simple, fundamental foundation of the entire Christian faith!

You could take the minds and learning of all the great pastors and scholars in the entire world—and roll them all into one. Next to the mind of God, they all have the intelligence of a learning-disabled fruit fly! I'm certain that all those men would agree with that statement, but then they turn around and correct His Book! Where is their common sense?

If the above scriptures are true, then there has to be a Bible somewhere which is absolutely and completely perfect and inerrant—the Word of God— that we can lay our hands upon and read from and preach with. Contrary to what your pastor might tell you, it cannot be a "consensus Bible," a mixture of parts of the KJV, parts of the NIV and parts of the NAS, because the modern Bibles contradict the KJV in about 30,000 places.

Logic tells us that a consensus cannot be arrived

at between two contradictory things. They would cancel each other out. Black blended with white equals gray! In simpler terms, does 1 John 5 have the 7th verse in it, or not? Either the Bible which deletes it is false or the Bible which leaves it in is false. Logic clearly shows that they both cannot be true Bibles!

Paul warns us in Galatians 5:9, "A little leaven leaveneth the whole lump." This means that even a tiny bit of sin or wickedness (leaven) quickly spreads to corrupt the entire system. Besides, who decides which parts from which Bible are right? Do we dare let any human being judge the Bible, no matter how wise, learned or Godly they are. Listen to what the Lord says about this issue:

> **"I will worship toward thy holy temple, and praise thy name for thy lovingkindness and for thy truth: for thou hast magnified thy word above all thy name."** Ps. 138:2

If God doesn't like you taking His name in vain (Ex. 20:7), imagine how unhappy He would be with someone who took His Holy Word in vain!

It is all a question of authority! If we say that God wrote only one Bible, and for us today it is the Authorized Version—1611, King James Version, then our problem is solved.

But if we say this version is nice, and that version is nice, and it is a matter of preference, then the authority becomes human opinion. Whether it is a Mormon prophet saying only they can interpret the Bible, or the pope or a Bible scholar with PhD's—let God be true, but every man a liar!

Without divine authority, the Bible becomes just another book, and ministers of the gospel might as well be Buddhists. But IF when you read God's Words, you KNOW that they are all God's Words (not just God's Word), just as He said them, perfect and singularly without error—just as Jesus promised us, consider what that does to your spiritual authority!

Contrary to what many Bible teachers say, you DO need the Words of God (all of them) not just something which is the Word of God. Every single word God has given us is indescribably precious:

> **"But he answered and said, It is written, Man shall not live by bread alone, but by every word that proceedeth out of the mouth of God."**   **Matt. 4:4**

We would be upset with any Bible scholar or teacher who tried to take JUST ONE of those words away, if we need them for spiritual life. Job said:

> **"I have esteemed the words of his mouth more than my necessary food."**   **Job 23:12b**

For a sampling of how powerful and vital every individual word which the Lord has given us is, see John 6:63, 68; 8:47; 14:23; 17:8, 1 Tim. 6:3, 2 Tim. 1:13, Rev. 1:3; 21:5; 22:18-19.

THE FINAL DETERMINATION

How do we know that the King James Version (KJV) is the Word of God? Here are some quick, "down and dirty" reasons why the KJV is the Word of God?[3] You can tell by...

• The incredible faith and character of the men who translated it. They spent hours in prayer daily and had no doubt that they were handling the true Word of God!

• How much the devil hates it!

• The fruit it has borne! Has any other Bible produced the kind of sin-killing, soul-saving, devil-chasing, snot-slinging, tavern-closing revivals that the KJV has?

• How many millions have saved by it? Wesley used it, Spurgeon used it, Bunyan used it, Jonathan Edwards used it, Finney used it, Moody used it, Billy Sunday used it, the "early" Billy Graham used it—and the list goes on!

• How it exalts the name, deity and the blood of Jesus Christ more than any other version by a country mile!

• The fact that it is universally despised by liberal, Pablum-drooling theologians who deny the inerrancy of scripture. (You can tell a Book by its enemies, NOT by its cover.)

• The fact that, in our many experiences, when you simply open it, demons begin to tremble.

• The fact that when you read it out-loud, you kick some serious slats right out of Satan's kingdom!

Why is all this? Because, like Jesus, those who preach or minister out of the TRUE Word of God, do so with authority (Mt. 7:28-29)! When we pray for people to be liberated, the people praying and reading the Bible out-loud behind us are using the one, true and perfect Word of God—and they KNOW it! Praise God!

This leads us to the bottom line in terms of spiritual warfare: The devil has a confusing mass of Bibles out there. Do you have the Word of God? Do you have the living Words of God? Or do you have a dead book?

> **"If ye abide in me, and my words abide in you, ye shall ask what ye will, and it shall be done unto you."** John 15:7

Jesus was able to minister with authority because He had no doubt about where His authority came from. Some Bible verses state that He cast out demons with His Word. When you pray, teach and preach out of that Book, the Holy Spirit is present in an unprecedented way. We have found repeatedly that when people we minister to study that Book, and memorize it religiously, their recovery time is sliced in half.

If you are using another book as your warrant of authority, what if it's an anti-Christ spirit? Please think about that!

Please understand, God will bless your work and your good intentions, even if you have been ministering out of a fake "bible." Praise the Lord, we live in an age of grace! If the Lord can use a donkey to preach (Num. 22:28), He can certainly get people Born Again or set free out of an apostate "bible."

However, we are in the last days, and the war is

heating up fast. Preachers are dropping like flies. Christians are wandering about, wrecked and wounded. Don't we need the sharpest, truest "Sword" we can get?

Now you are going to have to pray about this and see if it's time to toss your NIV, RSV or NAS in the bonfire of vanities. In this war, the Sword of the Spirit, the Holy Bible—is our only offensive weapon. What if yours shoots blanks?

> **"Whosoever therefore shall be ashamed of me and of my words in this adulterous and sinful generation; of him also shall the Son of man be ashamed, when he cometh in the glory of his Father with the holy angels."**
>
> **Mark 8:38**

17

Cursed Be the Tie That Binds

> "Know ye not that your bodies are the members of Christ? shall I then take the members of Christ and make them the members of an harlot? God forbid."
>
> **1 Corinthians 6:15**

One of the most common doorways through which demonic access is obtained is sex. God brought this home to us in a powerful way while we were young Christians, living in Dubuque, Iowa.

A church was advertising an evangelist who had supposedly been a Satanist before becoming saved. We felt led to attend one of the services.

During the altar call, the evangelist said that there were people in the congregation who had been deeply involved in Witchcraft. We were not known in this church, which made this "word from the Lord" remarkable. However, it could have been a lucky guess. The preacher said that those former witches needed to break all initiatic links between them and everyone they had initiated. He said they also needed to break all ungodly soul ties. Most of the higher level initiations in Witchcraft and Satanism were sexual in nature.

Since, between the two of us, we had initiated well over 175 people into Witchcraft, we felt that perhaps the Lord was speaking to us. As people went forward for the general altar call, we joined them. As we prayed, we felt almost audible "twangs" as we prayed and asked the Holy Spirit to sever all initiatic links and ungodly ties between us and any people we had initiated. It felt like a score of spiritual rubber bands snapping off of us. We felt incredibly freed up! Praise the Lord!

ONE OF THE BEST ARGUMENTS FOR CHASTITY!

No one denies that sexuality is a very powerful force. God created it as something good—as a way in which men and women could, within the bonds of marriage, participate in the creation of life!

Naturally, the devil understands this! Thus, one of the first things he did was pervert sexuality—both its physical and its spiritual aspects. Spiritually, it is vital to understand that whenever two people come together sexually, they become one flesh (Gen. 2:23-24). Jesus affirmed this important doctrine:

> **"For this cause shall a man leave father and mother, and shall cleave to his wife: and they twain shall be one flesh."**   Matt. 19:5

Though the Lord is talking here about marriage, Paul's writing in this verse and the verse at the heading of the chapter makes it clear that this is true in every sexual act—not just those between man and wife.

You see, a covenant link, originally intended by the Lord to cement the marriage act (Gen. 2:24, Matt. 19:6, 1 Cor. 6:15-19) is created by any sexual contact— tragically, even rape or child abuse. The additional problem is that in sexual abuse or SRA, the intense shame, agony and confusion created by this abuse is used to fixate into the child's mind certain vows, covenants and contracts that are made over her.

Satanists believe that the moment of sexual release for a sorcerer is one of the greatest points for releasing power and control into a child's soul. It is believed that statements or commands conveyed to the child (especially since she is often drugged and frightened) will have implacable vividness and power, if done while the child is being sexually terrorized. This is one of the major ways in which SRA survivors are demonized and held in bondage to their past—even if they become Born Again later on in life.

Even without the ritual satanic component, child abuse, incest, rape, fornication (including so-called "heavy petting,") adultery and homosexuality are ALL conduits for demonic oppression. It is a grotesque joke that demons are the ultimate sexually transmitted disease (STD)! Additionally, condoms do NOT protect you from demonic infestation!

The problem is that once this link is established, it cannot be broken, except through prayer to the Lord (Matt. 19:6). This means that if a child is sexually brutalized by either a Satanist or sex pervert, as that child grows up and becomes an adult, there is an invisible "conduit" connecting her to the molester. Every demon that the molester subsequently accepts into himself can travel through this conduit to the abuse survivor.

The story is the same for adults who engage in fornication, homosexuality or adultery. The only difference is that they went into the encounter of their own free will, but they still must reap what they have sown.

This is most often the cause of the "sickness" of sexual addiction, where a person is driven to encounter after encounter. Once they have had sex with a "swinging single," even a Christian man or woman will become infested with all the demons and perverse spirits their first "partner" already had from countless sexual encounters. Those spirits will then begin to whip their new "horse" into ever more and more profound levels of sexual excess.[1]

Unlike STDs, where one only has to worry about the people who have slept with your partner BEFORE you did—with the ungodly tie, you have to worry about all the sexual partners your partner fornicated with both before and AFTER your sexual contact! Do you see why the Lord wants us to be chaste before and after marriage?

Of course, victims of child sexual abuse had no say in the horrible things they were afflicted with. However, that does not necessarily protect them from the impact of the ungodly soul tie, anymore than it protects them from STDs. Therefore, we generally inquire about sexual history.

It may be traumatic to lead a person through these sorts of prayers, but it is essential. The survivor often feels intensely ashamed about these experiences. Fortunately, it is usually not necessary (in our experience) to have the person mention every person they have had sexual contact with. Frankly, most child abuse survivors might not be able to do that. Many Satanists force dozens of sexual contacts upon a child in one coven meeting, and often they are robed or masked! We feel that in most cases it is only necessary to make a broad statement (i.e., every person with whom I have had sexual contact).

Sometimes, there may be certain key people which the person may wish to mention by name. This can be both emotionally and spiritually liberating. However, this is only an option. It should NOT be considered a necessity.

IN THE GARDEN OF THE SUCCUBUS

Satan never leaves a stone unturned in his efforts to enslave us. Thus, there is a more bizarre twist to the problem of soul ties. In magic, this is called the "Mysteries of Solitude." In plain language, it is sexual self-stimulation or masturbation.

It is unfortunate that many Christian writers feel that this practice is not a serious problem. While it is not as serious a sin as adultery or homosexuality, it is still an adultery of the mind (Matt. 5:28). Since virtually all sexual self-stimulation is accompanied by either sexual fantasies or pornographic materials, it cannot be imagined that it is carried on without committing the sin of lust.

Also, it is one of the ultimate acts of selfishness. God intended sexuality to help relieve a person's loneliness (Gen. 2:18). Sexual self-stimulation does nothing to relieve loneliness. If anything, one feels more profoundly lonely than ever after this sin. We are not writing this to lay a "guilt trip" on anyone struggling with this habit, nor are we saying that it is some exceptionally heinous sin. However, it is a sin.

It is acknowledged that most adolescents mas-turbate, especially boys. While this might be a "normal" part of growing up in a fallen world, it is still a sin. However, it is a sin that can be repented of and forsaken—just like any other (1 John 1:9).

In seeking for ungodly ties or "open doorways" that might be troubling a person, our concern is if this is a "besetting" sin (Heb. 12:1). That's why we ask the question:"Is this a sin you are still struggling with? Or is it a sin which has hardly ever bothered you since becoming an adult?"

In our experience, if a person was ever involved

in sexual self-stimulation with great frequency or for a long period of time, there probably is a besetting sin involved, which may need to have its "doorway" slammed shut. If any sin is committed daily or every other day, it is certainly a besetting sin. This is especially true for married men or women.

Sexual self-stimulation is more understandable for a single person—not excusable, just understandable. However, for a married person to be doing such things several times a week indicates serious problems. We have prayed with Christians (mostly men) who were married and were practicing masturbation daily (or more often!). They had opened doors for demonic harassment and infestation. Usually their marriages were in trouble.

As to HOW OFTEN is often enough to constitute a besetting sin, it is better to err on the side of caution. Paul warns us that: "...whatsoever is not of faith is sin" (Rom. 14:23). Sensitivity is required, but if a person feels guilty about the practice, and is doing it with any degree of frequency, it is best to include it in the prayers for liberation. There are three basic reasons why:

1) Frequent sexual self-stimulation is a kind of idolatry—a door opening sin if there ever was one! This is because the oldest idols in human history were representations of the human reproductive organs. A person beset with this sin is worshipping at the oldest shrine imaginable, especially since pornography is usually involved.

2) Frequent sexual self-stimulation is creating a

covenant link—with yourself! You have bound yourself in a selfish covenant to serve yourself! Such people often cannot fully enter into relationships because they are already married to themselves! The person has covenanted with his or her sinful, fallen flesh to please it first—even before the spouse! Until it is renounced, the marriage is likely to run on only "half the cylinders."

3) Frequent sexual self-stimulation will often attract sexual spirits (those appearing to be men are called incubi, those looking like women are called succubi). These are spirits which will come and assume the form of impossibly perfect sexual partners. They will appear more flawless and desirable than even airbrushed centerfolds because Satan will have observed just what sort of person "turns on" his target. The spirit will exactly fulfill that fantasy.

As ghastly as this idea is, it is common practice in the higher levels of Satanism. They believe these "demon lovers" will come to men and draw seed from them. Then they will steal the resulting seed and go assault a human woman in male with or without her permission. Such spiritual "rape" is more common than most would think. The sick "hope" of such encounters is that the woman will conceive a child half-human and half-demon—a candidate for the anti-Christ!

Needless to say, once a man or woman has experienced "sex" with such a creature, normal marital relations with their spouse (however attractive) will pale into boring routine. Thus, the victim returns more and more to the spirit lover, and the bondage grows ever deeper.

This is not fiction from a horror novel. It is going on all the time. In high level Satanism, both of us were "married" to demons. We both had frequent "sex" with our Ascended Master spirit guides! We felt that this was the way we could gradually "evolve" into gods.

These beings do not have to be visible to be involved in your sin! Most of the time, especially with non-witches, they prefer to remain unseen. They do not want to give away their hand. However, they will weave a web of incredible bondage around the person which only prayer to the Lord Jesus can break. Thus, this is our recommendation to someone involved in frequent sexual self-stimulation:

1) Repent and forsake the sin. This must include the destruction by fire of any pornography in their home. You cannot play games with God on this!

2) Ask the Lord to break any covenants or soul ties made with their own flesh by the practice.

3) In the name of the Lord Jesus Christ, cut any ungodly soul ties with any sexual spirits, known or unknown, break any covenants made with such spirits, known or unknown, and finally command all sexual spirits to leave them at once.

This will often have a tremendous liberation on the person so victimized. There will also be "strong holds" which need to be torn down by frequent prayer, and there will probably be many indecent images burned into their memory. This, however, comes under the more normal heading of daily "crucifying the flesh" (Rom. 6:6, Gal. 2:20, 5:24), which all Christians must walk through. At least they will no longer have the demonic power driving them from within. Praise God!

NON-SEXUAL TIES

Sexual contact is not the only way soul ties (ungodly or otherwise) are formed. The Bible speaks of Jonathan's and David's souls being "knit" together, even though there is certainly no indication that they had a sexual relationship (see 1 Sam. 18:1).

This sort of soul tie can be any relationship in which a strong bond is formed. These can be parent-child relationships, sibling relationships, mentor-student relationships or friendships. All of these ties can be good, but they can also be ungodly. We all know of cases where a parent-child relationship has become unwholesome (without involving incest), or where any of these other relationships have become destructive—both emotionally and spiritually.

An ungodly soul tie in this sense is any relationship that stands between you and all that God wants you to be. Anytime a friend, relative or teacher begins to use your mutual bond of affection to manipulate or control you, there is the beginnings of the ungodly tie. It can be very subtle, which is why in our prayer (see Chapter 19), we have the person speak very generally of ANY ungodly tie, as it is seen by the Holy Spirit. That way, we let Him be the judge of which ties need to be cleansed. The Lord has the power to cleanse any part of a soul-tie that is displeasing to Him, as long as you invite Him to do it in prayer.

All marriages, parent-child relationships, etc. have something ungodly in them because they were forged between two sinful, fallen humans. Thus, these prayers can be an "open door" for the Holy Spirit to come in and cleanse anything sinful in a marriage or friendship and still leave the marriage bond, etc. intact—even strengthened! That kind of subtle and delicate emotional/spiritual surgery can only be done by the Master Physician! Praise His wonderful name!

In fact, the breaking of these soul ties can be incredibly liberating for a marriage. Over and above the breaking of lines through which sexual spirits can invade, tempt and harass (in the case of sexual ties), there is also the above-mentioned element of covenant keeping.

Think about it. You can only have a marriage covenant with one person at one time. If a person enters into marriage having committed fornication with others OR with an ungodly (non-sexual) tie to a parent, friend or sibling, it is virtually impossible for them to fully enter into a covenant with their spouse! They are already covenanted to someone else—even themselves. This is why the marriage seems so brittle and unsatisfying for both parties.

However, the good news from Jesus is that once you invite Him to come in and be the Third Partner in the marriage, and you let the Holy Spirit minister to those ungodly ties, both parties become freed up to enter into a full, rich and mature covenant with one another. Then—and only then—are the partners free to bless each other in all the ways the Lord intended.

18

Entering the Liberation Process

> "Blessed be the LORD my strength, which teacheth my hands to war, and my fingers to fight:" **Ps. 144:1**

We are ready to get into the process of setting people free through the Liberating Power of the Lord Jesus Christ. However, a few opening remarks are in order.

Many people are ministering in the area of deliverance. Many know what they are doing, and—unfortunately—some do not. We certainly don't claim to have the "one, true" method of liberating people from Satan's power. We aren't even certain if there is a "one, true" method, since all of God's children are unique. But we have prayerfully tried to stick as close to the Bible as possible.

However, just because we do it one way doesn't mean that if someone does it a different way, they are evil or messed up. Check out any practice with the Word of God. If you can find sound Bible principles behind it, use it. If you can't, then be very careful.

We are relative newcomers to a field in which many great saints have labored for years. We are not suggesting that we are "writing the book" on deliverance. There is only one Book on the subject—the Holy Bible. We acknowledge that we stand on the shoulders of earlier titans of the faith like Merrill Unger, Dr. Kurt Koch, Mark Bubeck and others.

However, we don't know of any other book that was written by people who have been through the occult, witchcraft, Satanism and liberation themselves. We want people to know that no matter how deeply they have been into the occult, they can get victory in their lives through Jesus Christ, just as we did.

This area of ministry is very deep, dark and complex. We are not the "experts." The only expert is the Holy Spirit. Presented herein are methods drawn from many sources—especially the Bible, and our own experience. It is our prayer that God can use us in our brokenness to minister to others of similar backgrounds and afflictions.

Finally, it is not our intention to debate whether or not a Born Again Christian can be demonized.[1] We know it is a controversy, with sincere people on both sides. Our position, based on years of Bible study and thousands of man-hours of prayer sessions with hundreds of people is that YES, Christians can be demonized, but not demon possessed, if the latter term means that the devil "owns" every spiritual "inch" of a Christian's "real estate."

Naturally, we feel that we are right and they (the no-Christian-can-have-a-demon school) are mistaken. However, we humbly suggest that the consequences of believing (wrongly) in our position are much less devastating spiritually than those of believing (wrongly) in their position.

We have seen the fruits of the no-Christian-can-have-a-demon doctrine. In many instances, a Christian who is suffering from serious demonic infestation will either:

a) Struggle fruitlessly against besetting sins until he or she is totally exhausted or demoralized, or:

b) Begin to doubt that they are saved at all!

Satan, the accuser, is only too happy to encourage the demonized Christian to believe they aren't saved. Perhaps they are too wicked, and God rejected them, even though they "went forward" and prayed the prayer. Such a Christian can end up in the "slough of despond" if everyone around them tells them "no, a Christian cannot have a demon!"

We have ministered to many such people, and it is truly a blessing to see the light of joy relit in their eyes when they are set free by Jesus. They now know that they are saved and that God really does love them. That knowledge alone is so incredibly liberating! These people are casualties of an all-too-academic "war" usually being waged by ivory tower theologians who would not know a demon from a doorknob!

In our reading of the Bible, Christians can have demons infesting them—inside of their bodies. If you disagree that is your right. Please read the Holy Bible and pray about it. We honestly believe that if you back away from "faith statements" or "denominational positions," and let the plain sense of scripture teach you, you will find that Christians can be demonized.

EXACTLY WHAT IS DEMONIZATION?

Just because it is possible for Christians to be demonized or oppressed, doesn't mean that every Believer is suffering in this manner. Probably, a comparatively large number of Christians do not have these problems. But the percentage is rising for several reasons:

1) More and more Christians are getting saved out of cults and the occult.

2) Fewer Christians are praying seriously. Thus the atmosphere of "prayer cover" and protection over Western nations is diminishing.

3) The destruction of sexual mores has led to a rise in the number of Christians who enter into marriages without prior chastity or with bondage to sexual sin.

4) Satan has stepped up his program because he knows that his time is running out.

5) Too many Christians are being distracted (or emasculated) by fake "bibles," fake "Christian" TV preaching, "Christian" entertainment, (which is about as Christian as a bordello) or by being linked unequally with cultists (Catholics, Masons, New Agers, etc.).

For these, and other reasons, the problem of demonic affliction and infestation is increasing among Believers. Just to clarify terms, we have this chart:

In which there are:

1) Fiery Darts: Thoughts and feelings fired at us by Satan. All Christians experience these. They are to be rebuked and resisted as soon as possible in the name of Jesus.

2) Mild oppression: More serious or chronic problems with the thought or emotional life: depression, anger, bitterness, impure thoughts, physical illnesses, etc. This is an invasion of the body (and occasionally the soul) by enemies of Jesus. Usually, at this stage, they cannot remain long without the person's consent.

3) Oppression: This is similar to the above, but more frequent, almost constant attacks on one's physical, emotional or moral well-being. Here, the "squatters" begin to stay longer in the body, and even in the soulish realm.

4) Mild Demonization: Involves more or less permanent occupation by demons, but usually only in a few key areas where the person has either consistently sinned or been sinned against. They remain in the body and the soul.

5) Severe Demonization: This involves an increase either in the depth of oppression or the number of spirits indwelling the person. Usually, radical and almost permanent changes in character occur here. Frequently the person begins to act in a manner which mimics psychosis. He or she may exhibit supernatural powers (telepathy, psychokinesis, etc.), knowledge (foreign languages, etc.) or strength.

6) Possession: Impossible for true Christians, but

common enough among unbelievers all over the world, especially those involved in habitual and serious sin, occultism or generational bondage.

7) **"Perfect Possession:"** This is rare, where there is almost literally "no-one home" except demonic strongmen. Usually, the human personality is so submerged that there is no sign of outward tension. Some of the great, supernaturally powerful leaders of our day were probably "Perfectly Possessed." They had so surrendered themselves over to Satan that he was able to work lying signs and wonders through them. Examples of such people would likely be Hitler, Charles Manson, "Rev." Jim Jones, Sai Baba, Saddam Hussein, etc.

OPEN DOORWAYS

These stages occur in the lives of Christians (to say nothing of unbelievers) for the following major reasons (often called open doorways):

1) Generational bondage (Ex. 20:5, Deut. 23:2) from ancestral involvement in idolatry or occultism. This is one of the most common ways in which people can be afflicted. Certain kinds of generational sin can affect a Christian all the way back ten generations (c. 400 years into your past!)

2) Being lured into occult or religious sin.

    a) Spiritism or trance channeling.

    b) Fortune telling or astrology.

    c) Magic, witchcraft, hypnosis, the development of "psychic powers."

    d) Idolatry (worship of any false god, involvement in cults, etc.).

  3) Serious and/or chronic, besetting sins:

    a) Anger, bitterness, unforgiveness, extreme jealousy.

    b) Gambling, greed, drunkenness, drug abuse.

    c) Abortion.

    d) Fornication, adultery or homosexuality.

    e) Gossiping, tale-bearing, etc.

    f) Rebellion against parents, cursing them, etc.

  4) Abuse, either emotional, physical or sexual can open doorways to oppression, even though the person was a victim, and not an active participant. This usually happens through:

    a) Anger, bitterness, unforgiveness.

    b) Loss of faith in God.

    c) Ungodly soul ties incurred through rape or incest.

    d) Use of hypnosis and triggers (more common in SRA survivors).

    e) Cursing of parents (Prov. 20:20).

    f) Incubus or succubus spirits (see Chapter 18).

  This list is not exhaustive, but it gives a good idea of things which can cause access points for satanic attack.

The Lord has blessed us with so many people coming to us that we have found it necessary to use a brief, crisis-oriented approach. Jesus' power is so awesome that we rarely have to see people more than two times. Once we understood the true authority of the Believer in Jesus Christ and got out of His way and let Him do the ministry, we have been wonderfully blessed to have people set free in three to four hours in most cases.

We do not feel that (in most cases) these six to twelve hour deliverance "marathons" are necessary or Biblical. Rather, they reflect a lack of under-standing of the consummate power of the Holy Spirit to smash the chains of darkness into flinders.

Sometimes we have people who think it is necessary to have hours of vomiting and growling in order to get REALLY set free. We meet those people where they are and minister to them as long and as tenderly as possible. However, we do not believe it is Biblical to permit demonic sideshows.

GETTING DOWN TO BUSINESS!

In our procedure, we have found it helpful to provide a kind of "intake form" in advance. Relevant parts of the form can be found in Appendix I. This form is designed to help him or her organize their thoughts and:

• To reveal the nature of the presenting problem (why they want help).

• Any relevant medical information: problems with drugs, etc.

• Any known ancestral or personal bondage to cults or the occult.

• Any known incidents of child abuse, rape, satanic abuse or contracts, or abortions.

• Any possible sinful sexual links (ungodly soul ties).

• Any serious, unresolved sins or emotional issues—especially unforgiveness.

Then we pray for the Holy Spirit's guidance in the session and for any lying or deceitful spirits to be bound from speaking or manifesting in any fashion.

Next we invite the person to ask any questions, and we teach about the process we are entering into. We fully disclose what is going to happen to alleviate as much stress and anxiety as possible.

"HONEY, I SHRUNK THE DEVIL!"

We emphasize that what we do is *not* exorcism. Exorcism is a magic ritual designed to cast out demons (see Acts 19:13ff) and is of dubious effectiveness. We do not recommend using the term, since it is not Biblically correct. This is especially true since Hollywood has (as usual) created a vast amount of misinformation about exorcisms.

Incidentally, we don't recommend using rituals or tactics which mock Satan or his minions. We have seen some ministers sing funny songs to the devil (or about him) during deliverances and make fun of him or belittle him—saying things like "Devil, you're a punk and we're going to kick your ****!"

This is dangerous and way out of order (Jude 8-9, 2 Pet. 2:10). Famed evangelist Mario Murillo calls this the "Honey, I Shrunk the Devil Syndrome,"[2] and we agree whole-heartedly with him. Anyone who does this kind of spiritual warfare is out from under the umbrella of protection of Jesus' gracious love, and may well get his clock cleaned!

Another current fad is discovering the name of the demon strongmen who rule over a city or nation and then taking them on. Unfortunately, such tactics have no Biblical or empirical support. They are dangerous. As Murillo points out:

> **"In Acts 8, Philip the Evangelist settled the question of how to win a city once and for all. The New Age village he entered boasted a great sorcerer who had amazed from the least to the greatest. Philip didn't search for the ruling demon's name; he proclaimed the Name that is above all names! ...Proclaiming Christ broke demonic power. The weapon of choice was, is, and always will be a vessel fully armed, who has the victory on three fronts (the world, the flesh and the devil)..."[3]**

This leads us into the importance of taking both the Lord Jesus Christ and the devil very seriously. Even if you have prayed for the liberation of a hundred people, you need to remain humble and still before the Lord and strive always for personal holiness. If you feel led by the Lord, fast at least one day before entering into this kind of ministry. Of course, keep your own prayer life active and vital, and spend a LOT of time in the Bible!

Additionally, we have found it incredibly helpful to have people praying for you during the ministry, as well as days before it—if possible. If this is done, nine times out of ten, the liberation will be a beautiful and gracious testimony to the power of Jesus.

It is wise not to do this kind of ministry alone, unless absolutely necessary! This is especially true with a person of the opposite sex, as demonized people sometimes become sexually provocative unless bound by prayer. It also avoids scandals or accusations of impropriety. A married couple ministering is ideal, but sometimes not possible. A good alternative is two (or more) men ministering to a man, and two (or more) women praying for a woman.

Beyond that, it is vitally helpful to have a prayer intercessor present, silently (or even not-so-silently) invoking the Holy Spirit's aid. Many times we have felt our arms lifted up, spiritually, by the prayers of our faithful prayer partners who sit silently beside us and pray for us. They are the unsung heroes of many a prayer session!

EMPOWERING THE BELIEVER!

In 99% of the people we pray for, the goal is NOT for *us* to cast demons out of the person, but to assist the person in asserting his or her own Christ-ordained authority over evil spirits! This encourages them, in the future, to depend upon Jesus for help, not on us. It brings empowerment and confidence into their lives. Occasionally, it has been necessary to pray FOR the person until they are "clear" enough to pray for themselves, but those are exceptions.

We have also found that it is necessary to have the person speak out loud. There is no Biblical evidence that Satan or his lackeys can read our minds, although they are obviously excellent judges of body language and character traits. This means that any affirmations, renunciations or rebukes of Satan or his demons must be done vocally. Even a whisper will do.

We have also found that, if possible, it is better to carry out this ministry in a church, or some other property set apart for the Lord's service. This gives a kind of "home court" advantage, and eliminates any anxieties about whether or not the place has been freed of any defiling influences. Some peoples' homes are not very spiritually tidy (see Chapter 11)!

An additional advantage to working in a church is the ability to keep all animals, children and unbelievers away from the vicinity of the liberation. Demons DO prefer any living form to being totally evicted from their "houses" (Mt. 8:31-32). In our early days, we had a demon leap into a cat. Of course, unbelievers have absolutely no protection against demonic attack. God seems to graciously and automatically protect infants, but we do like to be careful.

One final preparatory note is directed to those of the Pentecostal or Charismatic persuasion. We do not recommend allowing people to pray "in tongues" — in their prayer language—during a liberation session. This is especially true of the person you are praying for. Even respected Pentecostal ministers like Derek Prince have advised against this.

Our concern is that, even among sincere Christians, there is an increasing number of people with demonically generated tongues. We have frequently bound false tongues in the name of Jesus (under our breath) and had nearby Christians who were "prayer languaging" up a storm suddenly shut up for no apparent reason. Thus, we have found it better to ask everyone not to pray in their prayer language, rather than offend anyone unnecessarily.[4]

19

"Nuking" Satan's Strongholds!

"If the Son therefore shall make you free, ye shall be free indeed." John 8:36

Getting down to the actual "nuts and bolts" of liberation, here is how we proceed. First, we have the person for whom we are praying re-affirm their commitment to Christ.

It is a serious mistake to attempt to deliver an unregenerate person from demons without the express, clear leading of the Holy Spirit. Some have come away with broken bones trying to do so.

We have the person confess that either:

1) Jesus Christ is Almighty God come in the flesh (1 John 4:1-4). Or:

2) That they know (not hope) that they are going to heaven because they have faith that Jesus died on the cross for their sins and shed His blood to redeem them from their sins (1 John 5:13, Romans 10:9-10).

Don't settle for anything less than one of these! Believe it or not, Mormons and New Agers are able to say that Jesus is their Saviour, the Son of God, the Only-Begotten of the Father, etc. Then you need to make sure WHICH Jesus is being discussed! Keep it simple!

Rarely, we have had Christians who could not confess one of the two things above because of demonic resistance. Once, it took us over an hour just to get a Christian to say, "Jesus…is…Lord." If this kind of resistance occurs, the minister(s) and prayer warriors should pray to assist—binding Satan from interfering with God's process of freedom for the person.

They should persist, rebuking Satan in the name of the Lord (Jude 9) and reminding him that he is defeated and has no right to even be on the property, much less bothering the person. If there is serious resistance, sing praise choruses and hymns about the blood of Jesus, read aloud from Revelation 18-21 or Psalm 91. Keep at it until the demons buckle. It usually only takes a few minutes until the person is able to pray for themselves.

Resistance can be encountered at any level (sometimes surprisingly late in the session). Whenever it appears, deal with it as above. It is surprisingly effective.

Then we lead the person in speaking (in Jesus' name and authority) directly to Satan and his demons, commanding them to surrender ground they have gained. If resistance is encountered, proceed as above.

It is important to seek feedback. How do they feel? Are there any physical complaints—or thoughts which are not their own? The person needs to feel free to let you know about these sorts of problems. There are various ways in which Satan can throw stumbling-blocks in the path. These can be prayed against. They often include:

1) Acute headaches in the person (or others present)—often caused by the spirit of infirmity.

2) Panic attacks—can be caused by the spirit of fear.

3) Voices from within, telling the person not to trust the minister (spirit of fear).

4) Difficulty in hearing or speaking—caused by the deaf and dumb spirit.

5) Inability to concentrate—caused by the spirit of confusion.

6) Inability to remain awake—caused by the spirit of lethargy, OR by post-hypnotically implanted triggers.

If they report any symptoms, you need to pray against the afflicting spirit and bind it in Jesus' name.

Encourage the person in their self-reporting, as they sometimes feel they are being a bother. Assure them that this helps the prayer team discern what needs to be done. It is usually on this emotional level that Satan attacks, and through this we may discern what spirits remain and which are resisting the most.

Then we lead the person in a prayer asking the Lord to shut any doorways of demonic access which have been opened in the area of their life just prayed for, and to seal those doorways with Jesus' blood.

After you have finished, lead the person to pray for the Holy Spirit to fill and heal every aspect of their being that has been touched by the prayers that they have prayed. The prayer team should ask discernment for any further prayers needed.

To summarize, this cycle of:

1) Supplication to God for forgiveness (as applicable) and authority (with aggressive warfare from ministers and prayer team as needed).

2) Command Satan's demons to leave the person.

3) Prayer for the shutting of doorways of Satanic access.

4) Prayer for the Holy Spirit to fill and heal them.

Repeat whatever levels of ministry are needed.

MOVING THROUGH THE LEVELS

Levels of encounter are different for each person. During the diagnostic phase, we are usually able to determine what prayers are needed. The order

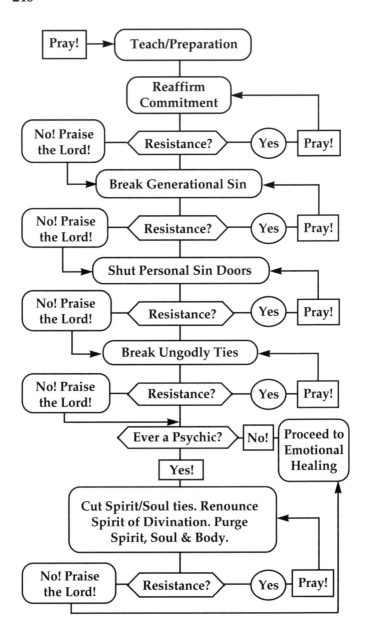

presented below is how we usually proceed, but individual needs and the Spirit's promptings may lead you in a different direction. You may need to move through the four-step cycle above with each level, although normally the person only needs to affirm the Lordship of Christ once, at the beginning.

I. Prayer for release of generational bondage: We usually do this first, since there is normally less resistance to it. Yet it can be very powerful. We normally have everyone who sees us do this one, since people seldom know much about their ancestors before their grandparents.

This should be prayed through at least four generations (Ex.20:5)—for the curse of illegitimacy, almost always through eleven generations (Deut. 23:2). Eleven generations is more than four centuries, and most of us have someone in our ancestry who was illegitimate.

The exact wording of the prayers is not as important as that the meaning be clear—especially to the person you are praying for. There is nothing "magical" about certain phrases, they just need to be Biblically correct.

II. Prayer for the renunciation of cult or occult activities (Personal Religious Sins): Idolatry is especially evil! Though the sin of idolatry is cleansed by the blood of Christ at salvation, its curse of demonic access can be carried on in our soul and body until specifically prayed against. "Cults" are false religions, usually those masquerading as Christian sects, but in the broader sense, major world religions (Islam, Buddhism, Hinduism, Cultural Spiritism, etc.) are also cults and need to be renounced.

It is helpful for the person to either make a list of possible cultic or occult practices or use a checklist like the one in our intake form, and specifically confess each form of idolatry to the Lord. We have found that certain cults and occult groups have specific thought-forms or egregores (demonic strong-men)— the worship of which has built up over centuries (See Deut. 32:17, Ps. 106:37, 1 Cor. 10:20-21, Rev. 9:20). These may need to be specifically renounced. A comprehensive list is in Appendix III.

Under this heading there are possible contingencies we need to mention:

• If the person was into the New Age Movement, cultural Spiritism or "regular" Spiritism[1] and successfully cultivated mediumship—i.e. "spirits" or "guides" spoke through them—they need to renounce, by name, the "spirits" (demons) which they channeled.

They also have to renounce the Spirit of Divination (Acts 16:16) and cast it out. They need to renounce their "psychic powers" or ability to astrally project, and ask the Lord to cut the link which the Spirit of Divination created between the soul and the spirit (Heb. 4:12).

Cultivation of psychic power, astral travel, psychedelic drug use or mediumship causes this link to be created by the Spirit of Divination—a link which God does NOT wish human beings to have at this time, except under specialized, Holy Spirit-ordained circumstances. Thus, the person needs to pray and ask for this link to be broken.

•People into upper level Satanism need to renounce their familiars, fetches and demon helpers by name.

•People who have joined cults which require oaths or covenants (i.e. Mormons, Masons, Catholics and many covens) need to renounce those covenants and ask God to forgive them for that sin (Matt. 5:34-37, James 5:12) and to break their power over them.

•SRA survivors need to pray especially against the Deaf and Dumb Spirit and its subsidiaries, the spirits of suicide and self-destruction. Renounce it and cast it out. This is because, as children, they are often programmed to "self-destruct" if they begin to talk about the cult. This is why so many people with this background are suicidal and indulge in behavior like wrist-cutting, head-banging and burning themselves with cigarettes. Once this renunciation and liberation is accomplished, the suicidal ideation and behavior should lessen considerably.

III. Prayer for repentance and renunciation of certain other specialized sins: These include abortion, drug abuse, drunkenness, homosexuality, adultery and pornography. Also any deep, sinful emotions (hatred, bitterness, lust, unforgiveness, etc.). These can all be doorways for demonic access.

A couple of specialized concerns:

•Abortion: In addition to the emotional trauma, and the killing of a child, this is an open doorway to two very mean and powerful "strongmen."

1) Molech, the god of infant sacrifice for the Ammonites (see 2 Kgs. 23:10, Jer. 32:35, etc.).

2) Lilith (see Chapter 8).

Usually, both of these strongmen must be renounced and cast out of a woman who has had an abortion. Occasionally, they must be cast out of a man who has pressured a woman into having an abortion.

•Drunkenness or drug abuse: If chronic, it may be helpful to renounce the specific strongmen associated with many drugs, including liquor (See Chapter 15).

•Unforgiveness and pent-up anger can be one of the most powerful and pernicious doorways to continued demonic infestation (2 Cor. 2:10-11, Eph. 4:26-32). It is very difficult to get full liberation from demonic oppression if unforgiveness is present. It is helpful to have the person prayerfully make a list of every person they need to forgive, and have them say:

> "Lord, through the power of the love of the Lord Jesus Christ, I forgive _____ for _____."

Sometimes people we cannot begin to think of forgiving in the natural man, we can forgive when we call upon the power of Jesus to help us forgive. This is essential, not only for liberation, but for emotional wholeness. It is also obedience to the Lord![2]

IV. Prayer for Breaking Ungodly Soul Ties: This can often be one of the most powerful moments in ministry. This is especially true for a survivor of child abuse or Satanic ritual abuse (see Chapter 18).

Since this is such a critical (and often misunderstood) part of the liberation process, here is a sample (or pattern) prayer for breaking ungodly soul ties. The wording is not "magical." Just the essential ideas are needed. However, we highly recommend that SRA survivors pray the third paragraph word-for-word because in most cases, it precisely utilizes the phrases used in original satanic ceremonies, and more effectively dismantles them:

> **"By the authority of Jesus' name, I ask you to cut any and all ungodly soul ties between myself and [name(s), if appropriate] and any person [or spirit] I have been sexually intimate with, known or unknown, remembered or forgotten. I ask you to use the Sword of the Spirit to cut any ungodly soul ties which may exist between us, right now! In Jesus' name, I ask you to cleanse those ties by the blood of Jesus of any possible access through which Satan can trouble me or my children.**

If appropriate: i.e. for voluntary adult behavior:

> **I confess (fornication, adultery, homosexuality, etc.) as sin and ask you to forgive me for committing them. I ask you to place all those acts under the blood of Jesus Christ which cleanses me from all sin (1 Jn. 1:7-9).**

[If there is suspicion that the person was ritually abused by Satanists as a young child, otherwise, omit:]

> **By the authority of the name of the Lord**

> Jesus Christ of Nazareth, I break the power
> of any and all covenants, contracts, dedica-
> tions or commissions made over me or my
> children [if any], known or unknown. I also
> ask the Holy Spirit of God to dismantle all
> triggers, post-hypnotic suggestions, implants
> or mind control and to destroy their power
> over me (or my children) forever!

> "I declare to Satan that he is a defeated foe
> in my life and in the lives of my family, and
> that by the power of the name of Jesus
> Christ, I shut any doorways of demonic
> access into my life and command him to get
> out of my life altogether. I ask you, Father
> God, to seal those doorways forever by the
> blood of the Lamb of God shed on the cross
> of Calvary.

Such a prayer will usually bring great release, especially for those victimized by child abuse or rape of any sort. For an explanation on "implants," mentioned above, see Appendix IV.

"Triggers" are post-hypnotic suggestions which are often planted in SRA survivors to help control them, manipulate them, or even drive them to suicidal acts. For more information, see Appendix VII.

V. Dealing with the Spirit of Divination: This step is needed for people who have used hallucinogenic drugs or been into the occult, Satanism, Witchcraft, or the New Age, and have tried to cultivate psychic powers, develop divinatory powers (i.e., Tarot cards, mediumship, palmistry, crystal balls, etc.) or achieve astral projection.

Here we pray and have the person renounce their powers and the Spirit of Divination—and ask the Lord to use the Sword of the Spirit to cut any links established by it (or any other demon) between their spirit and their soul.

We usually have them declare that they wish to send or receive NO messages from the spiritual world except what the Holy Spirit wishes them to receive, and then have them cast out the Spirit of Divination and any other demons.

VI. The "Full-Body Flush:" This is neither a medical condition, nor a car wash service. This is the catch-phrase we use for the final step in our process. We have the person go through their spirit, soul realm (will, emotions and mind) and their physical body and specifically repent for any sins committed in each of those areas.

Then we have them ask Jesus to forgive them, and have them command any strongmen that we (or they) have discerned to go where Jesus commands them to go—OUT of that area of their spiritual "anatomy." The list of these strongmen, their access points and their symptomology can be found in Appendix III, "The Taxonomy of Evil."

At three key points (after praying for the cleansing of the spirit, soul and body), we also have them ask the Lord to shut any doorways of demonic access opened by any sins, at any time, in any way—and ask the Lord to seal those doorways shut forever with the blood of Jesus.

These points are essentially between the spirit

and soul, between the soul and the body, and between the body and the outside world. Thus, body, soul and spirit are purged (or flushed) of any remaining demonic infestation. We then pray for a filling of the person with the Holy Spirit.

To explain this, we use the metaphor of a modern submarine. A submarine maintains its hull integrity through structural strength, but also through internal pressure going OUTWARD. The pressure of the ocean at certain depths is incredible, and the only way the submarine's hull can remain intact is through the use of bulk-head doors and maintaining air pressure within the vessel sufficient to help bolster the metal superstructure.

If any of the bulkhead doors are opened at the wrong time, the structural integrity of the sub can collapse.

We explain to the person that their body-soul-spirit is much like that submarine. By flushing each "compartment," then permanently shutting and sealing the "bulk-head door" with the blood of Jesus, and praying for the Holy Spirit to fill them, we create a supremely powerful internal pressure.

Even though, like the ocean, Satan maintains a constant pressure on a Christian, as long as the Holy Spirit is present with power (through daily prayer and Bible study) and the bulkhead doors remain sealed (which happens by keeping free of serious, doorway-opening sins), there is no way any kind of demonic forces can gain access. We explain that it is very difficult, if not impossible, for Christians to get

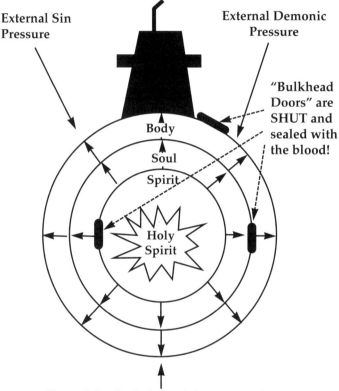

External Sin Pressure

External Demonic Pressure

"Bulkhead Doors" are SHUT and sealed with the blood!

Body

Soul

Spirit

Holy Spirit

"lust of the flesh, lust of the eyes, and
the pride of life." 1 John 2:16

The internal pressure of the Holy Spirit in a saved, newly liberated person is great enough to maintain the integrity of the "hull" against the world and the devil's fiery darts!

"re-possessed" because of these scriptural facts.

Thus, in the vast majority of cases, the liberation process is complete in a matter of hours. Sometimes, with more severe cases, it may be necessary to meet two or three times to pray against certain specific strongmen or strongholds, or to accomplish some emotional healing.

20

Aftercare

"But my God shall supply all your need
according to his riches and glory by Christ
Jesus."   Philippians 4:19

After the prayer session for liberation, some
aftercare considerations remain. Some people expect
more from a prayer session than is "delivered."

Sometimes this is because the expectations are
not entirely Biblical. Some people expect deliverance
from everything from athlete's foot to over-eating.
They forget that there is still "the flesh" to deal with.
Demonic infestation is not responsible for every sin
they ever committed.

Additionally, though the strongmen are gone, the strongholds might still be in place. These are the fleshly habit patterns which the demons have helped to reinforce.

Occasionally, in His gracious sovereignty, Jesus DOES deal with both the fleshly concerns and the demons in one mighty stroke. But that is not as common as any of us would like. We like to use the metaphor of the way the Lord helped Joshua take the Promised Land. They marched in and took Jericho in one mighty, spectacular swoop. The walls fell flat and city was taken!

This is much like the liberation process. Because our authority in the Lord is clear, liberation is almost always a matter of a couple of hours of ministry. However, just like the taking of Canaan, the process then often becomes more gradual. Obviously, God could have gone in and wiped out every Tom, Dick and Molech in the Promised Land immediately. Similarly, God could wipe out every demon, every demon stronghold, fleshly habit, wounded emotion and illness instantly.

That is usually not the case. The Lord IS in the character-building and humility business, and He wants us to understand the immensity of sin and its consequences. So while the liberation process is usually over quickly, the process of tearing down strongholds and bringing forth healing usually takes longer—however, not nearly as long as it would take had the demons been left within the person.

With that in mind, here are a few important facts

that the person who has just been set free needs to appropriate.

ELEMENTS OF AFTERCARE

It is important to remember that this liberation is an incredible miracle of God. In many cases, Jesus leap-frogs over years of therapy or torment and brings wonderful relief. The person needs to know that Jesus worked a wonderful miracle in their life.

They need to recommit themselves to walk more closely with their Lord and Deliverer. They need to build up good habit patterns to replace the sin strongholds which were crippled. This includes more frequent and serious prayer and Bible study, as well as other elements of the Christian life.[1]

Part of this involves (where practical) the open proclamation of the victory the Lord has given you! As the Lord told the demoniac in Luke 8:39:

> **"Return to thine own house, and show how great things God hath done unto thee. And he went his way, and published throughout the whole city how great things Jesus had done unto him."**

We are told that we overcome Satan by the blood of the Lamb and the word of our Testimony (Rev. 12:11). Thus, every time you share with others your victory in Jesus, it is an additional kick in the fangs to the devil. It weakens him still further, and does much to edify the faith of your friends. There are times when this is not wise, and sensitivity to the prompting of the Spirit is in order. Some people—

especially victims of abuse—may not feel comfortable telling the "whole story." Frankly, some Christians are not mature enough to handle such a testimony.

Just the same, most people can always share enough to glorify the Lord and affirm their own newly-found, Christ-ordained power over the forces of darkness (Luke 10:19). The testimony might give insight to listeners who are struggling with their own problems but don't know which way to turn.

Part of the demolition of strongholds involves everyone's favorite word, "discipline." This verse needs to be memorized and appropriated:

> **"And they that are Christ's have crucified the flesh with the affections and lusts."**
> **Gal. 5:24**

The person needs to be aware of the high calling to which they have been summoned and try to achieve a degree of holiness which keeps the strongholds ever lower on the horizon. They need to commit themselves to moral purity (1 John 1:7-9, 2 Cor. 7:1). Of course, no one can ever be perfect, but "short accounts" need to be kept with the Lord.

The person has to understand that one of the first things Satan will try to do is steal their victory. Though the demons have been cast out, Satan can still do what he does to every Christian: discharge "fiery darts." These are thoughts of doubt or defeat. He can whisper in their ear that the prayer session was a sham, a hoax. We convey to newly-liberated children of God the kinds of tactics the Deceiver uses to cast stumbling-blocks in their path. They need to:

•Realize that Satan can cause some of the same sights, sounds and tactile phenomena from outside them as he could from within. It's just much harder for him. He is like a prowler outside your house, hollering and throwing pebbles at the windows. He may be frightening, but he cannot come in without the Christian's express permission.

•Realize that just as they were saved by faith, not feelings, so they are set free by faith, and not feelings. They may or may not "feel" any different, but the heart is deceitful (Jer. 17:9). They should trust in God's promises, not in their own moods, and know that the victory is theirs in Christ.

•Realize that if they have been "straight" with the Lord Jesus and not held anything back that might give Satan legal ground, then there is no possible way he can access them, except through thoughts. They should not worry about minor things, God's grace is awesome.

If they forgot to mention something during the prayer session, and remember it later, they just have to confess it to Him, say they are sorry and ask Him to shut any doorways opened by the sin. Jesus gives us all a lot of "slack" if we are trying our best.

THE POWER OF PRAISE AND POSITION

God's Word assures us that He inhabits the praises of His people (Ps. 22:3)! Thus, where true praise and worship is offered, it is very difficult for Satan to gain the tiniest foothold. Adoration to God offered with heartfelt sincerity, or by a declarative act of will can never fail to unleash Christ's power and provision.

Many times we have watched "hell's foundations quiver at that shout of praise." We have seen demonic oppression melt away like morning fog before the sunlight of worship. It doesn't matter if the person feels like praising and worshipping or not. It is an act of will and faith to praise Him, even when we are under assault.

Following a prayer session, the person should learn to appropriate the precious realities taught in 2 Chron. 20, especially vs. 20-26. They should develop the habits enjoined by Psalm 103:1-2, Psalm 145, Eph. 5:19-20, Hebrews 13:15 and 1 Peter 2:9.

The person needs to learn that they have a special position in Jesus Christ. With the prayer team's help, they have seen that position in action during the session. They, like all Christians, are spiritually seated with Jesus Christ in the heavenlies. They have their victory, and will keep their victory through Him—and Him alone (Romans 8:31-39, 2 Cor. 4:7-15, Eph. 1-2). Nothing in all the universe can undo what Jesus Christ does. And what He does, He does perfectly!

> **"Wherefore he is able also to save them to the uttermost that come unto God by him, seeing he ever liveth to make intercession for them.** Hebr. 7:25**

Many Christians, especially those who have need of this sort of ministry, do not understand that Jesus Christ is praying for them every moment in heaven.

They need to realize, at a bone-deep level, that He is with them in their struggle—that He has been with them—and WILL be with them—every step of the way. Grasping that wonderful reality will bring them a peace which passes understanding (Isaiah 26:3; 30:15; 48:16-18, Jn. 16:33, Phil. 4:6-7 and 2 Thess. 3:16).

Beyond that, the person needs to recognize and guard against "Stylistic Approaches to Sin"— habitual sin patterns in their thoughts or actions. These are ruts of sinful thoughts or behaviors that have been plowed deeply into their soul either by their own sinful nature or by Satan. They need to understand that though the strongmen are gone, strongholds need to be yielded one by one to the control of the Holy Spirit.

Satan will almost certainly try to exploit or energize these strongholds to seduce the person into doubting their full liberation. Those kinds of fiery darts need to be sharply rebuked. The person must learn to study and appropriate the promises of Romans 6 and Ephesians 4:22-24. They need to make a daily sacrifice of their entire life afresh to God (Rom. 12:1-2) and let Him do the rest. He will transform their mind if they can stay out of His way and let Him do it.

RENEW YOUR MIND!

It is critically important that the person realize the dangers of a passive mind! One of the hardest things for many people to do after deliverance is use their mind effectively. Because of involvement in mystical practices, drugs or alcohol—or because of depending too much on evil spirits, their minds become flabby and lazy.

It is VITAL that they avoid anything which causes their mind to shift into neutral for any length of time. The best thing they can do is memorize scripture from the King James Bible. Mathematical tables can also be helpful—anything that forces their mind to exercise itself. When they find their mind drifting off, they should ask the Lord to help them claim the scriptural promises that we all have the mind of Christ (1 Cor. 2:16, Phil. 2:5, Rom. 12:2, Eph. 4:23, 2 Tim. 1:7, 1 Pet. 1:13).

Beyond all that, they need to appropriate the Armour of God daily, as discussed earlier—and realize the hell-cracking power of their one offensive weapon, the Word of God! With it, the new spiritual warrior can smash Satan's assaults with incisive "surgical strikes" of Bible-based tactical authority (Luke 10:19, James 4:7, 1 Pet. 5:8-9). It is important that the person pray for right discernment—because right discernment of demonic attacks, combined with faithful use of our weapons, *always* leads to victory through the blood of the Lamb!

21

Church-wide Issues

"He that hath an ear, let him hear what the
Spirit sayeth unto the churches..."   Rev. 2:7

Is your church under spiritual attack? If so, what
can be done about it? Let's take a look at some of
these problems, and see how best to dethrone Lucifer
from your church!

IS YOUR CHURCH UNDER
SPIRITUAL ATTACK?

Unless you are in a knot-hole dead church that is
doing nothing for the Kingdom, your fellowship is
probably experiencing incoming fire. This can take
any number of forms:

• Sickness or marital troubles among leadership and members.

• Children of leadership or members in trouble (drugs, rebellion, etc.).

• Infiltration of church by unsaved agents of the enemy.

• Gossiping and cliquishness.

• Preaching of a weak, wimpy gospel (never mentioning sin or hell) or "pop-psychology" gospel.

• Carelessness with the Word of God.

• Tendency towards excessive legalism or heavy-handed discipling.

• Besetting sin or cultishness among members (Masonry, New Age practices, etc.).

While some of these difficulties can be attributed to the dreaded old sin nature—both of the flock and the pastors—many can come from infiltrators and/or cursings from covens or New Age groups in the area.

For example, a lady who taught Sunday School in one of the largest churches in our area—a church with a nationally recognized pastor—was an associate of the second most powerful New Age leader in the world!

Another successful church never reprimanded or rebuked a fellow in its body who travels, doing seminars promoting occult healing techniques!

What can be done about problems like these? There is not just one answer, but one answer does loom large over all the rest:

PRAYER IS THE KEY!

Tragically, few pastors and/or churches pray enough. A recent survey showed the average pastor prayed only three minutes a day!!!

Your church should have an intercessory prayer team that can be contacted and galvanized into action with a few phone calls. This prayer must be aggressive and powerful, but Biblically appropriate. We feel that some unscriptural practices have crept into the spiritual warfare "camp." Be careful of these:

1) Don't try to manipulate people through prayer! That is not prayer, but witchcraft. In other words, don't try and arm-wrestle God into placing someone into a situation you feel they need to be in. Neither is it Biblically appropriate or possible to command people to do things in the name of Jesus.

2) It is not scriptural to curse people in the name of Jesus. Rather, pray frequently and bless those attacking you, claiming them for salvation. Pray that the REAL Jesus will be glorified before them. Also, pray to disarm the enemy's weapons. Daily:

• Ask the Lord to blind (and deafen) the enemy spirits to what goes on in and around church and homes of members.

• Ask the Lord to expose and cast out any spirits troubling the church building or property.

• Plead the blood of Jesus over your church, leadership and membership.

• Ask God to grant (or increase) discernment to

your pastor. Some have told us that their pastors confess to having absolutely no spiritual discernment. A pastor without spiritual discernment is like a sheriff with no bullets in his gun.

• Raise the Shield of Faith around your church, leadership and membership.

• Ask the Lord to bind Satan's ability to interfere with finances and programs.

• Ask the Lord to bind any false manifestations in the church, any false tongues, etc.

• Bind the lying and accusing spirit and the accuser of the brethren from sowing strife among the people.

• Bind all lying and seducing spirits from impacting the congregation.

Fasting is another key. It builds spiritual strength and increases discernment. It's good if a pastor exhorts his people to fast for key needs.

Additionally, encourage group intercessory prayer. Prayer meetings should be a weekly (or more frequent) part of the church's schedule. If they aren't, see about starting one—and stick with it!

SPARE YOUR FLOCK! (ACTS 20:29)

Without being paranoid, care should be taken that those in leadership or teaching positions be saved and doctrinally sound. Nobody is perfect, but no one should be allowed to teach or lead without meeting three criteria:

1) They can give, in their own words, an oral testimony of who Jesus Christ is (see Chapter 20).

2) They can demonstrate fundamental knowledge of and agreement with the doctrines of the church.

3) They have been set free from and/or renounced any past or present involvement in any cult or occult practices. (A common one these days is Freemasonry.)

We are continually amazed at how many bizarre people are allowed access to the church's most precious possession—its children!

We got a call from a woman whose evangelical church had a "terrific" youth leader who was deeply involved in "A Course in Miracles." This is a New Age course "channeled" by a demon, which denies most all the fundamentals of the Christian faith.

When concerned parents asked about this issue, he was brought before the elders. They asked him who he believed Jesus was. His reply, "the son of God." They asked him what Jesus had done for him, and he said something to the effect that Jesus had saved him by showing him that death was nothing to fear, and could be overcome and conquered!

That just isn't good enough! However, when a concerned mother pressed that issue, she was reprimanded for being unloving!

At another evangelical church, parents had no recourse but to pull their children out of the church because they were being sexually abused in childrens' church! It is enough to make you weep!

Some other concerns:

1) Every effort should be made to discourage gossip in the church. Sermons need to be preached against it periodically.

2) There should be accountability in the church leadership. No one should wield supreme authority except Jesus. Boards should check and balance pastors, and the Bible should be able to overrule the board or pastor if they step out of line (2 Tim. 3:16).

3) Manipulation of the members' lives should be avoided. However, members who are involved in cultic practices should be warned privately that what they are doing is out of order. In extreme cases, the format of Matt.18 should be used.

4) The church is a hospital for sick souls, therefore people who are in trouble spiritually should not be kicked out unless they are causing serious problems or scandal to the name of Jesus in the community.

5) Be careful about indiscriminate "laying on of hands" among members.

> **"Lay hands suddenly on no man, neither be partaker of other men's sins: keep thyself pure."** **1 Tim. 5:22**

There is a growing trend in evangelical (especially charismatic) churches called "body ministry." We have found many Christians have picked up demons by being prayed for by having hands laid upon them in churches.

There is a phenomenon of transference of spirits.

Many Christians do not understand that while it is Biblical for hands to be laid upon you for prayer, for healing, and for setting apart in the ministry, the preponderance of verses that deal with the laying on of hands is for the transference of sin (from a person to a sacrificial animal).

There is NO Biblical support for having members of a church body indiscriminately lay hands on one another. It is Biblical for church elders to do this (James 5:14-15), but these should be men who are proven servants of God.

If you allow a person to lay hands on you when your "spiritual immune system" is not prayed up and in full force (as when you are sick), it is highly possible for the spirits that are infesting the other person to come into you—without their knowledge.

Remember also that many churches have in their membership witches who pretend to be Christians. They will often be the first to lay hands on people for prayer and will deliberately impart evil spirits.

Some people may find this difficult to believe, but we have seen the casualties! People who have never dabbled in the occult and have no generational sin have come to us under heavy oppression.

You may be such a powerful, prayed-up Christian that if such people laid hands on you, the Spirit within you might prevent such transference. Praise God. However, not everyone in churches is a spiritual giant! It is Biblical for us to have a concern for what Paul calls the weaker brother (1 Cor. 8:9-13).

While God may frequently protect His children when they allow these sorts of unscriptural practices, we believe it is better to only let the pastor or elders lay hands on those who need prayer. In this day and age, it is certainly better "spiritual hygiene."

WE'VE DONE ALL THIS AND OUR CHURCH IS STILL UNDER SIEGE

If your church is under serious attack, and the above methods prove ineffective, we have found these possibilities to be effective:

1) Has the church and land been prayed for and set aside for the Lord's work in a spiritual warfare manner? Have the pastor and staff walked around the property, given it to the Lord in prayer and confirmed scriptural promises over it (Ps. 125:3, Josh. 1:3, Ps. 34:7)? Has the church building been anointed with oil recently?

2) Has the Holy Spirit been sought about open doorways within the church which are permitting Satan's fiery darts to get through?

• Witches (undercover) have been known to deliberately leave magical items on church property as "homing devices" for curses. These can sometimes be very mundane objects (gloves, scarfs, etc.).

• Watch out for odd looking graffiti on exteriors or in restrooms. Occasionally these childish-looking scrawls can be demonic writing. Plead the blood of Jesus over anything which is discerned.

• It is vital to ask the Holy Spirit for spiritual

discernment to expose anything in the property which the Lord does not want there. It is His church!

• Is the ministry of the Lord's Table being handled properly and reverently? We have noticed that many churches are getting quite casual about communion.

NOTICING WITCHCRAFT IN YOUR CHURCH

Subliminal Hypnosis: VERY strange things are going on at some supposed evangelical churches, evidently with the consent of leadership.

At one church, subliminal messages were being played through the sound system during the service. Back-masking was also used during the worship time. The pastoral staff said they believed the subliminal material would increase church attendance and that there was nothing wrong with it. The messages could not be understood so everyone had to take the staff's word for it.

Investigation revealed that these messages were (at best!) being used to "hypnotize" the people into giving more money, or getting friends to leave their own churches and attend this church (sheep-stealing).

The use of subliminal messages or back-masking is a form of hypnosis, and can be a major open doorway for demonic attack in the congregation (See Chapter 7).

The question must be asked: "Were other ungodly messages being hypnotized into the congregation without their knowledge?" And even if the staff's intentions were good, Jeremiah 48:10 warns us:

> **"Cursed be he that doeth the work of the Lord deceitfully..."**

HOW TO HAVE A CLEAN CHURCH

We know the scriptural requirements for elders and deacons from the pastoral epistles (cf. 1Tim 3). Their fruits need to be judged. Beyond that, here is how to discern who is from the Lord and who is not.

A pastor could announce in front of the church whom he serves, who Jesus Christ is to him, being lengthy and specific. Then he might say, "I'd like to invite you to join me in worshipping (and put it in first person terms) MY Lord and my God come in the flesh, the Lord Jesus Christ, my Savior... and I don't want you worshipping anybody else! (Ha! Ha!)"

Though it sounds funny as he's putting it in a humorous way, he's sending out a command: do not sing unless it is to MY LORD!

As he sings, he should watch and see who is not singing, or who's just lip synching the words. Or who is covering it up by looking holy and righteous with hands raised and eyes closed but are not joining in worship verbally!

When you make clear to infiltrators who the Lord is, who they're singing to and what the requirements are, you have them on the spot. They, of course, do NOT want to worship our Lord!

If the pastor (or worship leader) had said "I want

you to worship Jesus and nobody else," remember that there are different Jesuses out there. If he said "the lord," the "bad guys" will worship too, especially if the lyrics are in third person terms or vague enough. To a witch,"the Lord" COULD refer to Satan. So could "my Lord," "the One," "my Father" or "my Savior." Get them to sing "my Lord Jesus Christ" to separate the sheep from the wolves.[1]

What can help is singing some old-fashioned hymns about the blood of Jesus Christ. Watch the infiltrators start lip synching meaningful words like "MY lord, Jesus Christ," or "...died for ME", etc. Sometimes a Satanist will raise their hands, bypass those words, look holy and sing in tongues instead.

Or the pastor could ask, "Who will bow down with me in worshipping My Lord, Jesus Christ, the Saviour who is God come in the flesh, who died for my sins?" Or he could ask, "Will everybody get on their knees and join me in interceding to My Lord Jesus Christ for... (revival, or whatever)?"

TONGUES AND "CHARISMATIC" WORSHIP

That brings us to detecting lying, false tongues and binding all counterfeit gifts, signs and wonders. If you are in a Charismatic or Pentecostal church, you need to be very careful about the use of tongues. Infiltrators will be using demonic tongues. They will always sing to "my lord" in the third person, especially if its repetitious! Sometimes they will go out of their way to make it repetitious, repeating a song over and over. When does this become "vain repetitions?" (See Matt. 6:7.)

If your church believes in tongues, then you need to check tongues. We have been in charismatic churches where all manner of false tongues were tolerated. In one situation, a lady was repeating "Ave Maria, Ave Maria," which is Latin for Hail Mary! We find it difficult to imagine that the Holy Spirit was praying to Mary.

In another meeting, a woman was disrupting the prayer time with a loud, raucous tongue. She was so noisy that the prayer leader could not be heard. We prayed quietly (but audibly) and bound all false gifts, false tongues, lying signs and wonders in the name of the Lord Jesus Christ. She instantly shut up! She had no idea what we were praying because we were seated behind her. But the demons knew!

If you believe you should be praying in tongues, here is what you might do. Go to one corner of a room and pray in your tongue. From the other corner of the room, have a Christian friend—under his or her breath— bind all false gifts, false tongues, lying signs and wonders in the name of the Lord Jesus Christ. If your tongues ceases virtually at once, you know it is false and from the devil. If this happens, you need to renounce it and cast out the Spirit of Divination (see Chapter 19).[2]

Infiltrators in charismatic worship will also use distinctive hand signs (mudras) when they raise their hands in worship. They use this to signal others who know the sign that they are there, so others can come in to help infiltrate. The sign will vary from town to town, but in one church, we discovered that this sign was sticking their little finger out.

FELLOWSHIP TIME

Usually, when infiltrators first come into a church, they act very passive. They keep their ears open, gathering as much information as possible, like people's particular sin, how things are run, who is the strongest in the church, the weakest in the Lord. Once their plan is made, they begin to break down unity and prayer in the church.

MUSIC

When infiltrators take over they often go through the music department. The witch "music minister" is often quite good—a professional who knows how to manipulate and pick the songs that give a foothold to curse between songs.They especially like contemporary "choruses" that are in third person and very repetitious, no "blood" songs, no classic hymnody, but all rhythm and feel-good songs.

Your church should use music that uses words about Calvary, blood, etc. to make them show themselves. These truths make it very uncomfortable for them to be among God's people.

ANOINTING

Moses was responsible for anointing the tabernacle. He HAD to cleanse the sanctuary on a daily basis. The pastor, not just any men of the church, should be responsible for anointing the church and sanctuary. He should at least pray daily over the sanctuary and classrooms, if not anoint them daily.

Why? Because Satanists will use their oil, false

prayers, etc. to anoint and dedicate the church to Satan! There can be no evil power in the church if the Pastor's daily anointing has built up a depository of Holy Spirit power. This is one thing which will put teeth back into the church.

THE OIL ITSELF

Sharon and I pray over food because it's scriptural (1 Tim. 4:3) AND because people have attempted to poison us many times.

If we need to pray over our food in case it's been cursed, then shouldn't we also pray over our anointing oil, which represents the power in the blood of Jesus? EVEN if I've prayed over our oil when I fill the vial, I still pray over it and dedicate it to doing the will of God EVERY time I use it.

What to pray over oil? Ask the Lord what is needed. Forgiveness of sin? Healing? Ask God very specifically to anoint that oil to give that person whatever God needs to impart to them.

Often people will only give a general prayer when they put the oil in a container — a "buckshot" prayer. With a specific prayer, there is intercession going on both at the same time of the consecration and the anointing.

Pray for the oil's anointing. Infiltrators have been known to sabotage leftover oil, or defile it with salt, leaven, urine, etc. This is especially true if numerous members of the congregation have keys to the church. They will hunt it down and contaminate it. So it is best to pray over it every time, asking God to cleanse it if it has been defiled and empower it to do His will. His precious compassion is "new every morning (Lam. 3:22-23).

Finally, realize that Satanists will work as a team in the church. They'll collaborate each other's lies and slander. They will start rumors about the pastor or other prayer warriors in the congregation. If you don't have several eye witnesses, take it with a grain of sand (Deut. 17:6).

DISCIPLING ISSUES

How does your church deal with people getting saved from diverse backgrounds? An increasing number of people are being saved out of occult or cult backgrounds. We feel it is vital that these people get discipled—in the full meaning of the word—and get well-grounded in Bible study and prayer.

Sharon and I were truly blessed in that, during our earlier years in Christ, we had a pastor and his wife who were experienced in the Lord and who knew how to disciple. Much of whatever strength and doctrinal solidity we have came from that discipleship.

Sometimes ex-cultists for Jesus need additional spiritual and emotional support. Larger churches may wish to have support groups composed of ex-Mormons, ex-New Agers, etc. who have matured in their walk and can help newer Believers deal with their problems with compassion and patience.

A practice from the ancient church is worth looking at. When people were baptized, as a matter of course they were routinely led through prayers renouncing their former religious practices and were set free of any demonic bondages. Vestiges of this remain in the "high church" liturgies to this day. Be assured, today's culture is no less pagan than that of ancient Rome or Greece! Therefore, we recommend that medium to larger-size churches maintain a special prayer team which is able to minister liberation to these people.

Care should be taken to minimize the "weirdness" quotient involved. It should never be presented that you have to be a drooling demoniac or a tormented sex fiend to qualify. It should be presented as another normal part of the functioning of the church, like praying for the sick, childrens' church or a bus ministry. These prayer teams should be made up of mature, seasoned Christians, and must be accountable to the pastor.

It is our heartfelt prayer that ministry for liberation should be a normal part of any church's ministry. The fact that it has fallen, for the most part, to para-church ministries is a symptom of Satan's defanging and secularizing the church! We have bought into the world's view of reality!

YOU AND YOUR PASTOR

What about the spiritual warfare obligations of a church and its pastor? Many pastors and a lot of members do not understand an important element of their calling! Being a pastor doesn't mean just visiting the sick, preaching a sermon, counseling or fund-raising. A pastor should be a shepherd in the warfare of the heavenlies. In Jesus' day, shepherds fought off the wolves and protected the flock. Today, a pastor should function as the first line of defense for the local Body.

Pastors need to understand that God has given them a mantle of authority, but part of that authority is to lay down their lives for the sheep. This means that EVERY fiery dart Satan sends at a Christian should have to make it through the pastor first!

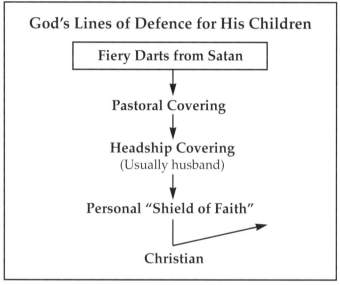

God's Lines of Defence for His Children

Fiery Darts from Satan

Pastoral Covering

Headship Covering
(Usually husband)

Personal "Shield of Faith"

Christian

The pastor is anointed of God to be the D.E.W. system for his flock, and God will mightily empower him to deflect most incoming fire. Obviously, all pastors get fatigued, overworked and occasionally neglect their prayer time. This is not to lay a guilt trip on pastors. If they try their best, our Great Shepherd will more than "take up the slack." And if a "sheep" deliberately wanders away from the flock and goes where it shouldn't, it is not the pastor's fault if the sheep gets bitten.

The flip-side of this truth is that churches have a vital obligation to pray for their pastor, staff and family members! Witches are praying and fasting for the fall of Christian leaders and the destruction of their families. This is all the more true if your church is making a difference in the community.

When we were in Elizabeth Clare Prophet's cult, C.U.T., the Church Universal and Triumphant, we went to one of their centers. In the basement was a room where members were on duty, 24-hours a day, 7 days a week, "decreeing" (their word for chanting repetitious prayers) against the pastors of the city.

A pastor friend of ours decided to oppose C.U.T.'s efforts to enter into their town. They picketed meetings and handed out tracts. Almost at once, key members of the church became deathly ill! Only when the pastor realized that he had a spiritual dragon by the tail and called for a fast and prayer session did the siege subside. The cult was driven from the community! Praise God!

Often these cultists are willing to spend much more time in their "spiritual warfare" than Christians spend in theirs. As a member of C.U.T. myself, we would rise before sun-up every day and "decree" for three or four hours! How many Christians pray for their pastor, intercede and do spiritual warfare for even one hour a day?

Church members should also support their

pastoral staff in other ways. For example:

• Do you have "roast preacher" for lunch after church on Sunday? Especially, don't undermine your pastor's authority in front of your children!

• Are the pastors more likely to die of sheep bite than the flock of wolf bite?

• Do you compliment your pastor on his work? He needs a good word as much as any other Christian.

• Do you pay your pastor a decent wage, or does he make the same pay as the kids who work at McDonald's. By the way, your pastor should not also have to be the custodian and grounds-keeper.

• Make it a point to pray for your pastor and his family daily, if not more frequently. If he is doing the job the Lord has given him, he needs your spiritual uplifting.

In closing, we want to express our heartfelt desire that spiritual warfare become part of the lifestyle of every Christian who reads this book! If you are not part of the solution, you may be part of the problem.

We believe that God is raising up Christians who want to be "armed and dangerous" to Satan's realm. Spiritual warfare is part of evangelism, it's part of worship, it's part of prayer and it's part of Bible study. There are few aspects of a Believer's life not impacted by it. Yet most Christians go blithely through their life unaware of these conflicts.

It is our humble prayer that this book will "turn

on" tens of thousands of Christians. They need to have "their ears on" and their "antennae up."

Secondly, we pray that this book will offer hope to people who are ensnared in demonic bondage. God really cares about their problems, and He has provided a solution through the cross, the blood of Jesus Christ and the power of His Word.

It doesn't take the proverbial rocket scientist to discern that, if the Lord tarries, we are going to need a new breed of Believer to survive in these days of "political correctness," gay rights, and New Age Bibles. It's going to take courageous, armoured up Christians who won't shirk the fight, and are unafraid of anything the devil can throw at them.

Christians bought by the blood and liberated from the chains of hell by the power of Jesus' Word can have a new quality of fearlessness. That is because they know that their Lord took everything in the devil's arsenal and still came out victorious and glorified. Christians may have been brushed by Satan's wings, but they've been healed by the Lamb of God! Such warriors fear nothing but their Lord!

Because He lives, we can live as well! Because He has set us free, we know that Satan cannot do anything to us that our Lord Jesus cannot set right. With that knowledge comes a holy boldness—and a faith that Jesus can empower us to take anything Satan has to dish out.

Our prayer, for ourselves and for all Believers, is that of Paul's at the end of the celebrated "armour of God" passage:

> "And as for me, that utterance may be given
> unto me, that I may open my mouth boldly,
> to make known the mystery of the gospel,
> For which I am an ambassador in bonds:
> that therein I may speak boldly, as I ought
> to speak." Ephesians 6:19-20

Even so, come quickly, Lord Jesus!

N.B. We want to acknowledge the help of Wayne Richard in compiling some of the material in this chapter.

Appendix I

Possible Demonic Access-Points

PERSONAL SIN DOORWAYS:
- Astral Projection
- Astrology
- Blood Pacts
- Channeling
- Clairvoyance
- Cursing Parents
- Divination
- Dowsing
- Dungeons & Dragons
- E.S.P.
- Eckankar
- EST (The Forum)
- Fetishism
- Fortune-telling
- Gurdjieff
- Homeopathy

- Homosexuality
- Hypnotism
- Incubi or Succubi (sexual spirits)
- I.U.D. (women only)
- Kabalah
- Levitation (table-tipping)
- Martial Arts
- Materialization
- New Age
- Occult books
- Ouija board
- Pacts with Satan
- Palm Reading
- Pornography
- Psychic Healing or Psychic Surgery
- Rosicrucians
- Sado-Masochism
- Satanism
- Séances
- Silva Mind Control
- Swedenborg
- Tarot Cards
- Telepathy
- Transcendental Meditation (TM)
- Voodoo (or Santeria, Camdoble, Palo Mayombe)
- Witchcraft
- White or Black Magick

CULTS AND ABERRANT RELIGIOUS GROUPS:

- Anthroposophy/Waldorf Schools (R. Steiner):
- Bahai
- Buddhism

- Children of God (Family of Love)
- Christian Science
- Church Universal & Triumphant
   (Summit Lighthouse)
- Elizabeth Clare Prophet
- Freemasonry
- Hari Krishna (ISKCON)
- Hinduism
- I AM Movement
- Islam
- Jehovah's Witnesses
- Liberal Catholic Church
- Liberal Theology
- Lodges (misc.)
- Mormonism
- People's Temple
- Process Church
- Rastafarianism
- Roman Catholicism
- Scientology
- Spiritualism
- Tara Center
- Theosophical Society
- Unification Church (Moonies)
- Unitarian Universalists Unity
- Way International
- Wicca
- Worldwide Church of God (Armstrong)
- Other cults

Appendix II

Procedures for Renouncing Strongmen from Various Cults

First, make certain the person is actually Born Again. Have them re-affirm their faith in Christ.

A. The ex-Mormon (Latter-day Saint)

1. Have them renounce the Church of Jesus Christ of Latter-day Saints as a false religion.

2. Have them renounce Joseph Smith as a false prophet.

3. Have them renounce the Book of Mormon as false scripture (if needed, as led by the Spirit).

4. Under personal sins:

    a. Have them renounce their baptismal covenants and any priesthood blessings they received.

    b. If they were temple Mormons, have them renounce their temple oaths and covenants and temple marriage as sin.

    c. Have them renounce their Melchizedek and Aaronic priesthoods as the sin of priestcraft (male only).

    d. Have them renounce their Patriarchal Blessing as the sin of mediumship (if they received one).

  5. Possible Strongmen:

    a. Mormo: god of the ghouls and of the dead.

    b. Moroni: a little-known demon frequently encountered on the Indian subcontinent.

    c. Spirit of priestcraft.

    d. Spirit of Bishopric.

    e. Perverse spirit (from following a false prophet. Isa. 19:14).

    f. Lying Spirit (from seeking false prophecies 2 Chronicles 18:22, Prov 6:16-19)

    g. Spirit of Error (1 John 4:6).

    h. Occasionally, Seducing Spirit (1Tim. 4:1) or Spirit of Whoredoms (Hosea 4:12).

B. The ex-Jehovah's Witness.

  1. Have them renounce the Watchtower Bible and Tract Society as a false religion.

  2. Have them renounce the Governing Body of the Watchtower as a false prophet.

  3. Have them renounce the New World Translation of the Holy Scriptures as false scripture (if needed, as led by the Spirit).

4. Under personal sins:

   a. Have them renounce their baptism as sin.

   b. Have them ask the Lord to forgive them for denying the deity of Jesus Christ and the Holy Spirit. Have them renounce their Arian "Jehovah-God" as an idol.

   c. Have them ask God to forgive them for denying the resurrection of Jesus Christ.

5. Possible Strongmen:

   a. Ra-Hoor-Khuit (Horus): Egyptian god of war.

   b. "Jehovah-God:" the mask of the false JW god.

   c. Perverse spirit (from following a false prophet. Is. 19:14).

   d. Lying Spirit (from seeking false prophecies. 2 Chronicles 18:22, Prov 6:16-19).

   e. Spirit of Error (1 John 4:6).

   f. Occasionally, Seducing Spirit (1 Tim. 4:1) or Spirit of Whoredoms (Hosea 4:12).

C. The ex-Christian Scientist:

1. Have them renounce Christian Science as a false religion.

2. Have them renounce Mary Baker Eddy as a false prophet.

3. Have them renounce the Science and Health and the Key to the Scriptures as false scripture (if needed, as led by the Spirit).

4. Under personal sins:

   a. Have them ask the Lord to forgive them for denying the unique deity of Jesus Christ and the Holy Spirit.

   b. Have them ask the Lord to forgive them for the sin of pride in seeking occult healing.

   c. Have them ask the Lord to forgive them for denying the reality of God's creation.

5. Possible Strongmen:

   a. Hermes: Greek god of the mind and founder of Hermetics.

   b. Spirit of divination: (from seeking occult power or healing, Acts 16:16-28).

   c. Perverse spirit (from following a false prophet, Isa. 19:14).

   d. Lying Spirit (from seeking false prophecies, 2 Chronicles 18:22, Prov 6:16-19).

   e. Spirit of Error (1 John 4:6).

   f. Familiar Spirit (from seeking occult power, 1 Sam.28:7-8).

   g. Spirit of Double-mindedness or Confusion (from denying the inerrancy of God's Word, James 1:8)

6. Specifically go through prayers to sever link between human spirit and soul, and cast out Spirit of Divination. This is needed for anyone who has cultivated occult or psychic power.

D. The ex-Freemason:

1. Have them renounce the Masonic Lodge as a false religion.

2. Under personal sins:

   a. Have them renounce their blood oaths and covenants taken in the Lodge initiations, and confess them to the Lord as sin.

   b. If they are Shriners, have them renounce as sin their temple oaths on the Quran in the name of Allah.

   c. If 32° Mason, have them renounce their Melchizedek priesthood as the sin of priestcraft.

   d. Have them renounce their false Masonic communion (both Scottish and York Rites).

   e. Have them declare emphatically that Jesus Christ is the only Worshipful Master, and and ask repentance for serving any other.

   f. Have them ask forgiveness for denying the Lord Jesus through Masonic initiations.

   g. Have them ask the Holy Spirit to cut the initiatic ties which they have to the fraternity forever and seal those ties with the blood of Jesus Christ.

5. Possible Strongmen:

   a. Ba'al: the actual god of Masonry.

   b. Jah-bal-on: secret name of Masonic god, revealed in York Rite Royal Arch.

   c. Tubalcain: secret Master Mason password, has become a strongman over the centuries.

d. Baphomet: secret name of the god of the Knights Templar, historic antecendant of Masons.

e. Dagon, Set, Molech and Lilith: all pagan gods or goddess involved with infant sacrifice (for women involved in Eastern Star).

f. Spirit of priestcraft.

g. Perverse spirit (from following a false prophet, Isa. 19:14).

h. Spirit of Error (1 John 4:6).

i. Seducing Spirit (1 Tim. 4:1) or Spirit of Whoredoms (Hosea 4:12).

E. The ex-Spiritist or New Age devotee:

1. Have them renounce Spiritism or the specific New Age group they belonged to as a false religion.

2. Have them renounce their medium, channeler or guru as a false prophet.

3. Have them renounce any "sacred books" they used (Urantia Book, OAHSPE, Aquarian Gospel of Jesus Christ) or "dictations" or readings from channelers as false scripture (if needed, as led by the Spirit).

4. Under personal sins:
   a. Have them ask the Lord to forgive them for denying the unique deity of Jesus Christ and the Holy Spirit.
   b. Have them ask the Lord to forgive them

for the sin of pride in seeking occult power.

    c. Have them ask the Lord to forgive them for trying to converse with the dead.

    d. Ask the Holy Spirit to cut any initiatic ties or ungodly ties with any guru, etc., and seal those ties off forever with the blood of the Lamb.

5. Possible Strongmen:

    a. Pythoness or Spirit of divination (from seeking occult power or conversing with "the dead" Acts 16:16-28).

    b. Hermes: Greek god of the mind and founder of Hermetics.

    c. "The Light:" a false term for the Force of the universe.

    d. Perverse spirit (from following a false prophet, Is. 19:14).

    e. Lying Spirit (from seeking false prophecies, 2 Chronicles 18:22, Prov. 6:16-19).

    f. Spirit of Error (1 John 4:6).

    g. Familiar Spirit (from seeking occult power, 1 Sam. 28:7-8).

6. Specifically go through prayers to sever the link between the human spirit and soul, and cast out Spirit of Divination. This is needed for anyone who has cultivated occult or psychic power.

F. The ex-Wiccan (white witch):

1. Have them renounce Wicca and Goddess-worship as a false religion.

2. Have them renounce their high priestess (or high priest) as a false prophet.

3. Have them renounce the Book of Shadows as false scripture (if needed, as led by the Spirit).

4. Under personal sins:

   a. Have them ask the Lord to forgive them for denying the unique deity of Jesus Christ and the Holy Spirit.

   b. Have them ask the Lord to forgive them for the sin of pride in seeking occult power.

   c. Have them ask the Lord to forgive them for trying to converse with the dead.

   d. Ask the Holy Spirit to cut any initiatic ties or ungodly ties (from sexual rites) with high priestess (or priest).

   e. Ask the Lord to forgive them for taking illegal drugs, and ask the Holy Spirit to shut forever any doorways of demonic access opened through those drugs.

5. Possible Strongmen:

   a. Diana, Aradia, Hecate, or other names of Goddess as worshiped in coven. The person will know the names.

   b. Herne, Cernunnos, Pan or other names of Horned God as worshiped in coven. The person will know the names.

   c. Pythoness or Spirit of divination (from seeking occult power, Acts 16:16-28).

   d. Hermes: Greek god of the mind and founder of Hermetics.

e. Perverse spirit (from following a false prophet, Isa. 19:14).

f. Familiar Spirit (from seeking occult power, 1 Sam.28:7-8).

6. Go through prayers to sever link between the human spirit and soul, and cast out the Spirit of Divination. This is needed for anyone who cultivated occult or psychic power.

G. The ex-Satanist (black witch or Setian):

1. Have them renounce Satanism as a false religion.

2. Have them renounce their high priestess (or high priest) as a false prophet.

3. Have them renounce any "sacred books" (*Satanic Bible, Book of the Law, Necronomicon, Book of the Coming Forth by Night*) as false scripture (if needed, as led by the Spirit).

4. Under personal sins:

a. Have them ask the Lord to forgive them for denying the unique deity of Jesus Christ and the Holy Spirit and worshiping Satan.

b. Have them ask the Lord to forgive them for the sin of pride in seeking occult power.

c. Have them ask the Lord to forgive them for making covenants, contracts, commissions or pacts with the devil.

d. Ask the Holy Spirit to cut any initiatic ties or ungodly ties (from sexual rites) with high priestess (or priest).

e. Ask the Lord to forgive them for taking illegal drugs, and ask the Holy Spirit to shut forever any doorways of demonic access opened through those drugs.

f. If needed (as in hardcore Satanism), ask the Lord's forgiveness for any abortions, infant, child, or adult sacrifices the person participated in. Ask Him to shut forever and seal any doorways of demonic access opened by those sins.

g. If needed (as in hardcore Satanism), ask the Lord's forgiveness for any sex rites done with demons, especially if done to conceive a "magickal child." Ask Him to shut forever and seal any doorways of demonic access opened by those sins.

5. Possible Strongmen:

a. Lucifer, Belial, Satan and Leviathan, as well as any specific "god-names" of high demons as worshiped in coven. The person will know the names.

b. If involved in human sacrifice or abortions: Lilith, Molech, Kali: all gods/goddesses of infant destruction.

c. Incubus or Succubus spirits: sexual demons involved in sexual magic, if (g. above) was done.

d. Legion (Luke 8:30) and/or Deaf and Dumb Spirit (Mark 9:25-26, Mt.17:14-18): Almost always present in survivors of SRA, or in anyone who was defiled as a child by sexual or occult abuse. Sometimes a "look-alike" for MPD.

e. Pythoness or Spirit of divination (Power demon): (from seeking occult power, Acts 16:16-28).

f. Hermes: Greek god of the mind. Founder of Hermetics.

g. Perverse spirit (from following a false prophet, Is. 19:14).

h. Familiar Spirit (from seeking occult power 1 Sam. 28:7-8).

i. Seducing Spirit (1 Tim. 4:1), or Spirit of Whoredoms (Hosea 4:12).

j. Spirit of Anti-christ (cf. 1 John 2:22, 4:2-3).

k. Spirit of Bondage (cf. Romans 8:15).

l. Spirit of Fear (cf. 2 Timothy 1:7).

6. Go through prayers to sever link between the human spirit and soul, and cast out the Spirit of Divination. This is needed for anyone who cultivated occult or psychic power.

7. They need to renounce any and all contracts, covenants, dedications or commissions made while in the cult, and ask the Lord to break their power.

8. They need to reveal and renounce any secret occult or demonic names they were given (if remembered). They also need to be clear of any occult or satanic books or artifacts (as mentioned above).

9. In rare occasions, it is also helpful to have them pray that the Lord would protect them as they sleep and would not allow them to be taken out of their bodies (ie. astral projection) for any purpose not of the Holy Spirit.

10. Breaking the power of Triggers can also be a concern. It will be dealt with in Appendix V.

Appendix III

The Taxonomy of Evil:

A Biblical Diagnosis of
Demonic Oppression

Sinful behavior in both Christians and non-Christians can be linked to demon influence. In looking for victory over behavior problems, health problems and even psychological problems—sometimes deliverance from demonic oppression can be of immense help.

This is especially true when the plagued person has a history of involvement in cults, the occult or ancestors who were involved in such practices (Exodus 20:5).

People most commonly suffering from such bondage include (in order of likelihood):

1) Former or current practitioners of the occult, witchcraft, spiritualism and Satanism.

2) Former or current members of cultic or heretical

groups which deny the deity of Jesus Christ as Almighty God (Mormonism, Jehovah's Witnesses, Freemasons, etc.)

3) Those descended from either #1 or #2.

4) Those who have been involved in homosexual behavior or chronic substance abuse, especially with psychotropic drugs (Marijuana, LSD, peyote, mescaline, etc.).

5) Those victimized by severe trauma (rape, child abuse, etc.).

6) Those practicing indiscriminate, promiscuous sexual intercourse with people other than one's spouse, particularly if the sexual partners have come from group #1 or #2.

The list below was compiled from several sources and represents years of empirical evidence in doing deliverance—such experience always being run through the filter of the Word of God. It shows various forms of evil supernaturalism, the symptomology they produce (Matt.7:16) and their likely entry point into the person.

Not everyone who has done or experienced these "entry points" is assured of having such-and-such spirit because the sovereignty of God frequently rids people of oppressive spirits at salvation. This is only a resource IF there are symptoms! We all must beware of spiritual hypochondria or "demon-hunting."

1. Spirit of Anti-christ: (cf. 1 John 2:22, 4:2-3)

Denies the Deity of Christ (1 John 4:3, 2 John 7).

Possible entry point: involvement in eastern religions, Yoga, martial arts, generational sin of parents.

Manifests as: a denial of the unique role of Jesus in human history:
- Against Christ and His teachings (2 Thess. 2:4, 1 John 4:3).
- Denies the Atonement (1 John 4:3).
- Humanism (2 Thess. 2:3,7).
- Teachers of Heresies (1 John 2:18,19).
- Attacks the testimony of Christians (2 Thess. 2:4, 2 John 7).
- Attempts to substitute self for Jesus (2 Thess. 2:3-12).
- Blasphemes the name of Jesus (1 John 4:5).
- Practices forms of salvation by works rather than grace (Rev 13:7).

2. Spirit of Bondage (cf. Romans 8:15):

Possible entry point: unrepented sin of lust of the flesh, generational sin of parents.

Manifests as: Lack of faith in their salvation (Rom. 14:23).
- All forms of addictions (2 Pet. 2:19).
- Anguish of spirit (Ex. 6:9).
- Uncontrolled lust, greed or ambition (Prov. 5:22, John 8:34).
- Besetting or compulsive sin, especially sexual enslavement (Prov. 5:22, Jn. 8:34).
- Bitter roots, bitterness (Job 7:14; 9:10, Prov. 14:10).
- Compulsive masochistic behavior, false martyrdom (same as besetting above).

- Captivity to Satan (2Pet. 2:19).
- Fear of death (Heb. 2:14,15).
- Serves the cause of corruption (Rom. 7:23, Acts 8:23, Rom 6:16, Lk 8:26-29).

3. Deaf and Dumb Spirit: (Mark 9:25-26, Mt. 17:14-18).

Possible entry point: early trauma in childhood, infancy or prenatal.

Manifests as: Hearing impairment, unwillingness to communicate.

- Self-punishing behaviors (cutting self), (Mark 9:18, 20, 26).
- Self-applied cigarette burns (Mk. 9:22).
- Head-banging, self abuse (Mk. 9:22).
- Suicidal ideation (Mk. 9:22).
- Foaming at mouth (Lk. 9:39 Mk. 9:20).
- Gnashing teeth (Mk. 9:18).
- Untreatable epilepsy, seizures; especially during times of satanic holidays (Mk. 9:20, 18, 26).
- Prostration, crying, ear problems, pining away (Mk. 9:26).
- Mental illness (Mt. 17:15, Mk. 9:17, 5:5).

4. Spirit of Double-Mindedness and/or Confusion (James 1:8).

Possible entry point:
- Lack of faith.
- Refusal to accept the Bible as the inerrant Word of God.
- Refusal to receive sound preaching.
- Unbiblical sexual relationships (Job 10:15, Ps. 44:15, Isa. 41:29; 45:16, Jer. 3: 25; 7:19).

Manifests as:
- Lack of assurance of salvation.
- Indecisiveness.
- Inability to get victory over sin.

5. Spirit of Divination or PYTHONESS (Acts 16: 16-28).

Possible entry point:
- Practice of fortune telling.
- Other methods of seeking high knowledge of wisdom, especially trance channeling.
- Hypnosis.
- Triggering.
- Generational sin of parents.

Manifests as:
- Mediumistic "skills" (channeling, etc.), (Micah 5:12, Isa. 2:6).
- "Second sight," psychic powers (Hosea 4:12, Ex. 22:18).
- Bondage to astrology, tarot cards, Ouija boards, palmistry, and other such practices (Ex. 7:11; 8:7; 9:11).
- Practice of hypnosis, water-witching, etc. (Deut. 18:11, Isa. 19:3).
- Drugs (Gal. 5:20, Rev. 9:21; 18:23; 21:8; 22:15).
- Astrology (Isa. 47:13, Lev. 19:26, Jer. 10:2).

6. Familiar Spirit: (1 Sam. 28:7-8).

Possible entry point:
- Hypnosis
- Attempting to conjure spirits
- Ventriloquism
- Dungeons & Dragons

- Ouija boards
- Tarot cards
- Palm reading etc.

Manifests as:

- Alleged communications from dead loved ones (Deut. 18:11,1 Chron. 10:13).
- Memory blocks or fragmented memory (Rev. 9:21; 18:23; 21:8; 22:15).
- "Voice" mediumship (channeler who speaks without lips or vocal chords) (1 Sam. 28:7,8, Isa. 8:19; 29:4).
- Peep & mutter (Isa. 8:19, 29:4, 59:3).
- Severe dyslexia/or Yoga (Jer. 29:8).

7. Spirit of Fear: (2 Timothy 1:7)

Possible entry point:

- Extreme terror experience from childhood.
- Parental neglect.
- Use of psychedelic drugs.
- Generational sin of parents.

Manifests as:

- Phobic behaviors or paranoia.
- Profound anxiety, inability to trust God or relate to Him as Father (1 Peter 5:7).
- Nightmares, night terrors (Ps. 91:5).
- Heart failure (Ps. 55:6, Lk. 21:26, Jn. 14:1, 27).
- Inordinate fear of death (Ps. 55:4, Heb. 2:14, 15).
- Untrusting, doubt, fear of man (Mt. 8:26, Rev. 21:8, Prov. 29:25).
- Torment (Ps. 55:5, 1 Jn. 4:18).

8. Spirit of Haughtiness: (Prov. 16:18-19)

Possible entry point:

- Excessive pride or gossiping.
- Boasting
- Envy

Manifests as:

- Pride, snobbishness.
- Unteachable, obstinate, idle (Prov. 29:1, Dan. 5:20, Ezek. 16:49, 50).
- Rebellious to pastoral authority (1 Sam. 15:23, Prov. 29:1).
- Bragging or boastfulness (2 Sam. 22:28, Jer. 48:29, Isa. 2:11,17, 5:15).
- Argumentative or contentious (Prov. 13:10).
- Extreme self-righteousness or religiosity (Lk. 18:11,12).
- Reject God (Ps. 10:4, Jer. 43:2).

9. Spirit of Heaviness: (Isaiah 61:3)

Possible entry point:

- Tragedy in life or traumatic experience.
- Generational sin of parents.

Manifests as:

- Depression.
- Despair.
- No urge to praise God.
- Unpacified, a root of bitterness.
- Morbid grief (Neh. 2:2, Prov. 15:13).
- Loneliness, inner hurts (Lk. 4:18).
- Gluttony, insomnia (Neh. 2:2).
- Self-pity (Ps. 69:20).
- Hopelessness (2 Cor. 1:8,9).

- Broken hearted (Ps. 69:20, Prov. 12:18; 15:3, 13; 18:14, Lk. 4:18).

10. Spirit of Infirmity: (Luke 13:11)

Possible entry point:

- Generational sin of parents.
- Bad health practices.

Manifests as:

- Chronic illness or deformity.
- Bent body or spine.
- Asthma, chronic colds (John 5:5).
- Frailty or weakness (Lk. 13:11, John 5:5).
- Severe feminine disorders in women, impotency in men (John 5:5, Acts 3:2, 4:9).
- Arthritis (John 5:5).
- Cancer (Lk. 13:11, John 5:5).
- Oppression (Acts 10:38).

11. Spirit of Jealousy: (Numbers 5:14)

Possible entry point:

- Sexual defilement
- Rage
- Anger (Gen. 4:5-6, Prov. 6:34; 14:29; 22:24-25; 29:22-23).
- Lack of discipline from parents.
- Strife (Prov. 10:12).

Manifests as:

- Rage, jealousy, resentment, hatred of partner.
- Cruelty (Song of Solomon 8:6).
- Murder, hate (Gen. 4:8; 37:3,4,8).
- Extreme competitiveness (Gen. 4:4-5).

- Selfishness, causing divisions (Gal. 5:19).
- Revenge, spite (Prov. 6:34; 14:16-17).

12. Spirit of Lethargy: (Isaiah 29:10)

Possible entry point: Can be a curse from God for:

- Refusing to listen to and obey the preaching of His Word.
- Improperly criticizing pastors or elders.
- Refusing to obey the Lord.
- Generational sin.

Manifests as:

- Sleep disorders, narcolepsy.
- Apathy, sluggishness, sleepiness (Job 30:17).
- Chronic exhaustion, "chronic fatigue syndrome" (Lam. 2:18).
- Clinical depression (in absence of medical or environmental causes) (Prov. 29:9).
- Spiritually "deaf" to God's truth: counterfeit "covering," a false shield is keeping God's spirit from flowing and giving its life (Ps. 88:17).

13. Lying Spirit: (2 Chronicles 18:22, Prov. 6:16-19)

Possible entry point: This can also be a curse from God for seeking false prophecies or for "ear-tickling" preaching. Or it can be generational sin of parents.

Manifests as:

- Compulsive lying, delusional behavior.
- Flattery or insincere praise (Ps. 78:36, Prov. 20:19; 26:28).
- A religious or ecclesiastical spirit (Gal. 5:1).
- Profanity, hypocrisy, accusations (Rev. 12:10).

- Excessive or idle chatter, gossip (1 Tim. 6:20, 2 Tim 2:16).
- Superstitions, false Prophecy (1 Tim. 4:7, Jer. 23:15-17; 27:9-10).
- Slander (Prov. 10:18).

14. Perverse Spirit: (Isaiah 19:14)

Possible entry point:
- Curse from God for following false priests or prophets.
- Idolatry
- Generational sin

Manifests as:
- Sexual perversion.
- Addiction to pornography.
- Any indulgence in repeated disobedience to God (Prov. 17:20, 23; 12:8; 14:2; 29:8).
- Teaching false doctrine, perverting the Word of God (Isa. 19:14, Rom. 1:22, 23, 2 Tim. 3:8,2).
- Scripture twisting, heresy (Acts 13:10, 2 Pet. 2:14).
- Stubborn, unreasonable (Prov. 19:2).
- Ingratitude, foolish (Prov. 1:22; 19:1; 15:4).
- Filthy minded (Prov. 2:12; 15:23, 33).

15. Seducing Spirit: (1 Timothy 4:1).

Possible entry point: Following false prophets or teachers who are involved in carnal sins. Seducing spirits seem to be messengers sent from Satan to deceive believers.

Manifests as: searing of the conscience.
- Seduce, tempt or beguile the person into false doctrine.

- Causes double-mindedness (see above).

16. Spirit of Whoredoms: (Hosea 4:12)

Possible entry point:
- Worshipping false gods.
- Offering sacrifices to false gods.
- Other harlotries against the true God.
- Generational sin of parents.

Manifests as:
- Satanism
- Making pacts with the devil.
- Unfaithfulness
- Adultery (Ezek. 16:15, 28, Pr. 5:1-14, Hosea 4:13-19).
- Prostitution of soul or body (Ezek. 16:15, 28, Prov. 5:1-14).
- Self-idolatry (Jud. 2:17, Ezek. 16, Hosea 4:12).
- Love of the world, money, food, glamour (narcissism, compulsive concern with physique—body-building, etc.) (I Cor. 6:13-16, Phil. 3:19, James 4:4, Ezek. 16:28).
- Spiritual idolatry (Hosea 4:12).

17. Spirit of Slumber (cf. Romans 11:8)

Possible entry point: Following legalistic religions, serious parental neglect, especially neglect by the father.

Manifests as: Inability to love, or be truly sexually intimate.
- Inability to worship.
- Spiritual torpor or stagnation.
- No internalized sense of right or wrong.

18. Spirit of Error: (1 John 4:6).

Possible entry point: Refusal to hear the warnings, counsel of God or Word of God. Refusal to apply Biblical tests to doctrines.

Manifests as: (Primarily institution-wide) heretical cults.
- Contentious (James 3:16, 2 Peter 2, 1 Jn. 4:6.
- Running after false doctrines (1 Tim 6:20-21, 2 Tim. 4:3, Titus 3:10, 1 Jn. 4:1-6).
- Denial of the deity of Jesus Christ (2 Thess.).
- Aberrant or heterodox Christian teachings, (2 Peter 2:10).
- Inability to understand simple Biblical truths, (Prov. 10:17; 12:1; 13:18; 15:10, 12, 32, 1 Jn. 4:6, 2 Tim. 4:1-4).

19. Devouring Spirit: (Malachi 3:8-12)

Possible entry point: Disobedience to God, especially in the area of tithing. Or generational sin of parents. The only way to be delivered of this spirit is to obey God's law and tithe.

Manifests as: Chronic poverty, deep indebtedness.
- Financial or real estate calamities (natural disasters).
- Inability to ever save money.
  (Be sure to tithe time—in the form of Bible study and prayer—as well as talents and finances).

20. Buffeting Spirit: (2 Corinthians 12:7)This is a specialized problem because this spirit works against ministries. It torments the minister or causes the needs of the ministry to go unmet. God seems to allow this to keep his servants humble. Intercessors are often faced with this but having the covering of your pastor as well as prayer partners often renders it less effective.

21. Legion/Unclean Spirit: (Mark 1:26; 3:11; 5:3 ff, Luke 4:33; 8:27 ff).

Possible entry point: The defilement of a child's spirit. This may be the result of physical or sexual abuse, incest or involvement of the child in occult practices or ritualized abuse. Sometimes "imagined" child abuse can also open doorways if the child feels deep within themselves that they have been defiled or violated.

Manifests as:
- Insomnia
- Suicidal ideation, self-mutilation.
- Supernatural strength
- Morbid fascination with death, human waste, putrefaction or grave-yards.
- Extreme inner torment, hears voices, has nightmares.
- Exhibitionism, nudity, homosexuality, promiscuity, perversions.
- Perfectionistic, extreme performance orientation, compulsively clean.
- Extremely precise, block-like handwriting.
- Reclusive, very rigid and controlled.
- Anorexia, Bulimia, compulsive over-eating.
- Has trouble seeing God as Father.

Appendix IV

Implants

Implants, also known as "inserts" or "object links" are common in SRA survivors. These are usually tiny foreign objects which are inserted subcutaneously in the child during rituals after being "blessed" on the altar of Satan. We have seen metal, bone, stone and even seeds so used.

These objects—often no larger than a pin-head—form a "homing device" so the Satanic cult can trace the person, wherever they may go as an adult. The implant, having been used in idolatrous worship, also constitutes an "open door." It would be like the person wearing a pentagram around their neck.

Usually these people are ignorant of the existence of these implants, although in Christians they will sometimes cause rashes on the skin surface over the area where the thing is implanted.

One woman we counselled with had a strange, ring-shaped rash develop over her sternum after we prayed for her. She went to a doctor, and he discovered and removed a thin, stainless-steel ring from under her skin. There was no medical reason for such an artifact, nor did she have any memory of it being implanted.

Sometimes, when the normal prayer session does not bring immediate victory, we suspect the presence of these implants—because they may constitute a "legal ground" for Satan to keep his troops within the person until the implant is removed.

Then we really begin to pray in earnest for the Lord to either destroy the implant from within the person, or to have the person's body expel or discharge it. While implants are found in virtually any part of the human body, they are most commonly found in:

1) Areas corresponding to occult chakra points. These include:

    a) Crown of head.

    b) "Third Eye" region (between and above eyebrows).

    c) Throat

    d) Sternum

    e) Around the navel.

    f) Reproductive organs (more common in females).

    g) Anal area

2) Nasal passages

3) Ear cavities

4) Vicinity around vaccination scars, or any surgical scars. Sometimes a satanist doctor recommends "surgery" for a child. During the appendectomy or tonsillectomy an implant is also added. The scar is explained by the surgery, and the scar tissue helps conceal the implant.

5) Teeth: Sometimes dentists get "in on it" and when they fill a cavity, they also place a tiny implant in the person's filling.

Usually implants cannot be medically detected. Therefore, we must rely upon the Lord—praise God! We have had many people seek God about removing implants, and the Lord is gracious to comply.

Sometimes, they just vanish, although a strange heat or rash is felt on the surface of the skin. Other times, if it is near the surface of the skin or near an orifice, the body will discharge it. It may be so small that it is unnoticed in the bedclothes in the morning. It may simply look like a tiny sliver of metal or bone—nothing to attract attention.

If you do find it, simply pray over it and destroy it. Usually, victory will follow almost immediately. Praise the Lord!

Appendix V

Triggers

A trigger is any event that precipitates a response. The triggers we refer to have been purposely placed, usually to control the behavior of a person at a later time and place. Interestingly enough, some commonly used triggers are spoken of in Proverbs 6:12-13:

> **"A naughty person, a wicked man, walketh with a froward mouth. He winketh with his eyes, he speaketh with his feet, he teacheth with his fingers."**

Suggestions and associations made during emotional trauma (such as child abuse) can surpass our ability to file them in a way they can be recalled at will. Very severe trauma sometimes embeds people so deeply they mimic the autonomic nervous system (ANS) of the human body. Repetition of the suggestion thus enforces their power to cause the desired reaction.

TYPES OF TRIGGERS

Triggers may fall into one or several categories of response correlating to the five senses: sight, hearing, feeling, taste and smell. These BASIC TRIGGERS are association/response-oriented and, though simple in form, are often difficult to discover because they ARE so common.

The next category of intensity holds what are called COMMAND TRIGGERS. These verbal triggers are set to activate when certain specific conditions arise. Two of the most common are passive mind and fear (usually of death.)

1. An example of the passive mind triggering would be the person beginning to have a memory, or receiving healing during The Lord's table, or even beginning to repeat some renunciation prayers when, in an instant, they may fall into a deep sleep, faint, or become so disoriented and confused they cannot hold a thought.

2. The fear trigger is also a command trigger but can be set at any level, from conscious conditioning to being so deeply embedded in the psyche they are comparable to functioning like the human autonomic nervous system.

EXAMPLE ONE

For instance, baby John tries to play with his toy by plugging it into the electrical outlet when he hears his father's loud voice yell "NO!" followed by a few giant steps across the room in an amazingly short period of time. Then he receives a serious explanation as to why we do not play with electrical sockets. This is considered a good parenting technique yet with young children part of the response is because of shock and reinforcement. This trigger is usually on the conscious level.

EXAMPLE TWO

We find another fear trigger embedded slightly deeper. Johnny is now about five with an older brother who enjoys teasing him. One day while the older kids have him blindfolded they force him to eat spaghetti, telling him it is worms. It was only one of many incidents of teasing and little Johnny has long forgotten it. Yet, throughout the rest of his life he refuses to eat spaghetti. He just doesn't like it.

These two examples are innocent. Can you imagine what might be accomplished if a devil-influenced or drug-crazed person intended to purposely program someone?

3. A very common trigger among SRA victims is what we have come to call **Death Trigger.** During the abuse or ritual the victim is literally driven out of her body either by physical abuse, drugs or suggestions given her through hypnosis which are as real to her as though they were really taking place. While she is out of her body only the ANS keeps her alive. Her will has left or closed down temporarily because of severe strain on the psyche. Taking advantage of this weakness the abuser now implants the suggestion that if the victim ever tells of the incident or who the abuser was she will die.

As the victim overcomes her programming and

remembers, she is literally afraid for her life. She must be convinced that her panic attack, or worse, out of control body, is reacting to a lie that can be broken only by her own faith in the fact that it IS a lie! This is where the real battle for liberation and healing takes place and is an area that intercessors focus on in prayer a great while. Only when Biblical principles are understood and the battle is already won in the spiritual realm should one proceed to the actual process of breaking this type of trigger.

OUT-OF-THE -BODY VERSUS PERSONALITY FRAGMENTATION

Earlier we spoke of someone being forced out of their body (astral projection). There is another phenomenon called personality fragmentation. Why some victims react one way and other victims in another way is not known. We can only assume that those with generational doorways (especially familiar spirits) are more predisposed to leave their bodies since the pathways are already there and convenient, whereas creative victims seem inclined to dissociate resulting in the fragmentation of their personalities.

The next command trigger is fairly simple, yet reaps much havoc. We refer to it as CONTRARY PROGRAMMING. Like some Amerindian shamans and most Satanists who learn to act and think backwards, some victims are given programs which cause them to do this. They can vary from a broad range which appear as general rebellion (usually against authority) to specific topics. For example,

"Whenever you hear the words 'I love you,' you will process the thought as 'I hate you, you are not worthy to be loved.'" Another one often used to prevent the clients from getting free is "When you hear 'The blood of Jesus has set you free' you will process it as 'Jesus lost on Calvary, Satan rules'".

The last type of programming we will talk about is "MOLES" popularized in *The Manchurian Candidate* and other films and TV shows. These are persons with seemingly normal lives but all of a sudden they commit sabotage, treason or murder but they don't realize what they have done until the act is completed (if they realize it at all!).

When it seems they may be discovered they will commit suicide, which has also been pre-programmed into their psyche. If they have accomplished their task undiscovered the program will tell them to forget everything about what they have done.

DISCOVERING TRIGGERS

If you have reason to believe you have triggers you may want to pray to the Lord Jesus Christ and ask Him to remove them. If you are the curious type you may want to know what they are. In this case, it would be wise to first pray and ask if it is SAFE for you to know. It is NOT necessary for you to remember before the Lord can remove them!

Sometimes the discovery process works in reverse. You find yourself a bit disoriented and wondering why you just did what you did. Again, it is good to pray and ask the Lord Jesus Christ to neutralize anything not in His perfect will for you.

If you want to know more specifically, first ask if it is safe for you to pursue this. If so, replay the events of the last ten to fifteen minutes to see if you were staring at some object, or if a phrase was playing over and over in your head, etc.

God will bring triggers to your memory if He wants you to know, and He wants you to know what they are because just by exposing them with His love to your conscious mind their power is broken.

Sometimes these suggestions are chained together to form a string of reactions and are embedded in the personality in such a way as to cause emotional trauma as they are being removed. In these cases the Lord is merciful and often heals without any participation from us at all. Do not be disappointed if He heals without you remembering. Consider it a blessing!

SPIRITUAL CONSEQUENCES

It is often the intent of the abusers who have programmed the person with these triggers to both control and dishearten the survivor.

Such victims of triggers often feel as if they have lost control of their lives. This is especially true of those who fear that their triggers have caused them to do sinful, evil things either with or without their conscious knowledge.

A person who has gone through a wonderful and liberating prayer session might be completely demoralized if they feel that a trigger may have caused a memory "black-out" during which they might have sinned. One woman we prayed for later experienced a trigger-induced black-out and awoke in the back of a car being homosexually raped by two witches from her old coven. She felt utterly defiled and fled the car screaming.

Such people often believe that they have committed "doorway-opening" sins such as fornication and that all their prayers for liberation are undone. It may seem to them to be an impossible task to rebuild their lives. The "accuser of the brethren" is working overtime on them, making them think that they have failed mightily and will never get free. IT IS VITAL TO UNDERSTAND THAT THIS IS A LIE FROM THE PIT!

GOD'S WORD BRINGS COMFORT. PAUL TELLS US:

> "There hath no temptation taken you but such as is common to man: BUT GOD IS FAITHFUL, WHO WILL NOT SUFFER YOU TO BE TEMPTED ABOVE THAT YE ARE ABLE; but will with the temptation also make a way to escape, that ye may be able to bear it."   1 Cor. 10:13

Please understand! Since triggers are inflicted without the person's conscious consent (in most cases) and since they by definition force the person to do things without their consent, THERE IS NO ELEMENT OF THE PERSON'S WILL INVOLVED.

Triggers are designed to operate below the level of moral choice! God will NOT hold a person responsible for actions done under coercion. Nor will He allow Satan to claim access through such triggered responses. That is the clear sense of this verse.

On a more mundane level, a person is not judged for what they do in their sleep. If a Christian has a dream with violent or sexual content, that is not a sin, or else the Lord would have provided them a way to resist or escape (1 Cor. 10:13). They do not need to confess it as sin, no matter how real or vivid it was. Similarly, the woman survivor mentioned above would not be held accountable by the Lord for what she did while under the influence of a trigger. No open doorways would be created by her rape, no matter how awful the experience was emotionally or physically.

> **"Shall not the Judge of all the earth do right?"**   **Gen. 18:25**

Other passages amplify this very point:

> **"And whosoever lieth carnally with a woman, that is a bondmaid, betrothed to an husband, and not at all redeemed, nor freedom given her; she shall be scourged; they shall not be put to death, BECAUSE SHE WAS NOT FREE.**   **Lev. 19:20**

> **"But if a man find a betrothed damsel in the field, and THE MAN FORCE HER, and lie with her: then the man only that lay with her shall die: BUT UNTO THE DAMSEL THOU SHALT DO NOTHING; there is in the damsel no sin worthy of death: for as**

> **when a man riseth against his neighbor, and slayeth him, even so is this matter: For he found her in the field, and the betrothed damsel cried, and there was none to save her."** **Deut. 22:25-27**

Thus, no man or woman is held accountable by the Lord for things that they were forced to do beyond their ability to resist. If they couldn't resist it, then it wasn't a temptation to sin! This is not to diminish the emotional turmoil such triggers may cause. However, we want to encourage the person who is struggling with these issues that God is NOT judging them for their actions, no matter how much Satan might whisper in their ears that He is. There is NO GUILT! Any guilt they may experience is false, and from the deceiver!

We close then, with a prayer which we have found enormously effective in ministering to people that seem to be suffering from the trigger phenomenon:

AFFIRMATION OF LIFE

I declare that Jesus Christ is my Lord and Savior. I declare that every aspect of my life is under the protection of Jesus Christ (2 Cor. 10:4-5).

I declare that all my memories are under the protection of Jesus Christ. I declare that I will remember only what Jesus wants me to remember, when He wants me to remember it. When I have memories that Jesus wants me to remember, I am safe and I will live.

(Depending on the individual needs or concerns of the person, the following additional paragraphs can be added:)

a. I declare that Jesus Christ is in control of ALL MY MUSCLES AND BODY MEMORY. I declare that when I relax my muscles or have body memory, I am safe and I will live.

b. I declare that Jesus Christ is in control of MY IDENTITY AND PERSONALITY. Because Jesus knew who I was before I was knit together in the womb (Ps. 71:5-7, 139:13-15), He is in total control of my identity and personality. I therefore have the identity and personality that Jesus wants me to have and I am safe and I will live.

c. I declare that Jesus Christ is in control of WHOM I LOVE, and that I will love whomever Jesus wants me to love. In that love, I am safe and I will live.

d. I declare that Jesus Christ is in control of WHAT I SPEAK, and that I will speak whatever Jesus wants me to say. In that speaking, I am safe and I will live.

e. I declare that Jesus Christ is in control of MY EATING. I will eat whatever Jesus wants me to eat, when and as often as He wants me to eat. I ask our Father to bless my food and He will bless it as He promises, for Jesus is in control of my eating, I am safe and I will live.

f. I declare that Jesus Christ is in control of MY SLEEPING. I will sleep when Jesus wants me to sleep, as often as He wants me to sleep and as long as He wants me to sleep. As Jesus is in control of my sleeping, I am safe and I will live.

I declare that Jesus Christ is in control of my actions, and that no event, action, memory or thought will trigger me to do anything that is not in the will of Jesus. I declare that because my actions are controlled by Jesus Christ, I am safe, I will live, those around me are safe, and they will live.

Under the power of the name of Jesus Christ, my Lord and Savior, I break all mind control, triggers, hypnosis, and post-hypnotic suggestions made over me (Matthew 6:31-33, John 14:6).

(We gratefully acknowledge the work and contributions of Rachel Jacobsen, who contributed much of the material in this appendix.)

Appendix VI

A Slander on the Word of God!

From the very beginning, Satan and his servants (those serving him knowingly or unknowingly) have attempted to slander the inspired Word of God (see Gen. 3:1)! This is especially true when considering the question, "Can a Christian have a demon?"

This topic is hotly debated, with the modern day "Pharisees and Sadducees" weighing in heavily on the side that says, "Gracious no, a Christian cannot have a demon within." Even among those (reputable scholars all!) who defend the idea of demonic infestation among believers, there is a common canard being pushed on the unsuspecting public.

This cheerful lie is that much of the confusion about "demon possession" and the Christian originates with the unfortunate translation of the King James Version using the words "demon possession" where a better rendering might be phrased differently. Basically, they have blamed the Authorized Version (KJV) for much of the misunderstanding. The sad fact is that if they had stuck with the KJV, they would have cleared up this entire issue!

It might surprise many to know that nowhere does the Holy Bible (i.e. the Authorized Version—1611 KJV) talk about anyone, Christian or otherwise being "demon possessed" or being "possessed by a demon." That is partly because the word "demon" is studiously absent from the KJV text.

Instead, the Bible refers to evil spirits as either devils or unclean spirits. The word "demon" has been added to all the major "bible" versions since the 19th century and its presence in those texts is intentional and NOT to be trusted. There is not space here for an examination of the reasons for that change.

However, leaving the devil/demon issue behind, there is STILL no verse in the entire Bible which says that one can be devil-possessed or possessed by a devil. Note that closely and bear it in mind the next time you hear some "Bible teacher" or "deliverance minister" slander the KJV.

To the contrary, the Authorized Version is very careful to say that people being afflicted or infested by evil spirits are "possessed with devils" (Matt. 4:24). For further support, see Matt. 4:24; 8:16,28,33; 9:32, Mark 1:23, 32; 5:2, 15-16,18; 7:25, Luke 4:33; 6:18; 7:21; 8:2,30,36, Acts 5:16; 8:7; 16:16 and 19:12-13!

Anyone who can read plain English can see that there is a world of difference between being possessed BY devils and being possessed with devils. The phrase "possessed with" is a slightly old fashioned way of saying "has." In other words, someone who is possessed with devils simply "has devils."

A person might just as readily say that someone is possessed with great strength, meaning that they have great strength, not that they are possessed BY their muscles.

Nowhere does the Holy Bible teach that a person can be possessed by a devil in the sense that every inch of their "spiritual real estate" is owned by Satan. The only possible deviation from this is Judas, who is obviously the exception that proves the rule.

Thus, Christians can relax about being "demon possessed" or "devil possessed" because the plain English of the Bible never says that anyone could be so possessed! You don't need to be a Greek scholar to figure that one out. However, that does not mean that a demon cannot inhabit a Christian. The issue is: A devil (demon) cannot have a Christian, but a Christian CAN have a devil (demon).

Again, turning to the plain English of the King James Version, almost every time devils are discussed in their relation to people, they are spoken of as being geographically located INSIDE a person:

> "When the even was come, they brought unto him many that were possessed with devils: and he cast out the spirits with his word, and healed all that were sick:"
>
> **Matt. 8:16**

Clearly, these people were infested (possessed) with evil spirits! This same phenomenon is found in 34 other places in the New Testament: Matt. 8:31, 9:34, 10:1, 10:8, 12:24, 12:27-28, 12:43, Mark 1:26, 1:39, 3:15, 3:22, 5:8, 5:13, 6:13, 9:38, 16:9, 16:17, Luke 4:36, 4:41, 8:2, 8:29, 8:30, 8:33, 9:49, 11:15, 11:18, 11:19-20, 24, 26, 13:32, Acts 8:7, 19:12.

In a comparative handful of verses, (Matt. 4:24, 12:22, Luke 6:18, 8:2, 8:36, 9:42) people with evil spirits are described as being "healed." However, the preponderance of verses are on the side of those who actually had the devils within them. Virtually ALL of these cases were people who were Jews, and thus under the Covenant of Moses. They could be viewed analogously to Christians in the New Testament under the New Covenant.

Therefore, the vast majority of those afflicted with evil spirits (even Christians) will probably have a greater or lesser degree of infestation inside them. It doesn't make them evil or unsaved, it just means that they need ministry!

That is what the Bible teaches, and don't let any Greek "scholar" tell you differently (Mal. 2:12).

Footnotes

CHAPTER 1

1. For a complete account of our extraordinary tale of salvation and deliverance from Satanism, see *Lucifer Dethroned* (Chick Pub. 1993).

2. *Michelle Remembers,* Michelle Smith and Lawrence Pazdur, M.D., Congdon & Lattés, 1980. This was the first book to present a case history of a female survivor of SRA who remembered being horribly abused by her parents and others after she reached adulthood. It was the book which brought SRA to public consciousness. It's chief flaw is that the Catholic church is presented as having a valid answer to Satanism, which it does not.

3. See *Lucifer Dethroned,* especially pp. 161-170 and pp. 184-200 for a fuller discussion of this controversy.

CHAPTER 2

1. The use of the word "exorcism" is unfortunate, but at that point, we didn't know better. Exorcism is actually not Biblical. It is an occult ritual and is found in many ancient magical texts as well as the ritual books of the Roman Catholic church. The only "exorcists" in the Bible tried to use the name of Jesus in a magical way without being truly saved. Thus they had no authority. They got the tar beaten out of them by a demon possessed man. (See Acts 19:13-19.)

2. See *Lucifer Dethroned,* (Chick Pub., 1993) especially pp. 97-108, for a fuller discussion of Aleister Crowley and his *Book of the Law.*

CHAPTER 3

1. **The Myth of Mental Illness**, Dr. Thomas Szasz, Harper & Row, 1974; Szasz, *The Myth of Psychotherapy*, Doubleday/ Anchor, 1978; Martin & Dierdre Bobgan, *The Psychological Way/The Spiritual Way*, Bethany House, 1979; Martin & Dierdre Bobgan, *Psychoheresy,* Eastgate Publishers, 1987, among others.

2. *Diagnostic and Statistical Manual of Mental Disorders* (Third Edition - Revised) American Psychiatric Association, Washington DC, 1987, p. 272.

3. Ibid. p. 269.

4. *The Baker Encyclopedia of Psychology*, David C. Benner, (editor), Baker Book House, 1987, p. 318.
5. *DSM-III-R,* p.271.
6. *The Psychological Way/The Spiritual Way,* Martin & Dierdre Bobgan, Bethany House, 1979, pp. 65-85.
7. *Satan's Children,* Dr. Robert S. Mayer, (Putnam's, 1991) for an example of how this can work in secular therapy.

CHAPTER 4
1. See *Lucifer Dethroned*, pp. 317-318 for a fuller account of this.
2. *Spiritual Warfare*, Dr. Timothy Warner, (Crossway, 1991), pp. 79-80.
3. *The Handbook on Spiritual Warfare,* Dr. Ed Murphy, (Thomas Nelson, 1992) p. 110.

CHAPTER 5
1. *The Handbook for Spiritual Warfare,* p. 134.
2. A more complete explanation of our actual prayer methodology is included in Appendix 5.

CHAPTER 6
1. Divination is the sin of trying to learn unknown things or the future by any supernatural means. Necromancy is the sin of trying to get information from the dead (i.e. from demons masquerading as spirits).

CHAPTER 7
1. *The Baker Encyclopedia of Psychology*, p. 545.
2. Ibid. p. 543.
3. *The Hermetic and Alchemical Writings of Paracelcus the Great* (ed. A. E. Waite) University Books, 1967 (1894 original English edition).
4. *Encyclopedia of Occultism and Parapsychology*, Leslie A. Shepherd, Vol. 2, Avon Books, 1980, p. 687.
5. Ibid.
6. *The Baker Encyclopedia of Psychology*, p. 543.
7. Somatization is a psychological term for when emotional distress is transferred to the body in the forms of pains or aches. A headache caused by stress is a familiar example. With hypnosis, one can make the physical body feel pain that isn't there and also make it NOT feel pain that is there. There is no clear explanation for why this is. It might be rooted in the spiritual realm (i.e., demonic).

8. *Webster's New World Dictionary,* College edition, 1966, p. 1187.
9. *The Baker Encyclopedia of Psychology,* p. 558.
10. "Prime Time Live," ABC News, original telecast, 1/7/93.

CHAPTER 8
1. Satan is not omniscient or omnipresent. Therefore he is dependent upon receiving information from his demon servants. If you pray for the Lord to cut off those lines of communication, it will facilitate matters greatly!

CHAPTER 9
1. The Associated Press, June 27, 1992.

CHAPTER 10
1. *Mormonism's Temple of Doom,* Bill Schnoebelen and James R. Spencer, Triple J Publications, 1987.
2. A talisman is an occult artifact which has been "loaded" or "charged" in a magic circle and is believed to carry intrinsic power with it. Any power a talisman has would have to be given to it by demon spirits placed in it, by a knowing or unknowing magician.
3. *Whited Sepulchers: The Hidden Language of the Mormon Temple,* Bill Schnoebelen and Jim Spencer, Triple J Publications, 1990, pp. 25-34. *Mormonism's Temple of Doom,* Triple J, 1987, pp. 31-32 and footnote #43.

CHAPTER 11
1. Write the authors for a short paper — "Straight Talk on D&D."
2. Ninja (Ninjitsu) is the most highly occult of all Japanese Martial Arts. Ninja are said to be able to turn invisible, walk up (or through) walls, and disappear like magic. Also, the T.M.N.T have an occult "master" or "sensei," a talking rat that teaches them Eastern/occult meditation practices and astral projection. The casual, teen-oriented dialogue and characterization of the Turtles mask a heavy occult world-view and teaching philosophy.

3. There are several possible reasons for the weird effect C-P dolls have on kids. They all have "birth-certificates" and are "Christened" and given names. The naming and/or baptizing of dolls or poppets is a witchcraft practice. Also, many of the names are quite odd, and relate to pagan deities. Finally, in an informal (non-scientific) poll we took among parents in our community, we found that all the dolls' birth certificates were dated October 31— Halloween! That can hardly be a coincidence. We wonder if

demons are placed in the dolls, just as witches do when they "baptize" their poppets. Parents need to pray about this, since we have noted that many little girls get almost demonic in their ferocity if their parents try to take their C-P dolls away.

4. The question, "What is a cult?" is a hot topic. However, here are some common cults: World-wide Church of God, (formerly run by Herbert W. Armstrong), Unification church (Moonies), Scientology (Dianetics), Children of God (or Family of Love), Way International, Transcendental Meditation, Hari Krishnas, United Pentecostal Church, Christian Science. This is not an exhaustive list. Cults spring up like crab grass. If you have doubts, contact your pastor or write the authors for help.

5. Other famous supposed "apparitions" of the Virgin Mary include: Our Lady of Lourdes, Our Lady of Fatima (the most influential one of the 20th Century), Our Lady of Garabandal, plus lesser known apparitions such as those of Necedah, WI. (1952-1978).

6. For a thorough analysis of Martial Arts, contact the authors and request: "Straight Talk #41: Should a Christian Practice the Martial Arts?"

7. This is an extremely controversial issue among some Christians. For comprehensive information, contact the authors for "Straight Talk #37: Homeopathy."

CHAPTER 12

1. *The Christian in Complete Armour* (vols. I & II), *The Banner of Truth Trust,* William Gurnall, Box 621 Carlisle, PA 17013. Or 3 Murrayfield Road, Edinburg, Scotland EH12 6EL.

2. *The Believer's Guide to Spiritual Warfare,* Thomas B. White, Frontline Ministries, Box 786, Corvallis, OR 97339-0786. This book is excellent!

3. *Bible-Believers' Commentary on Galatians, Ephesians, Philippians and Colossians,* Dr. Peter S. Ruckman, Bible Baptist Bookstore, Pensacola, FL, 1980, p. 339. We are deeply indebted to Dr. Ruckman for many of the insights in this chapter.

CHAPTER 13

1. For more on these seven church periods, see *The Second Coming of Christ,* Clarence Larkin, Larkin Estate, 1922, p. 52.

CHAPTER 14

1. Shamanism is just a fancy New Age term for a witch doctor. A shaman can be defined as a pagan priest, in theology usually

either pantheistic (God is all and all is God) or animistic (every-thing is alive and has a soul). An integral part of most shaman's discipline is the acquiring of the consciousness of plant and animal spirits, often through drugs or meditation.

2. The Third Eye, called the Ajna Chakra in Yoga, is an occult "gland" which allegedly exists between and slightly above the eyebrows. A major goal of occultists and Witches is the opening of the Third Eye, which, they believe, gives them the ability to see into the spirit realm. This power is actually triggered by demonic power, a Spirit of Divination to be precise (Acts 16:16).

3. *Encyclopedia of Occultism and Parapsychology*, vol. 1, Leslie A. Shepherd, p. 234.

4. Ibid., vol. 2, p. 927.

5. Webster, p. 400.

6. Ibid.

7. New Age leader David Spangler has declared that Lucifer is the primary Initiator. (See Spangler, *Reflections on the Christ*, Findhorn, 1977, pp. 36-39, 40-44.

8. We have found that when praying and invoking the authority of the name of the Lord Jesus Christ, it is helpful (though not essential) to use His full title, as above. There are thousands of Jesuses—especially in Hispanic nations—and there are many "christs" (Matt. 24:24, Mark 13:22). Indeed, Lucifer himself is a "christ" in that he is anointed (Christ means "anointed one"—see Ezek. 28:14). There are also many lords (1 Cor. 8:5), but in all the universe, there is only ONE Lord Jesus Christ!

9. It may surprise those who think of Muslims as very temperate people to learn that their idolatrous god, Allah, is one of the strongmen behind Hashish. That is because Hash was invented by a heretical Muslim leader, Hassan i Sabbah.

10. There are several excellent books which examine this sensation that is sweeping evangelical churches. Among the best are Dr. Cathy Burns' *Alcoholics Anonymous Unmasked*, Companion Press, 1991, Martin & Deidre Bobgan's *12 Steps to Destruction: Codepndency Recovery Heresies*, Eastgate Publishers, 1991, and Dr. William L. Playfair's, *M.D., The Useful Lie*, Crossways, 1991.

CHAPTER 15

1. This is an occult doctrine which is not supported by the Bible. God's Word says nothing about "Arch-dukes" in hell, although it does indicate a kind of demonic hierarchy of throne, dominions, principalities and powers (Col. 1:16). Thus, we cannot vouch for

the certainty of this belief. We only know that the several high-level Satanists we have prayed for have all manifested this Arch-duke, and that whatever he or it is, it is less than nothing next to Jesus Christ our Lord. That is all we need to know.

CHAPTER 16

1. Beware of the "New" King James Version, which is also full of pitfalls. Also, its "logo" is a disguised seal of the anti-Christ, a 666. Satan is such an ego-maniac, he loves to "sign" his work.

2. Stewart Custer, *The Truth About the King James Version Controversy,* Bob Jones University Press, 1981, pp. 12-13, provide a good example of this position.

3. For more on the superiority of the King James Version over other modern "Bibles," see *Let's Weigh The Evidence,* Barry Burton, Chick Pub., 1983; *Which Bible?,* Dr. David Otis Fuller, Grand Rapids, Intl. Pub., 1970; *The Answer Book,* Dr. Samuel Gipp, Bible Literature & Missionary Found., 1989; *New Age Bible Versions,* Gail Riplinger, AV Publications, 1993; *The Christian's Handbook of Manuscript Evidence,* Dr. Peter S. Ruckman, Pensacola Bible Press, 1976.

CHAPTER 17

1. Male homosexuals are usually much more promiscuous than heterosexuals or lesbians. This soul-tie conduit explains the powerful bondage under which these people labor. They might have literally thousands of demons. However, while they cannot fight against such bondage in their flesh, a few simple prayers to the Lord Jesus can usually set such people free. Praise God!

2. For example, see Norman L. Geisler, *Ethics: Alternatives and Issues,* Zondervan, 1975, p.201.

CHAPTER 18

1. Especially see Merrill F. Unger, *What Demons Can Do to Saints,* Moody Press, 1991, and C. Fred Dickason, *Demon Possession and the Christian,* Moody, 1987.

2. Mario Murillo, *Fresh Fire,* Anthony Douglas Publ., 1991, p. 29-36.

3. Ibid. pp. 33-34.

4. A demonic tongue is actually a kind of channeling or mediumship. Thus, the tongue needs to be confessed, renounced, and the Spirit of Divination cast out and doorways shut.

CHAPTER 19

1. By "regular" Spiritism we mean the 19th century cult started by

the Fox sisters in which people hold seances to contact dead relatives through mediums who are often "ordained" Spiritist ministers as we were.

2. For excellent material on this, see Neil Anderson's *The Bondage Breaker,* Harvest House, 1990, esp. pp. 194-196.

CHAPTER 20

1. Much of the material is this chapter is from the wise insights of Thomas White of Frontline Ministries, P.O. Box 786, Corvallis, OR 97339-0786. His excellent book, *The Believer's Guide to Spiritual Warfare* (Servant Publications, 1990) is highly recommended!

CHAPTER 21

1. The concept of choruses, prayers and "Bibles" which deliberately avoid talking about Jesus or God the Father, and use vague terms instead is dealt with extensively in G.A. Riplinger's excellent book, *New Age Bible Versions,* AV Publications, 1993, especially pp. 39-97.

2. A special note to Pentecostal brothers and sisters. Just because you have a friend pray and bind false tongues and your tongues still continue, does not mean that those tongues are from the Holy Spirit. They could simply be from your flesh, your own human nature. This is a psychological phenomenon called "glossolalia." Caveat emptor!

3. See Riplinger's *New Age Bible Versions,* for astonishing proof of how "New Age" and occult the NIV, NASB, Good News for Modern Man, The Living Bible, and even the "New" King James Bible really are. We cannot afford to play games with the Word of God, or Satan will run over the denominational world like a steam roller!

About the Authors

William and Sharon Schnoebelen have been in full-time ministry since 1986. In response to a growing need for a prayer and counseling ministry to people coming out of Satanism, cults and the occult, they founded *With One Accord Ministries* in 1992.

This ministry is dedicated to winning souls out of the kingdom of darkness through the preaching of the gospel of Jesus Christ. It is also involved in a teaching ministry in churches, Sunday Schools, Bible Colleges and seminaries — teaching churches and individual Christians to meet the challenges of cults.

This involves training Christians how to evangelize cultists, and how to defend the Bible as the perfect and authoritative source for all matters of faith and practice. To these ends, *With One Accord* publishes a bi-monthly newsletter called "The Liberator."

Finally, as ex-cultists themselves, Bill and Sharon pray and counsel with people coming out of cults. They, along with the *With One Accord* prayer team, have prayed for literally hundreds of people to be set free by the liberating power of Jesus Christ.

As more and more people are freed from cults and the occult, it is Bill and Sharon's prayer to some-day establish a "Safe House" and Retreat Center, where survivors of cults can receive prayer and discipleship in a shielded environment.

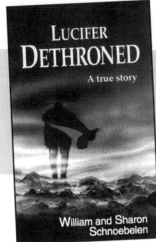

LUCIFER DETHRONED
A true story

Also in Spanish!

William and Sharon Schnoebelen

He tried the occult, and even vampirism... Then Jesus Christ made everything new!

For millions of young people, vampire movies is the current fad. Interest in the occult is on the rise worldwide. Here is the amazing story of a man's descent into vampirism, and how Jesus Christ set him free.   350 pages

"You can ignore almost everything you have seen from Hollywood about vampires. They are NOT undead corpses who turn into mist or become bats. They are severely disturbed people (Biblical translation: demonized). They get relief from stress by drinking their own blood or the blood of animals or other people. Psychiatric literature is full of cases of people who drink other's blood.

"Members of the Orthodox clergy introduced me to the vampire cult... I developed a genuine addiction to fresh blood, more powerful than bondage to any drug. Only Jesus could heal me of this. To Him goes all glory, honor and praise!"

William Schnoebelen

By William Schnoebelen

Straight Talk Booklets

by Bill and Sharon Schnoebelen

• **Straight Talk on Homeopathy**

Is it a form of harmless herbalism or "alternative medicine," or is it something much more sinister? Find out the truth from Sharon (a former holistic doctor) and Bill (a former radiathesiast).

• **Straight Talk on Dungeons & Dragons**

This challenging game has been sweeping the country for years. Find out why it is actually "entry-level witchcraft."

• **Straight Talk on Masons and the Ku Klux Klan**

Are these two secret societies related? The answer may surprise you.

• **Straight Talk on the Job's Daughters**

This Masonic order for young women seems innocent enough, but is very deceiving. Learn how young Christian girls could actually be deceived into bowing their knee to a Luciferian priesthood power.

• **Straight Talk on the Grange**

You will discover that ancient and sinister pagan deities lurk beneath the apparently harmless facade of this lodge group, often dubbed "Masonry for Farmers."

Videos

by Bill and Sharon Schnoebelen

• Exposing the Illuminati from Within (2 tape set)

Powerful 4 1/2 hours of video, in which Bill reveals
hidden components of Satan's new world order from
a former insider's point of view: discusses Masonry,
Illuminism, ritual abuse, government black
operations, UFO's, and the Alexandrian cult, in end
times deception. Provocative!

• The Battle Belongs to the Lord

New 90 minute video! Learn how to protect yourself
and your family. Bill shows how you can effectively
engage the enemy.

"Straight Talks" and videos are available from:

With One Accord Ministries
P.O. Box 457
Dubuque, IA 52004-0457

www.withoneaccord.org